Research Guide
to Musicology

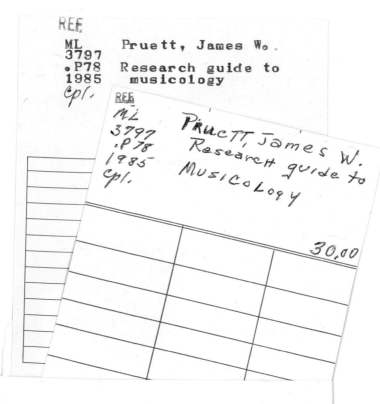

Research Guide
to Musicology

James W. Pruett and Thomas P. Slavens

SOURCES OF INFORMATION
IN THE HUMANITIES
NO. 4

CHICAGO
American Library Association
1985

Sources of Information in the Humanities
Thomas P. Slavens, series editor

Research Guide to Religious Studies by John Wilson
and Thomas P. Slavens

Research Guide to the History of Western Art by W. Eugene
Kleinbauer and Thomas P. Slavens

Research Guide to Philosophy by Terrence N. Tice
and Thomas P. Slavens

Designed by Harvey Retzloff

Composed by Huron Valley Graphics, Inc.
in Sabon on a Text Ed/Linotron 202
phototypesetting system

Printed on 60-pound Glatfelter, a pH-
neutral stock, and bound in
C-grade Holliston Roxite cloth
by Braun-Brumfield, Inc.

Library of Congress Cataloging in Publication Data

Pruett, James W.
    Research guide to musicology.

    (Sources of information in the humanities ; no. 4)
    Includes index.
    1. Music—Bibliography. 2. Musicology. I. Slavens,
Thomas P., 1928-   . II. Title. III. Series.
ML113.P83 1985   780'.01   84-24379
ISBN 0-8389-0331-2

CONTENTS

Preface to the Series   vii

Introduction and Bibliographic Note   ix

Part I.   INTRODUCTION TO RESEARCH IN MUSIC

1. *The Field of Music Scholarship*   3

2. *The Ways and Means of Musicology*   16
   Historiography   16
   Periodization   24
   Analysis and Method   27
   The Documents for Music History   34
   Performance Practice   41

3. *The Periods of Music History*   46
   Origins and the Music of Antiquity   46
   The Middle Ages   51
   The Renaissance   58
   The Baroque Era   69
   The Classic Era   78
   The Romantic Era   86
   The Twentieth Century   94
   American Music   100

Part II. REFERENCE WORKS

Dictionaries and Encyclopedias   107
General   107
Biography, International   110
Biography, National   112
Biography, Jazz, Popular, and Folk Musicians   113
Musical Instruments   114
Terms   115
Opera and Theater Music   116
Music Industry   118
Musical Themes and Devices   119
Musical Film   120

Histories and Chronologies   120
Histories   120
Music History in Pictures   121
Chronologies   122

Bibliographies of Music Literature   122
General   122
Current or Annual   123
Special and Subject Bibliographies   123

Bibliographies of Music   128
General   128
Current or Annual   130
Special and Subject Bibliographies   131

Catalogs of Music Libraries and Collections   136

Discographies   137
Yearbooks and Directories   138

Miscellaneous Bibliographical Tools   139
Guides to Music Librarianship and Research   139
Bibliographies of Bibliographies   140

Annotated Listing of Selected Music Periodicals   141

Author-Title Index   147

Subject Index   167

PREFACE TO THE SERIES

The purpose of this series is to help librarians, students of library science, and other interested persons in the use of resources in the humanities. The series encompasses art, music, philosophy, and religion. These fields share an interest in the creative, aesthetic, and imaginative impulses of human beings and the cultures in which they live. Individuals find joy in music and art; philosophy and a basic religious impulse have prompted the quest for emotional and intellectual fulfillment. Scholarship in the humanities has been produced with the goal of enhancing the quality of human life while seeking to understand it more adequately, and those who seek information about the humanities make use of libraries; often, however, they become confused by the large quantities of available materials.

This series, then, is intended as a guide in the search for information in the humanities. Each volume basically has two parts. The first features a survey of the field by a specialist, and the second is an annotated list of major reference works prepared by the series editor. The survey includes a history of the field, a description of methodology, and current issues and research. The descriptions of issues and research summarize critical assessments of significant monographs, with an emphasis on modern scholarship. They do not cite primary sources, such as the Bible or a particular painting or piece of music. Rather, the essays focus on the concepts presented in key secondary works. They stress Western subjects and titles. Citations are given in full following each section.

The second part of each volume lists and annotates major reference works. The list relates subject scholarship to bibliography, thus expediting information retrieval.

Many people have assisted in the preparation of this series. They include the Publishing Services staff of the American Library Association, without whose encouragement the series would not have been produced. The collaborators are also grateful for financial assistance from the University of Michigan which granted us the first Warner G. Rice Faculty Award in the Humanities for the purpose of assisting in the preparation of this book. These funds were used to employ Marjorie Corey, Anne Deason, Richard Heritage, Margaret Hillmer, Patricia Kirschner, Karen O'Donnell, Robert Krupp, Gail Davis, Nancy Green, Rex Miller, Mary Beth Sasso, Barbara Vaccaro, Charlene York, John Berens, and Janice McIlwain as research assistants in this project; their endeavors are very much appreciated. We also take pleasure in thanking the professors who wrote the essays. They represent the best of humanistic scholarship in the United States and have made a major contribution to the organization of information in their disciplines.

THOMAS P. SLAVENS

INTRODUCTION
AND BIBLIOGRAPHIC NOTE

The history and development of research in music are two of the threads running through chapters 1 and 2. Modern research principles and methodologies of musicology are best seen in the light of their origins and early applications. Musicology can no longer be accurately termed a "young" discipline, and I hope that the comments and readings that follow reflect its current degree of maturation.

By no means are all aspects of research in music either discussed or even mentioned in this book. My aim has been to select ideas and research that seem to be most influential, most revealing of the history of music, most helpful towards understanding what it is that scholars do, and what is simply interesting and intriguing. Occasionally only one side of a debated issue is mentioned; a host of issues, problems, and people is completely lacking.

The bibliographic citations are representative of research in music, the listings are only small samplings. In no case is any sort of comprehensiveness sought. English-language references predominate, in keeping with the aims of this series; with *The New Grove* widely available, additional readings can be easily found.

References to articles in *The New Grove* (*The New Grove Dictionary of Music and Musicians*, edited by Stanley Sadie. 20v. London: Macmillan, 1980) are shortened to author, title, and *The New Grove*.

JAMES W. PRUETT

PART I

INTRODUCTION TO RESEARCH IN MUSIC

1

The Field of
Music Scholarship

Musicologists, like most humanists and social scientists, give order to their work through conceptual frameworks that reflect relationships among the various activities they engage in and the research that results from them. These schemata offer more than simply a justification for types of research and methodologies; they offer conceptualizations of a field of research that aim to show a kind of gestalt for the discipline, to suggest a general meaning for the entire endeavor, and to demonstrate the interrelatedness of the parts of the field.

Definitions of the field of research for musicologists have varied, but from the earliest beginnings of music scholarship in the late eighteenth century, distinctions have prevailed that separate the work into categories, historical and systematic, distinctions that exclude the artistry and genius of active composing and performing. This is not to say that artistry is of no interest to the scholar, or that it may not be a part of his or her own endowment and makeup.

The founders of modern musicology in the late nineteenth century—in addition to numerous monographs, editions of music, and bibliographic contributions—offered conceptualizations for the discipline that have, to a greater or lesser degree and with greater or smaller modifications, persisted to the present day. Guido Adler's "Umfang, Methode und Ziel der Musikwissenschaft" (1885; incorporated later into his *Methode der Musikgeschichte*, 1919) was a logical outgrowth of the methodology that he and his contemporaries employed, and it reflects not only his thought, but also his rationalistic inheritance from earlier nineteenth-century historians.

In general, Adler (1885–1941) grouped under historical musicology the common activities of researchers that reveal aspects of the history of music through time, such as the study and deciphering of

3

old musical notations, the translation of early documents, the history of musical forms in all their various stages, and any similar study that seeks to place music within a historical context or within a given period. Systematic musicology was characterized as embracing study of the "laws" that govern research in branches such as acoustics, psychophysiology, psychology, aesthetics, and the principles of education in music. He and all other scholars since realize that many parts of each division cross and recross between the historical and the systematic.

The historical and systematic orientations are often seen as the two principal axes that organize scholarly thought. Although the axes may be represented horizontally and vertically (as historical and systematic, respectively) the intersections of the resulting historico-systematic grid are numerous and the main divisions that the lines represent should be understood as complementary, not as exclusive or totally separate endeavors.

Adler's schematic aimed at exhaustively organizing the field and subfields of research, and his hierarchies of areas of study must be regarded as the most important and influential organization of musicology, incorporating its explicit and implicit aims. It was the blueprint that guided scholars for the first half of the twentieth century, appearing most clearly in a book by Glen Haydon (1896–1966). His *Introduction to Musicology* was influential in its time in the United States and abroad, and was the first extensive description of the field of research by an American, although a number of less comprehensive statements had been made earlier. Adler's view, rarely accepted in its entirety, has been subjected to additions, deletions, and redrawings since it was first offered, though the types of research described have been carried forward without abatement, albeit almost always with refinements in method and technique. It might be fair to say that musicologists have, since Adler, gone about their work aware of the problems of organizing a field of learning, while at the same time doing the immense original research that itself reorganizes the discipline. The lack of a complete philosophy of musicology has rarely impeded the research itself. The published work of scholars in the early decades of the twentieth century continued in the traditions of research carried on before and after Adler's statement. What differences can be observed are ones of detail and breadth, not those of basic assumptions that determine the direction of the work.

Nevertheless—perhaps even because of the great quantity and high quality of musicological research—contemporary scholars are again reflecting, to a significant degree, on the organization and meaning of their research activities. The historical and systematic axes still dominate, in general, as by nature they do in almost all humanistic research; but the ultimate purpose of some activities is being questioned, the essential values challenged.

Scholars in music have instigated or endured certain divisions in the general field of research, notably the division of music research into musicology and ethnomusicology (formerly termed comparative musicology). It should be noted that not all specialists in either field are happy about either the division or the term *ethnomusicology*. As musicology usually denotes the Western European artistic tradition that is typically traced from Classical Greek times to the present, ethnomusicology usually denotes a study of orally transmitted music, the music of nonliterate or primitive societies, and music of cultures whose musical styles lie outside the European fine art heritage. How to deal with and explain these musics, and how to relate them and the powerfully dominating Western musical ideas, are fundamental problems for both musicologists and ethnomusicologists as they work towards concepts of music as a phenomenon of human life and expression. A gap—some would say a genuine schism—lies between the two disciplines, and attempts to close it and meld the groups have been unsuccessful. Some musicologists maintain that a lack of methodological rigor weakens ethnomusicological work; some ethnomusicologists identify a failure to place music in the proper cultural framework as a primary deficiency of musicologists' research.

Musicology, by Frank L. Harrison, Mantle Hood, and Claude Palisca, vitalized discussion of the field of learning, especially as practiced in the United States. The essayists—a medievalist and ethnomusicologist, an ethnomusicologist, and a historical musicologist, respectively—proved to be lodestones for immediate praise and criticism. First, simply by appearing in a series named Humanistic Scholarship in America, the book instantly reconfirmed musical scholarship's place within the broadest conception of human activities. Second, by including the thought of a leading ethnomusicologist, an implicit plea was made for uniting all musical research under the title *Musicology*. In his contribution, "American Scholarship in Western Music," Palisca sees musicology as work carried on mainly (but not entirely) under the heading of music history, a notion that has drawn criticism and praise. Some criticism arises because of his exclusionary view that acoustics, physiology, and other sciences are not within the proper scope of musicology, although they do remain related and relevant. By saying that "the musicologist is first and foremost a historian" and by adding that the scholar is not *only* a historian, Palisca gives great breadth to the researcher's activities—and on a worldwide basis, a point sometimes misunderstood by his critics.

Alan Merriam (1923–80), an anthropologist by profession, argues in *The Anthropology of Music* that since the study of humanity in all its contexts is indeed the work of anthropology and its allied sciences, an anthropological approach may be a key to unite the polarized fields of ethnomusicology and musicology. As Gilbert Chase notes in "American Musicology and the Social Sciences," Glen Haydon came remarkably close to Merriam's essential notion that anthropology holds important keys to developing a sound scheme for the entire range of scholarly inquiry in music. Chase, in other writings as well and joined by John Blacking and others, is generally aligned with Merriam in an anthropological-sociological conceptualization. Walter Wiora, in *The Four Ages of Music*, seeks a universal design for viewing music and its history, but the brevity and incompleteness of his argument casts doubt upon its validity.

American musicologists have shared with their foreign colleagues an interest in determining the values that are inherent in their work, just as Adler, Hugo Riemann (1849–1919), and other early pioneers did. There is an astonishing degree of interest today in providing guiding philosophies and schemata, though the plans are typically less broadly inclusive of all scholarly activities in music than those of European counterparts. Contemporary comment seems to be less interested in a unified field theory such as Adler's—with the notable exception of Charles Seeger—than in a redirection of the ends of musicological research.

The study of Western music still largely depends on musical scores, but, to use Palisca's pithy phrase, "the blind pursuit of the banner of style criticism" is being questioned. Style criticism, as defined and utilized by many scholars in this century, depends on detailed analysis of the elements of a composition, directed towards the goal of understanding how the music of a composer, era, or genre works, towards defining the essential qualities of the music in a rigorous, systematic, even scientific way. Hugo Riemann and Guido Adler laid the foundations for style criticism, seeing in such work the essential task for scholars in their efforts to trace and relate evolving—at least changing—musical styles, as the primary means of telling the history of music. Nowadays, say the critics of Riemann and his disciples, contextual and aesthetic considerations are too often left out of the researcher's methodology, aims, and writings, and too often the report is only enumerative or descriptive, devoid of interpretation, criticism, and historical context.

The extraordinary growth of musicology since World War II, most especially in the United States, to whom leadership in research has passed, is marked not only by quantity and breadth of subject but increasingly by new methodology and critical approaches, and by disagreement from within as well. The influx of scholars fleeing Nazism in the thirties and forties energized the young American branch of the discipline, and the teaching and research of these emigrés provided models and inspiration; the quickening force they exerted is difficult to overestimate. The differences in a governing philosophy of musicology that are now arising do not necessarily derive from opposing views of the basic procedures of editing, analysis, historical research, and so forth, but from a challenge to the ultimate ends of musicological work that once were thought securely defined.

One of the areas demanding attention is the relationship of musicology to performance, which—though sometimes misunderstood— is necessarily close. Through editions and through the studies of how music was performed in its time of origin (performance practices), through the study of the history of musical instruments (organology), through the study of historical settings in which music was presented (from medieval castle halls to Wagner's Bayreuth), and through the study of old tuning systems—among many examples—musicologists offer to performers standards of authenticity previously not thought possible, as music is recreated in modern performances. They also offer an ever-expanding repertory of music for the performer's selection. Performance is an essential consideration for much musicological work, but the humanist's inquiry remains a more than equal partner. Contemporary debate often centers around the extent to which old music should be recreated, the extent to which authenticity should be sought, given modern ears and modern society, and the ultimately impossible achievement of total "recreation."

Few scholars argue against cultivation of performance-oriented research. Many actively combine performance participation with their scholarship, thus following along the lines advocated by Blume and older scholars such as Adler and Riemann, who consistently view performance considerations as an essential part of the research view of the scholar, including personal participation. Richard Taruskin, a prominent younger member of a group of performer-scholars, presents a stimulating view of how musicology should relate to performance. His questioning of the degree to which authenticity should reign supreme and to what degree a "reconstructionist" attitude should prevail, will undoubtedly be questioned in turn by many scholars and performers.

Musicology in service to performers is the dominant theme in *Musicology*, by Denis Stevens. Although Stevens tends to understate the aspects of pure research in musicology and overplay the destiny of musicology as residing in the service to performance, he nonetheless joins the ranks of those advocating what might be termed applied musicology. Edward Kottick reviews the place of the *collegium musicum* within the training of scholars, properly a concern of many who are organizing the field.

Because music is an art, a number of scholars—Joseph Kerman, in particular—have offered the concept of criticism as a final governing factor in the way interpretations and reports of research are made. Historical context, causality, value, and the language used in writing about music are all components of the musicologist's narratives. Analysis must not be seen as an end, especially enumerative analysis that describes "facts" about music's structure and form; it should be seen as a means towards establishing value and understanding for the music under consideration. Analytic criticism tends to be the term that best satisfies the requirements of those devoted to analysis as an essential tool, but who also seek interpretation and consequent expression of value. Another effort to reorder the ends of musicological research concerns how music is to be described and the role that explicative analysis plays in scholarly discourse.

Within, roughly, the two decades of 1960–80, the purposes, character, and methods of musicology in the United States, and with full implications for other countries as well, have been debated energetically in the setting of annual meetings of the American Musicological Society; *Musicology*, by Harrison, Hood, and Palisca (1963), may be seen as the primary catalyst. The debates have focused attention on how scholars see themselves within a field of inquiry. Kerman has, since 1964, been the most articulate advocate for a reshaping of research, one that seeks to establish criticism as the end result of musicological work. Critics, notably his principal respondent, Edward Lowinsky, see in such efforts a negating of the value of much scholarly activity that may be an end in itself, for example, bibliography, aspects of the process of preparing editions of music, and other pursuits that employ criticism very little or not at all.

Leo Treitler, searching for a comprehensive approach to understanding music "*in* and not *of* the past," is developing for scholars a mode of thinking that draws on work in linguistic theory, in philosophy, and on concepts in criticism. He argues that the mode and aims of the analytic process chosen by the scholar influence and determine what is discovered, and that any mode of analysis that hinders illumination of a given music's context is suspect, even "antihistorical." He calls for a consideration of music in all of its historical contexts, and pleads for development, or perhaps recapture, of a language that represents in words the expressive elements in music, much along the lines of Peter Kivy in *The Corded Shell.* Kivy also seeks a theory of musical expression and aesthetics, and he calls for a language to account for expressivity in music. His orientation derives from theories of musical expression in the seventeenth and eighteenth centuries, times that were rich in attempts to develop overarching theories of expression in music. The result of this orientation is an "emotive criticism of music," a means whereby the "criteria of human expressiveness can be identified with those of human expression. . . ."

Since 1956, when he published *Emotion and Meaning in Music,* the ideas of Leonard Meyer have helped direct and shape discussion of what language and analytic theory might best be used to describe expressive elements in music. Meyer's attention to a fair sampling of the musics of the world—his ethnomusicological view—seems to nod in the direction of Seeger's unified field theory. It is important to note that Meyer, as well as Treitler and Kivy, among many others, never isolate their theories and constructs from the music itself: their explanations and proposals always use concrete musical examples to illustrate specific ideas and notions.

The issues of how musical scholars should view the general field of research and the relative values among its subfields and methodologies still are the subject of debate, nationally and internationally. For example, the International Musicological Society (IMS), at congresses in 1977 and 1982, sought the most comprehensive format for papers and discussion by adopting themes that stressed "world music." At the 1982 congress of the IMS, Ludwig Finscher, the president, sounded a cautionary note. He observed that, in his view, the Strasbourg conference treated ethnomusicology less well than in 1977. Which is mainly to note here that the tug between the two areas continues.

As recently as 1981 the American Musicological Society (AMS) organized a special forum whose papers were judged so provocative of thought that immediate publication has ensued. The publication, *Musicology in the 1980s* (Holoman, ed.), finds a good part of its relevance and meaning as a long-delayed response to the Kerman-Lowinsky debate of 1964 and the publication of Harrison/Hood/Palisca's *Musicology* in 1963. The report of the AMS forum is in two parts: "Current Methodology: Opportunities and Limitations" and "The Musicologist Today and in the Future." Although a schematic design for musicology was neither sought nor accidentally attained, the statements reveal an increasingly questioning attitude of scholars towards both methods and goals. The canonized virtues of style criticism and enumerative analysis and description, for example, are again somewhat desanctified. The processes and roles of analysis are reexamined, and the burgeoning interests in iconography and music within the history of ideas are discussed critically.

The inaugural issue of *The Journal of Musicology* (January 1982)—like the AMS forum—uses "Musicology in the 1980s: Points of Arrival and Goals" as a rubric for a dozen articles that are descriptive and prescriptive in relation to the general field of musicology. Taken together, they review scholarly progress in the United States. Separately, they discern flaws in musicology's perception of itself, some principal defects lying in lack of breadth, occasional superficiality of research, and, by implication, too narrow a view of music within the human context. The contributors do reaffirm the traditional roles of analysis, criticism, philological source criticism, and the traditional research areas, particularly as desiderata in various eras are noted.

Although attempts to provide complete, Adlerian schematics are out of fashion in presentday musicology, one scholar in particular— Charles Seeger (1886–1979)—persisted in trying to develop a multi-faceted model. Seeger repeatedly presented brilliant, praised, but largely unaccepted proposals for a unified field theory for music and its scholarship. The grandeur and sweep of his models are unmatched among modern scholars. He holds a unique position in the academy by virtue of his work as historian, philosopher, musicologist, ethnomusicologist, laboratory scientist, and first American teacher of musicology (at Berkeley). He, as few others, took Adler's original outline of the field and enlarged its scope according to the changes in thinking and methodology that have been contributed in the twentieth century. Seeger rather tenaciously acknowledges Adler's essential soundness and sets about to modify rather than reject. He regularly opposes the division of research into the two disciplines of musicology and ethnomusicology. He contends that since all musics are a part of human activities, using *ethnomusicology* to refer to music other than one's own clouds the issue by inadvertently establishing false values and relationships. Furthermore, Seeger conceives the broadest possible definition for music itself, devoid of initial comparative evaluations, other than what might be interpreted as the general value that a given culture ascribes to its own music. Such an "absence-of-assigned-value" approach has been an essential part of studies in the history of American music, especially as presented by Gilbert Chase, a supporter of Seeger's world view. Although Seeger's efforts in formulating a unified field theory for scholarship have not resulted in general acceptance, his work has undoubtedly contributed much to the renewal of interest in how the disciplines and their subdivisions are related and defined.

Intense—some say narrow—specialization, not only between the main branches of musicology and ethnomusicology but also in the many subdivisions, has led to comment not unlike that of C. P. Snow in *The Two Cultures and the Scientific Revolution* (New York: Cambridge Univ. Pr., 1959). As Snow bemoaned the fact that a gap of communication lay between science and other intellectual activities, so musicologists often find gaps of both communication and relevance among the scholars in music. What is sometimes seen as crippling specialization is largely a postwar phenomenon, and older scholars such as Friedrich Blume (1893–1975) have warned against alienation of research from the broad view of music history. The efforts of Treitler and others to place music in contexts argue for specialization to at least find relevance to the broad stream of music history.

During the last decade of his life Blume made two forceful pleas, not explicitly against specialization as such but for three considerations: first, for expansion of research activities into more of the byways of music history, including the lesser composers. (Marxist scholars tend to disagree. They hold that musicology's most pressing task is to develop comprehensive theories for historiography and musicology, thereby enabling scholars to deal more effectively with data already at hand.) Second, he hoped for a lessening of the hypnotic fascination for the works of the great masters, when there are so many gaps in our knowledge. Third, Blume, who himself may have closed the era of great humanist encyclopedists in music, pleaded for research of breadth and scope and for comprehensive surveys, knowing full well that such research has to be founded on detailed and usually narrow studies, but nonetheless still objecting to "outrageous perfectionism." The tone of Blume's exhortation finds resonance in comments from Alexander Ringer to the effect that musicology "made a veritable fetish of objectivity" in striving to find its place "in an academic environment that was dominated by the exact sciences." And Ringer's criticism is echoed, in turn, in those statements offering reexaminations of how we deal with the expressive content of music.

Muted appeals asking that musical scholarship in America have more of an effect on precollege students have had little effect (see Palisca and Lippman, among others). This contrasts with some efforts in Europe where the geographic problems are smaller and the cultural climate more amenable to influence. The frequent lack of a humanistic orientation in American college students in some ways affects their breadth of learning as they become historians. These views must be taken with caution, however: it is incontestable that some of the best and most broadly based contemporary research is by American musicologists, born and trained.

The decade of the 1970s and the first years of the 1980s show concern about how the field of research is conceptualized, how scholars report their work, and about the historiography of musicology. Music historiography has been repeatedly mentioned in this overview of the discipline; it receives extended treatment in chapter 2.

Acta Musicologica, Basel: Bärenreiter-Verlag, 1928– . (The journal of the International Musicological Society has included for a number of years a series of articles reporting on musicological activity in various countries. In addition to bibliographic coverage and a report of the activities in a given country, the series offers a kind of pulse-taking of the state of the discipline.)

Adler, Guido. *Methode der Musikgeschichte*. Leipzig: Breitkopf & Härtel, 1919.

———. *Der Stil in der Musik*. Leipzig: Breitkopf & Härtel, 1911. 2nd ed., 1929.

———. "Umfang, Methode, und Ziel der Musikwissenschaft." *Vierteljahrschrift für Musikwissenschaft* 1 (1885): 5–20.

Arnold, Denis. "The Profession of Musical Scholarship." In *Modern Musical Scholarship*, pp. 1–14. Ed. by Edward Olleson. Boston: Oriel Pr., 1980.

Blacking, John. *How Musical Is Man?* Seattle: Univ. of Washington Pr., 1973.

Blume, Friedrich. "Historische Musikforschung in der Gegenwart." In International Musicological Soc., *Report of the Tenth Congress, Ljubljana 1967*, v. 1, pp. 13–25. Ed. by Dragotin Cvetko. 2v. Kassel: Bärenreiter-Verlag, 1970.

————. "Musical Scholarship Today." In Brook, *Perspectives in Musicology*.

Brook, Barry, ed. *Perspectives in Musicology. The Inaugural Lectures of the Ph.D. Program at the City University of New York*. New York: Norton, 1972. (See especially the addresses of Friedrich Blume, Gilbert Chase, Vincent Duckles, Paul Henry Lang, and Gustave Reese.)

Bukofzer, Manfred. *The Place of Musicology in American Institutions of Higher Learning*. New York: Liberal Arts Pr., 1957.

Chailley, Jacques, ed. *Précis de musicologie*. Paris: Presses Universitaire de France, 1958. (New edition in preparation.)

Chase, Gilbert. "American Musicology and the Social Sciences." In Brook, *Perspectives in Musicology*.

————. "Musicology, History, and Anthropology: Current Thoughts." In Grubbs, *Current Thought in Musicology*.

Chrysander, Friedrich. "Vorwort und Einleitung." *Jahrbücher für musikalische Wissenschaft* 1(1863): 9–16.

Dahlhaus, Carl. *Esthetics of Music*. Tr. by William W. Austin. New York: Cambridge Univ. Pr., 1982.

Dreyfus, Laurence. "Early Music Defended against Its Devotees: A Theory of Historical Performance in the Twentieth Century." *The Musical Quarterly* 69 (1983): 297–322.

Grubbs, John, ed. *Current Thought in Musicology*. Austin: Univ. of Texas Pr., 1976. (See especially the articles by Gilbert Chase, Vincent Duckles, and Charles Seeger.)

Harrison, Frank L., Mantle Hood, and Claude Palisca. *Musicology*. Englewood Cliffs, N.J.: Prentice-Hall, 1963.

Haydon, Glen. *Introduction to Musicology. A Survey of the Fields, Systematic and Historical, of Musical Knowledge and Research*. New York: Prentice-Hall, 1941.

Holoman, D. Kern, and Claude Palisca, eds. *Musicology in the 1980s: Methods, Goals, Opportunities*. New York: Da Capo, 1982. (See especially the articles by Claude Palisca, Maria Rika Maniates, Joseph Kerman, Leo Treitler, and Richard Taruskin.)

Hood, Mantle. *The Ethnomusicologist*. Rev. ed. Kent, Ohio: Kent State Univ. Pr., 1983.

International Musicological Society. *Report of the Eighth Congress, New York 1961*. Ed. by Jan LaRue. 2v. Kassel: Bärenreiter-Verlag, 1962. (See especially "The Employment of Sociological Methods in Music History," v.2, pp. 146–49, and related papers, v. 1.)

Kerman, Joseph. "A Profile for American Musicology." *Journal of the American Musicological Society* 18 (1965): 61–69.

Kivy, Peter. "*The Corded Shell*": *Reflections on Musical Expression*. Princeton Essays on the Arts, 9. Princeton: Princeton Univ. Pr., 1980.

Kottick, Edward. *The Collegium: A Handbook*. Stoning, Conn.: October House, 1977.

Lippman, Edward. *A Humanistic Philosophy of Music*. New York: New York Univ. Pr., 1977.

————. "What Should Musicology Be?" *Current Musicology* pp. 55–60 (Spring 1965).

Lowinsky, Edward. "Character and Purposes of American Musicology: A Reply to Joseph Kerman." *Journal of the American Musicological Society* 18 (1965): 222–34.

Maniates, Maria Rika. "Applications of the History of Ideas to Music (II)." *The Musical Quarterly* 69 (1983): 62–84.

Merriam, Alan. *The Anthropology of Music.* Evanston, Ill.: Northwestern Univ. Pr., 1964.

Meyer, Leonard. *Emotion and Meaning in Music.* Chicago: Univ. of Chicago Pr., 1956.

"Musicology in the 1980s: Points of Arrival and Goals." *The Journal of Musicology* 1 (1982): 1–66. (Articles by a dozen American musicologists; see especially the contributions by Paul Henry Lang, James Haar, Alejandro E. Planchart, and Gilbert Chase.)

"Musicology Today." In International Musicological Soc., *Report of the Eleventh Congress, Copenhagen 1972,* v. 1, pp. 167–218. Ed. by Henrik Glahn et al. 2v. Copenhagen: Wilhelm Hansen, 1974. (Formal papers and round table discussion.)

Nettl, Bruno. *The Study of Ethnomusicology: Twenty-nine Issues and Concepts.* Urbana: Univ. of Illinois Pr., 1983.

————. *Theory and Method in Ethnomusicology.* Glencoe, Ill.: Free Pr., 1964.

Olleson, Edward, ed. *Modern Musical Scholarship.* Boston: Oriel Pr., 1980.

Palisca, Claude. "Reflections on Musical Scholarship in the 1960s." In *Anthropological and Historical Sciences, Aesthetics and the Sciences of Art,* v. 1, pt. 2, sec. III, pp. 791–802. Ed. by Jacques Havet. The Hague: Mouton, for UNESCO, 1978. Reprinted in Holoman, *Musicology in the 1980s.*

Price, Kingsley, ed. *On Criticizing Music: Five Philosophical Perspectives.* Baltimore: Johns Hopkins Univ. Pr., 1981. (Contains: Charles Rosen, "Influence: Plagiarism and Inspiration"; Joseph Kerman, "The State of Academic Music Criticism" (revision of "How We Got into Analysis, and How to Get Out," in *Critical Inquiry* 7 (1980): 311–31); Monroe C. Beardsley, "Understanding Music"; Rose R. Subotnik, "Romantic Music as Post-Kantian Critique: Classicism, Romanticism, and the Concept of the Semiotic Universe"; Karl Aschenbrenner, "Music Criticism: Practice and Malpractice.")

Riemann, Hugo. *Grundriss der Musikwissenschaft.* Wissenschaft und Bildung, 34. Leipzig: Quelle & Meyer, 1908. 4th ed., ed. by Johannes Wolf, 1928.

Ringer, Alexander. "A Question of Commitment." In "Musicology Today."

Seeger, Charles. *Studies in Musicology, 1935–1975.* Berkeley and Los Angeles: Univ. of California Pr., 1977. (Selected essays by Seeger, some rewritten or edited.)

Spiess, Lincoln, ed. *Historical Musicology.* Musicological Studies, 4. New York: Institute of Medieval Music, 1963.

Stevens, Denis. *Musicology; A Practical Guide.* London: Macdonald Futura, 1980.

Taruskin, Richard. "The Musicologist and the Performer," in Holoman, *Musicology in the 1980s*, pp. 101–17.

Tomlinson, Gary. "The Web of Culture: A Context for Musicology." *19th-Century Music* 7 (1984): 350–62.

Treitler, Leo. " 'To Worship That Celestial Sound': Motives for Analysis." *The Journal of Musicology* 1 (1982): 153–70.

———. "What Kind of Story Is History?" *19th-Century Music* 7 (1984): 363–73.

Wiora, Walter. *The Four Ages of Music*. Tr. by M. D. Herter Norton. New York: Norton, 1965. (Tr. of *Die vier Weltalter der Musik*.)

2

The Ways and Means
of Musicology

The origins of modern music historiography lie in the eighteenth century. Although philosophers, composers, theorists, and a host of other writers before the Enlightenment had written more or less systematically about music and had commented on its history, it was not until the early and middle decades of the eighteenth century that a coherent and rational approach to music historiography began to develop, as indeed it did in most areas of learning.

Towards the middle of the 1700s writers began to realize that analysis of styles, examination of primary sources, and—above all—the processes of verification and accuracy had to play important roles in any determination or speculation about music and how it came to be what it is. This era saw the final shucking of the notions that either divine intervention or natural origins had to serve as "Prime Mover" in the activities of humanity, whether they be artistic, technological, political, or whatever. The humanism of the Renaissance, with its abiding interest in human beings, might be seen as having moved inexorably to a time when reason, abiding confidence in human rationality, was the guiding principle.

In a spirit identical to that which compelled the great French Encyclopedists, the music historians of the eighteenth century sought to gather all musical knowledge, distill it, examine it systematically and scientifically, and reveal the progress of music. The idea that music had moved more or less continuously from primitive to advanced stages, from inferior to superior music, is present—usually to a great degree—in practically all writings on music in the eighteenth century. Indeed, such an evolutionary, or genetic, concept has tended to

16

dominate music historiography until modern times. Not until the twentieth century, when the minor composers in music history are often studied as intensely as the major ones, has the evolutionary concept come close to being abandoned, along with certain philosophical theories of value in music and its historiography.

While developing the early techniques of examining sources, that is, establishing a philological basis for portraying music history, the early historians of music had little timidity in expressing their opinions about the music itself. In general, the explicit (or implicit) theme is that humans have struggled to perfect music, and the best music is that of the eighteenth century. The two centuries since the Age of Reason have established a more dispassionate historiography for music.

Remarkably, eighteenth-century music historians, and other writers as well, wrote about what today we would call world music; that is, they included music outside the European artistic tradition. Thus, while detailing as far as possible the progress of music from antiquity and the Middle Ages to their time, they often went to great lengths to rationalize folk and primitive music. Jean-Jacques Rousseau (1712–78), for example, mentions folk and ethnic (including North American Indian) music in his *Dictionary*.

The ground for eighteenth-century music historical writings was prepared by such works as the *Traité de l'harmonie* (1722) of Jean-Phillipe Rameau (1683–1764). In this work, and others that followed in the next four decades, Rameau fundamentally reshaped music theory. He combines the science of acoustics with a theoretical system to account for harmony (chords and their inversions), consonance and dissonance, and major and minor tonalities. His arguments, refined by successors, remained dominant until the disintegration of tonality in the twentieth century. Rameau's work ranks with the greatest intellectual achievements of music theorists, with, for instance, that of Tinctoris in the late fifteenth and Zarlino in the middle sixteenth century. Present-day scholars—historians and theorists—still mine Rameau's treatises as they seek to determine and understand the principles of music governed by tonality.

Two more publications from about the same time as Rameau's *Traité* that wielded a comparable influence on early music historiography are by Johann Mattheson (1681–1764): *Der vollkommene Capellmeister* (1739) and *Grundlage einer Ehren-Pforte* (1740). The former is noted for its breadth and detail of what Mattheson believes the first-rate musician should know and be able to do, and for its position as a principal source for the doctrine of musical affections

(*Affektenlehre*). This doctrine holds that specific musical idioms and styles can elicit specific human emotions and reactions; that is, it is a musical rhetoric; the topic is of considerable contemporary interest among musicologists. Mattheson's *Grundlage* is a compilation of biographies of deceased and living musicians, and it reflects a generally careful methodology of research. He drew as far as possible on what he considered to be authentic documents and on correspondence with those still living or living within the memory of others. If the technology had been available, no doubt he would have qualified as an oral historian.

The first large-scale histories of music come from the Enlightenment, those by Charles Burney (1726–1814), *A General History of Music*, and John Hawkins (1719–89), *A General History of the Science and Practice of Music*. Hawkins's five volumes were published entire in 1776; Burney's four volumes over thirteen years, 1776–89. Characteristic of the era, a lively debate regarding the merits of each ensued; contemporary and modern thought unquestionably gives the greater merit to Burney, a professional musician, well-traveled and sensitive. Hawkins, a lawyer, was musically talented, resourceful, and industrious, but simply lacked Burney's superior gifts. Burney's judgment that music is but an innocent diversion, an ornament in the life of men and women, rankled then as now, although his opinion was shared by many; Hawkins's dismissal of all non-Western music as barbaric was unworthy of his acknowledged ability and intellect.

Essentially all of the elements of modern scholarship appear in these two histories: use of original sources; presentation of earlier music in notation and in score formats that modern musicians can easily read; profuse use of illustrations; the scholarly appurtenances of footnotes, bibliographic citations, and indexes; evaluative and interpretive opinion; quotation—sometimes very extensive—from original sources, oftentimes in lengthy translations; and editions of entire compositions (especially in Hawkins) that provide something of a musical supplement. From the time that the two histories were issued until today, they have continued to serve as invaluable resources for practically all historians of music.

Two other histories of music roughly coeval with Hawkins and Burney, and equally products of the Enlightenment, are the *Storia della Musica* (3v., 1761–81) by Giovanni Battista Martini (1706–84) and the *Allgemeine Geschichte der Musik* (2v., 1788–1801), by Johann Nikolaus Forkel (1749–1818). Unlike both Burney and Hawkins, neither Martini nor Forkel completed their planned surveys of the entire history of music.

Martini's three large volumes trace the history of music only through ancient Greek times. The sheer bulk of his work far outweighs the musical fragments that were available to him, although his volumes do bespeak a formidable attempt to grapple with ancient music theory. Forkel, on the other hand, does discuss music up to the end of the sixteenth century. And, more importantly, he surpasses his three contemporaries in his superior systematic and controlled approach to the telling of music history. Most especially, Forkel established standards of bibliography that have generally prevailed until modern times. And perhaps more than any previous scholar, he carefully evaluated the bibliography that was available to him through painstaking examination and criticism. Modern music historiography and its reliance on sound bibliographic control can be said to begin with Forkel.

A confluence of forces and interests seems to appear in the early and middle decades of the nineteenth century, leading directly to the founding of modern music research. Sound philological approaches were established; the music of J. S. Bach was rediscovered, provoking interest in the music of all earlier times; the romantic movement caused scholars and others to look longingly—if often incorrectly—at the past; and various reform movements in church music created a desire to restore that music to what was considered past glory by reusing former aesthetic ideals in composing new music. Important early milestones in nineteenth-century music historiography are the first scholarly journals, the first notable biographic monographs in music such as Forkel's Bach (1802), Carl Winterfeld's Gabrieli (1834), Otto Jahn's Mozart (1856–59), and Alexander Thayer's Beethoven (1866–79), as well as the beginning of the first complete edition of Bach's works in 1851.

François-Joseph Fétis (1784–1871), though known to modern scholars primarily as the compiler of *Biographie universelle des musiciens*, was in many respects forward-looking in his *Histoire générale de la musique* (1869–76). The history is among the largest essayed since those of Hawkins and Burney a century earlier. In Fétis's history, "progress" is now totally discarded and historiography is based firmly on investigation of the changes scholars can discern in music's history. Influenced perhaps by the growing interest in orientalism and other non-Western cultures, Fétis seeks to expand the music scholar's role to all music systems. Hugo Riemann, though offering a varying methodology (see chapter 1), reflects—as Fétis—a solid conviction that stylistic change is the key element in music historiography.

Our understanding of nineteenth-century music historiography, and its continuing influence, has been notably enhanced by the work of Vincent Duckles. He interprets music historiography as "not merely the writing of music history, but the historical examination of all the processes of musical scholarship." He continues to draw attention to both historiography and the history of musicology, particularly through tracing the bibliographic history of the discipline. By identifying the underlying themes of scholarly publications through musicology's relatively short life, Duckles comes close to characterizing the evolution of music research. By identifying the natural biases of early scholars as well as their genius, he presents cogent reasons why the field has developed as it has. A signal service of his approach lies in reinforming colleagues and students of the basically sound foundations upon which their work rests.

Still another service offered by Duckles is his identification of specific schools of historical thought that have dominated at certain times and then been abandoned, or continued with modification. For example, in "Patterns in the Historiography of 19th-Century Music," Duckles distinguishes between two approaches that were (and still are) problems to music historians: the cultural-sociological and formalistic-structural. The former finds meaning and value within the context of a music; the latter, in "the forms and structures inherent in the nature of the medium." These two approaches or trends are identified by Duckles as persisting until the end of the nineteenth century and as being heavily influential on those scholars who produced the basic bibliography of editions and monographs at the turn of the century.

Since the beginning of the twentieth century and most particularly since the 1940s, literally thousands of editions and studies have appeared, and they incorporate less of a new historiographical orientation than they do a wealth of new data and interpretation. Whereas the earlier musicologist may have felt—and been—competent to write a history of music from its origins to the present, since World War II it simply is no longer within the grasp of an individual to do so. Indeed, it may be fair to say that the single-author comprehensive histories of music effectively ended with the *Geschichte der Musik* (vols. 1–3, 1862–68) of August Wilhelm Ambros (1816–76), who himself carried the work only into seventeenth-century music history, the remainder of the study being completed by colleagues; unlike the history of Fétis, Ambros's cultural approach and more solid research sustained its place in scholarship through a third edition (5v., 1887–1911). The occasional single-author history of today tends to be the comprehensive textbook, such as *A History of Western Music*, by Donald J. Grout; but the comprehensive textbook may also be the effort of several specialists, such as the *Schirmer History of Music*, edited by Leonie Rosenstiel.

The ambitious, multivolume collaborative historical surveys that begin to appear early in the century illustrate the changes in musicology's historiography. Among these works are the *Handbuch der Musikwissenschaft* (13v. in 10, 1927–31), edited by Ernst Bücken (1884–1949) and *The Oxford History of Music* (6v., 1901–5) with its subsequent heavily revised editions (by new authors) in 1928–34 and 1954– . Style criticism, especially as demonstrated by German musicology, joined with cultural history makes much of the writing in the *Handbuch* of interest today, though many historical details are out-of-date. The first edition of the *Oxford History* reflected the maturation of English scholarship in a generally uniform viewpoint and method; in the last edition it might be said that data seem to have outstripped interpretation and synthesis, resulting in some contributions being brilliant summations, some less so.

Data synthesis is a clear hallmark of much twentieth-century historiography, particularly in American musicology. The two most important contributions of Gustave Reese (1899–1977), *Music in the Middle Ages* (1940) and *Music in the Renaissance* (1954; rev. ed., 1959), offer unique contributions to the study of Western music in those eras. Drawing on practically all published work—editions of music as well as monographic and periodical literature—Reese offers (as of their publication dates) state-of-the-art summations that provide both findings of past research and judicious judgments of his own. The books had an enormous influence on both mature and younger scholars and have done as much as any other publications to establish medieval and Renaissance studies as particular areas of excellence in America.

If the synthesis of data seems to have been Reese's special contribution to musicology and its historiography, breadth of interpretation belongs to Paul Henry Lang (1901–), whose *Music in Western Civilization* is unique in twentieth-century publishing. Lang's contribution is as much a cultural history of music as it is a tracing of the specific events in music's history. The interpretive and cultural nature of Lang's approach in this book and elsewhere continues to provide a model and goal for researchers and music historiographers in the late decades of this century.

Duckles's "cultural-sociological" orientation looms large in many musicologists' narratives of the history of American music. In general, studies in American music have relied much more heavily on context than on style criticism or aesthetic value. For example, Gilbert Chase's first two editions of *America's Music* clearly incorporated his continuing interest in contextual history and it is symptomatic that the forthcoming third edition will bear the subtitle, "A Cultural Interpretation."

By and large, musicologists have proved unable to shake fully either all traces of a lingering nineteenth-century Darwinism or remnants of *Geistesgeschichte*. Although the movement of music history is no longer seen as passing through stages of growth that lead to "better" or "more complex" music, scholars seem unwilling to remove charged words and phrases such as "influenced," "resulted in," "advanced," or "declined" from their descriptive vocabularies. Paradoxically, while discarding attempts to define spiritual unities in the various eras, scholars are searching with renewed energy for musical and extramusical forces or stylistic elements that can serve to reveal unity and cohesion in music of a given time or place.

Scholars use ordinary language to write about music, although, of course, the technical jargon of music and history is necessarily included. An essential problem, as Donald J. Grout has pointed out in "Current Historiography and Music History," is to understand the values of the past, insofar as the modern writer is able to do so, without losing the important level of objectivity that should be maintained. Music historians—as all humanists—have to be selective in the choice of materials to be examined and the facts to be described, and in the weight they give to facts in interpretations and evaluations.

Arthur Mendel (1905–79), in "Evidence and Explanation," states that musicologists are interested in facts and relationships, and "in musical works themselves, as individual structures and as objects of delight." Drawing on the ideas of a number of historians and philosophers outside music—such as Benedetto Croce, Isaiah Berlin, Karl R. Popper, R. G. Collingwood, and Carl Hempel—Mendel challenges colleagues to put the empirical elements of their work in proper perspective; that is, to accept empiricism as an essential part of research in music but not to overplay its role. In addition, scholars must not omit what he terms the "fictive" part of historical narrative, the part that derives from "insight and imagination." He adopts

Croce's well-known instruction to the effect that if one wishes "to understand the true history of a neolithic Ligurian or Sicilian," then one must try to become a neolithic Ligurian or Sicilian; one must enter the Ligurian's mind, his mental processes. To arrange only the Ligurian's relics (to arrange only the elements of music or historical facts) is only to create "a tidy order," not history. Analysis provides much significant information, but Mendel argues that something beyond analysis and historical fact still remains, something still puzzles the musicologist: "Perhaps our delight in the work [the composition] consists partly in being baffled by it, and perhaps there is no theoretical reason to believe that analysis cannot eventually remove our bafflement: but then it would at the same time have removed our delight." Mendel further argues that the musicologist who has lost touch with the aesthetic component in music has indeed lost touch with its history as well.

Musicologists' historiographic methodology tends to be cautious of linear explanation, whereby one event results from, or is conditioned by, some earlier event; whereby an event is explained by referring to earlier ones. Mendel's caution against "pre-dated prediction" equates roughly with Grout's "post-dated prediction," although the latter tends to justify such explanation as valuable since historians must investigate the surroundings of a historical event, such as the creation of a composition.

Carl Dahlhaus's *Grundlagen der Musikgeschichte* (1967) is now available in a fine translation by J. B. Robinson, as *Foundations of Music History* (1983). Until now the work has been largely ignored by English-speaking scholars, owing partly to its density of thought and partly to the complexity of its German philosophical heritage and style. Because the translation will undoubtedly have an important influence on concepts of music historiography outside German-speaking countries, it warrants close attention.

Dahlhaus attempts to reconcile the practical difficulties that music historians face as they practice their craft, not to devise only a philosopher's perspective on music history. He believes that "Music historiography has a different legitimization from political history. It differs from its political counterpart in that the essential relics it investigates from the past—the musical works—are primarily aesthetic objects and as such represent an element of the present; only secondarily do they cast light on events and circumstances of the past." He sees flaws in Guido Adler's theory that style is the key with which to make music history intelligible: style criticism does not necessarily reveal the organic nature of music history, if indeed music does have such a nature (see chapter 1). Historians, while discarding organicism, do admit to "evolutionary gradualism."

Dahlhaus, in the company of many musicologists, sees the fundamental problem as consisting of how to relate art (i.e., music) and history. Hermeneutics, historical truth, and musical and historical value are blocks with which Dahlhaus constructs a theory of music historiography. He challenges some aspects of "structural history," wherein "historians have let themselves be browbeaten into adopting an analytical and discursive style to replace, or at least augment, the epic style of traditional history, where readers were meant to sense the awareness of actual events." A proper role for structural history, in his view, is to mediate between social and cultural history. Dahlhaus presents a lucid, usually sympathetic account of reception history—how an artwork is received by its public—noting the necessarily close dependence on journalism. His closing caveat is that reception history cannot replace textual criticism with respect to the "authentic version" of a work.

PERIODIZATION

To be intelligible, music history—like all history—must be organized in some fashion. Typically, a chronological framework to organize the passing of centuries is made, according to various principles. Musicologists are as wary as other historians of the dangers in labeling chunks of time, but—given that requirement of making a long history comprehensible—designations have been applied in order to segment music history. More or less common agreement has established the following periods: *Antiquity*, to about 450 A.D.; *Medieval*, to about 1450; *Renaissance*, to about 1600; *Baroque*, to about 1750; *Classic*, to about 1820; *Romantic*, to about 1910; *Modern*, or Twentieth Century, to the present.

Argument over the periodization of music history is usually conducted along lines parallel to those in many fields of research. As the names given above for the periods of music history suggest, music historians have borrowed terms from other humanistic disciplines, notably art and literary history. The eras' years of demarcation do not necessarily coincide with sister areas of research: for example, extending the Medieval Era to 1450 and the Renaissance to about 1600, long beyond the periodization for literature and art. Indeed, scholars seriously question whether, for instance, the Classic Era actually can be defined clearly enough to be called a period in music history at all. At least one very distinguished modern musicologist, faced with writing a history of music in the Classic Era, could not find the requisite boundaries and unifying elements to continue the project.

But as the first paragraph points out, some sort of organization for eras seems to be mandated. Musicologists, knowingly or not, often accept the commonsensical notion of Louis Batiffol when he struggled with the word *Renaissance:* "There is no reason to modify a vocable which expresses what everybody understands." (As presented by W. L. Wiley, *The Gentleman of Renaissance France* [Cambridge: Harvard Univ. Pr., 1954, p. 3], glossing Batiffol's *Le Siècle de la Renaissance* [10th ed., Paris, Hachette, n.d., p. 106].)

As with all efforts at segmentation, the beginnings of these eras of music history are flexible; especially does contemporary scholarship tend to see the antecedents and consequents of an era more clearly, thereby making cutoff dates even fuzzier. The astonishing quantitative and qualitative growth in music scholarship since World War II has contributed to a much fuller understanding of the music, styles of composition, and the spirit that all combine somehow to unify a given age, or, indeed, to dismember it. The result is that often smaller chronological periods are now being offered as units of organization. This tendency does not, however, revert to the old nineteenth-century devices of characterizing an era in terms of "the great musician" or of the single form ("the symphonic age") or style ("the thorough-bass era").

Revealing the boundaries of eras was, before World War II, largely based on discovery of musical documents, especially musical scores. Although new finds have not ceased entirely, the great age of discovery was effectively over by the 1950s, as Manfred Bukofzer (1910–55) once pointed out. A corollary to his statement might be that the principal task remaining is to refine our understanding of periods, styles, composers, and the like, to sharpen our investigative methodologies and techniques, and to develop new ones.

A renewed interest in controlling the bibliography of music research materials, more widespread interest in the humanistic study of music, and the coming of age of musicology as a discipline have all combined to provide new scholarly editions of known and unknown music, new studies of famous and obscure composers and schools, new monographs on the various eras, and so forth. A vast expansion of information coupled with new directions for research is generating new ideas on the validity of periodization, or at least is causing significant refinement.

Striking are the changes, for example, in the views of composers' lives. For instance, Georg von Dadelsen completely revamped the sequence in which J. S. Bach's works were thought to have been composed. Dadelsen's *Beiträge zur Chronologie der Werke J. S. Bachs* reviews evidence that had been available for many years, applies creative critical and investigative procedures with regard to musical sources, and offers new results. For Beethoven, another example, the latest organization presents no fewer than eight subdivisions, in contrast to the three—long and justly criticized—that had dominated thought about his work (see Kerman and Tyson, "Beethoven").

Refining the organization of music history has led scholars to draw not only on subtle and gross stylistic changes as markers and milestones, but also on the appearance and disappearance of musical forms, on what appear to be epochal compositions, and, to a somewhat lesser degree, on what are perceived to be important political, social, technological, or economic landmarks. The "great musician" approach—now abandoned—chose individuals to delimit or characterize a period, an approach now seen to be more fallacious than truthful. For example, it proved to be more of a curse than a convenience that J. S. Bach, the greatest representative of the Baroque era, died in 1750, the bisecting year of the eighteenth century, and a year that provided excessively neat pigeonholes for classifying musical styles as pre- and post-Bach. Modern scholars now more clearly see in music contemporaneous with Bach's last decades the beginnings of musical styles that flow more or less smoothly into the Classic Era. The notion that individual composers, through unique gifts, may almost singlehandedly shape the course of music history has provoked both drivel (Robert H. Schauffler, *Beethoven: The Man Who Freed Music* (New York: Tudor, 1944), and remarkable insight (Leo Schrade, *Monteverdi: Creator of Modern Music*). Indeed, Schrade (1903–64) is among a very small coterie of musicologists who aim at describing the history of music within the large framework of the history of ideas.

Music periodization may be seen as simply a general taxonomic aid, a means of grasping what otherwise would be ungraspable. This viewpoint is typically present in textbooks where the overview may be valued more highly than concepts. But mere taxonomy is exceeded when relationships within a body of music can be established, permitting scholars to regard the music as a part of a whole within a certain span of time.

ANALYSIS AND METHOD

Throughout the history of scholarship in music, musical style has been the primary means of defining change and, consequently, defining the eras of music. The ways in which composers use pitch, rhythm, melody, harmony, counterpoint, musical forms—these and all the other elements that go into a composition—serve as fingerprints and roadmaps. It is held that analysis of music, especially when coupled with biographical, economic, social, and whatever other data come forth, leads ineluctably to our greater understanding of the music under consideration, and inevitably to our greater understanding of the course of music history. Through analysis of the musical styles of individuals, of groups or schools of composers, and of repertories of music, music history is ordered, made comprehensible.

Heavy reliance on style analysis, or style criticism, has been present to some degree for the roughly more than 100 years that music scholarship has been actively carried on, and has been an integral part of the investigator's methodology since Guido Adler's "Umfang, Methode, und Ziel der Musikwissenschaft" in 1885 and *Der Stil in der Musik* in 1911 (see chapter 1). A pioneering and hugely influential study, derivative of Adlerian concepts of style analysis, is *The Style of Palestrina and the Dissonance*, by Knud Jeppesen (1892–1974), which appeared first as a dissertation approved by Adler at the University of Vienna in 1922. Its subsequent translation from Danish to German, and later translation into English (two editions), gave an extremely wide dissemination of Jeppesen's methodology and ideas, as well as a wealth of new and important data. In Jeppesen's study a composer's entire musical output is analyzed in exquisite detail to determine precisely the ways in which a particular style trait—musical dissonance—is treated. To accomplish his task, Jeppesen was compelled to determine the melodic, rhythmic, and harmonic (vertical) features of Palestrina's works. His results provided, for the first time in the history of musical scholarship, a convincing summary of musical style firmly based on empirically derived information; his results have influenced a great number of stylistic studies since 1922, both in Renaissance researches and other eras as well. While Jeppesen's detailed analytical methodology has been utilized often, scholars have sometimes failed to incorporate into their own studies an element that he considered essential: the aesthetic effect that a particular style trait may have on our perception of a given musical work. It is increasingly clear that this aesthetic component, central to Jeppesen's work, is assuming (or reassuming) its importance in contemporary thought.

Even if there may be more or less common agreement on the general validity of style analysis, there is less agreement as to the method of analysis that should be employed. Ian Bent, in "Analysis," presents an excellent survey of the history and controversies surrounding musical analysis. He also restates a fundamental principle—now more broadly endorsed—that the gathering of empirical data through analysis should ultimately serve the aesthetician. That is, analysis leads to our greater understanding of the art of music in all its many aspects, and consequently to a greater understanding of mankind and human values. (Bent surveys all of the various "schools" of analysis and gives brief and lucid explanations of each. The details of these approaches are too formidable for the present volume, but the interested reader will find Bent particularly helpful, with bibliography as well.)

Jan LaRue is among those scholars (who include Jeppesen) who consider "feature analysis" an important element in determining musical structure. In *Guidelines for Style Analysis,* LaRue establishes five categories of features to be examined: sound, harmony, melody, rhythm, growth. These categories, along with their numerous subdivisions, allow the scholar to develop a profile of a single piece of music or group of pieces. Such detailed analysis may generate a wealth of data and make generalization difficult, especially if the repertoire is large. LaRue recognizes the difficulty, and provides additional means of synthesizing the data with a system of generalization. Identification of pattern, based on frequency of occurrence, is an important result of LaRue's approach, as indeed it is in the analytical systems that have feature analysis as the essential component.

Some analytical theories do not seek to result necessarily in giving support to historic periodization on stylistic grounds, but rather seek to find an "analytic common ground" that might be valid in several periods. The revolutionary concepts of Heinrich Schenker (1868–1935) with respect to musical analysis have had a profound effect on twentieth-century scholarship, no matter whether an individual musicologist or theorist accepts Schenkerian thought. Adherents of Schenker's methodology are compelling opponents to rethink their own methodology and results, with the consequent enlivening of scholarly debate.

Schenker developed his ideas in a series of publications; one of the most important has only recently been published in an official English translation for the first time, *Free Composition*. Through this volume and its predecessors, Schenker developed a new and rich vocabulary for equally new and rich ideas. In essence, Schenker sees counterpoint as a more basic element in music than harmony. Through his method of analysis for tonal music, Schenker offers a means of discerning very large-scale structure in a piece of music; his means utilizes a revolutionary reductive process that culminates in a graphic representation. Such a graphic representation reveals the essential nut of a composition's structure, and can be presented in highly abbreviated form. Visually, Schenker's graphic analyses resemble in kind and brevity the models offered by scientists as representations of molecular structures—though not in the arrangement of lines and symbols, since Schenker's graphics use music staves and modified note symbols. Schenker's legacy is felt most strongly among American scholars; in European countries his influence is often slight, even totally absent in some areas.

Allen Forte is in the forefront of those scholars who have combined Schenkerian theory with personal and creative approaches to musical analysis. Forte, adding the potential of the computer, is developing new ideas for the analysis of both tonal and atonal music. Eugene Narmour's *Beyond Schenkerism* is a spirited view of the flaws he perceives in Schenker's thought and influence on contemporary research in music theory.

Recent statements have criticized what might be called a strictly formalist approach to musical analysis. Leo Treitler, in " 'To Worship That Celestial Sound': Motives for Analysis," an expansion of his contribution to Holoman, *Musicology in the 1980s* (see chapter 1), enlarges his argument for the contextual approach to history and to analysis. In this article Treitler offers a concrete example of the methodology he advocates by giving "interpretative reflections about Beethoven's Ninth Symphony," a work that for him "*demands* interpretation." The language that Treitler uses embraces music's usual technical terminology and, more importantly, expressive and sometimes dramatic language to underscore and make emphatic the expressive content he finds in the symphony. Additionally, he repeatedly brings in elements of the historical context for the work. Altogether, the article serves as a model for the approach to analysis that Treitler and others advocate.

A semiological approach to musical analysis is being advocated by a few scholars who see in its application great potential for fuller understanding of music as a structure of signs. If a musical work can be broken down into segments and signs of designation applied to them, then further relationships among the segments will reveal themselves. Semiotics derives from a structural approach to linguistic analysis, an approach that defines the signs of a society and leads to generalizations of considerable magnitude. A new language of description evolves, a "meta-language." The use of such a structuralist approach to music, its analysis and meaning and its overall history and smaller eras, is in very early stages and no predictions of its further development and effectiveness are possible.

Jean-Jacques Nattiez founded, in effect, musical semiotics. His *Fondements d'une sémiologie de la musique* is a complex, often obscure statement of the field. Patricia Tunstall offers an introduction to the ideas and difficulties of musical semiotics in "Structuralism and Musicology: An Overview"; but, her view is challenged by Roger Scruton's "The Semiology of Music." Jonathan Dunsby, "Music and Semiotics: The Nattiez Phase," provides the most lucid analysis of where semiotics now is among the various approaches to musical analysis and description. His survey of the various points of view among scholars is carefully drawn.

Marxist "dialectical materialism," associated mainly with the Eastern political bloc, has yet to make a significant impression on the broad range of musical scholarship in the West. In spite of Western scholars having expanded their interests into economic, social, and political history as they relate music history, they have not generally accepted the economic and social "laws" that Marxist colleagues profess to see as determining factors of human experience. Nor, for example, have they yet accepted the view of society as an "organic system." Nonetheless, Eastern and Western researchers do share a renewed interest in viewing music as a part of society and within the broadest historical context. The divergence of view begins again when the Marxist writers define the ultimate aim of scholarship as improvement of society and its members. Among the relatively few Western examples of attempts to incorporate the ideals of Marxist dialectical materialism in writing music history is *English Chamber Music*, by Ernst H. Meyer.

Adorno, Theodor. *Philosophy of Modern Music.* Tr. by A. G. Mitchell and W. V. Blomster. New York: Seabury Pr., 1973.
Allen, Warren D. *Philosophies of Music History.* New York: American Book Co., 1939.
Ambros, August Wilhelm. *Geschichte der Musik.* 5v. Leipzig, 1862–82. Rev.

ed. Hildesheim, 1968. (Vols. 4 and 5, partly written by Ambros, were published posthumously.)

Beach, David. *Aspects of Schenkerian Theory.* New Haven: Yale Univ. Pr., 1982.

Bent, Ian. "Analysis." *The New Grove.*

Bücken, Ernst, ed. *Handbuch der Musikwissenschaft.* 13v. in 10. Potsdam: Athenaion, 1927–31. Repr.: New York, 1949.

Burney, Charles. *A General History of Music.* 4v. London, 1776–89. Repr.: New York, 1935.

Cannon, Beekman C. *Johann Mattheson, Spectator in Music.* Yale Studies in the History of Music, 1. New Haven: Yale Univ. Pr., 1947.

Chailley, Jacques. *40,000 Years of Music.* Tr. by Rollo Myers. London: Macdonald, 1964.

Chase, Gilbert. *America's Music.* 2nd ed. New York: McGraw-Hill, 1966. (3rd ed. forthcoming.)

Coussemaker, Edmund de. *Scriptorum de musica medii aevi novam seriem.* 4v. Paris, 1864–76. Repr.: Berlin, 1931; Hildesheim, 1963.

Coover, James. "Music Theory in Translation." *Journal of Music Theory* 3 (1959): 70–96.

Crocker, Richard. *A History of Musical Style.* New York: McGraw-Hill, 1966.

Dadelsen, Georg von. *Beiträge zur Chronologie der Werke J. S. Bachs.* Tübinger Bach Studien, 4/5. Trossingen: Hohner, 1958.

Dahlhaus, Carl. *Foundations of Music History.* Tr. by J. B. Robinson. Cambridge: Cambridge Univ. Pr., 1983.

―――. *Analysis and Value Judgment.* Tr. by Siegmund Levarie. New York: Pendragon Pr., 1983.

Dickinson, George Sherman. *A Handbook of Style in Music.* Poughkeepsie, N.Y.: Vassar College, 1965.

Duckles, Vincent. "Johannes Nicolaus Forkel: The Beginning of Music Historiography." *Eighteenth-Century Studies* 1 (1967–68): 277–90.

―――. "Musicology at the Mirror: A Prospectus for the History of Musical Scholarship." In *Perspectives in Musicology,* pp. 32–55. Ed. by Barry S. Brook et al. New York: Norton, 1972.

―――. "Patterns in the Historiography of 19th-Century Music." *Acta musicologica* 42 (1970): 75–82.

Dunsby, Jonathan. "Music and Semiotics: The Nattiez Phase." *The Musical Quarterly* 69 (1983): 27–43.

Eggebrecht, Hans Heinrich. "Historiography." *The New Grove.*

Fétis, François-Joseph. *Biographie universelle des musiciens et bibliographie générale de la musique.* 2nd ed. 8v. Paris, 1873–78. *Supplément et complément,* by Arthur Pougin. Paris, 1878–80. Repr.: 10v. Brussels, 1972.

―――. *Histoire générale de la musique.* 5v. Paris, 1869–76.

Forkel, Johann Nikolaus. *Allgemeine Geschichte der Musik.* 2v. Leipzig, 1788–1801. Repr.: Graz, 1967.

―――. *Ueber Johann Sebastian Bachs Leben, Kunst und Kunstwerke.* Leipzig, 1802. Repr.: Augsburg, 1925; Frankfurt, 1950; Kassel, 1950. (Engl. tr. by Charles S. Terry, New York, 1920.)

Forte, Allen. *The Compositional Matrix.* Monographs in Theory and Composition, 1. Baldwin, N.Y.: Music Teachers National Assn., 1961.
———. *The Structure of Atonal Music.* New Haven: Yale Univ. Pr., 1973.
———, and Steven E. Gilbert. *Introduction to Schenkerian Analysis.* New York: Norton, 1982.
Georgiades, Thrasybulos. *Music and Language: The Rise of Western Music as Exemplified in Settings of the Mass.* Tr. by Marie L. Göllner. New York: Cambridge Univ. Pr., 1982.
Grout, Donald J. "Current Historiography and Music History." *Studies in Music History: Essays for Oliver Strunk,* pp. 23–40. Ed. by Harold Powers. Princeton: Princeton Univ. Pr., 1968.
———. *A History of Western Music.* 3rd ed. New York: Norton, 1980.
Haar, James. "Music History and Cultural History." *The Journal of Musicology* 1 (1982): 5–14.
Hawkins, John. *A General History of the Science and Practice of Music.* 5v. London, 1776. Repr.: London, 1935; New York, 1963; Graz, 1969.
Jahn, Otto. *W. A. Mozart.* 4v. Leipzig, 1856–59. Tr. by Pauline D. Townsend, London, 1882; repr.: New York, 1970. 7th ed., rev. by Hermann Abert. Leipzig: Breitkopf & Härtel, 1955–56. (Engl. tr. by Traute Marshall in preparation.)
Jeppesen, Kund. *The Style of Palestrina and the Dissonance.* 2nd ed. Tr. by Edward J. Dent. London: Oxford Univ. Pr., 1946.
Journal of Music Theory. New Haven: Yale Univ., School of Music. 1957– , v. 1– .
Kerman, Joseph, and Alan Tyson. "Beethoven." *The New Grove.*
Lang, Paul Henry. *Music in Western Civilization.* New York: Norton, 1941.
LaRue, Jan. *Guidelines for Style Analysis.* New York: Norton, 1970.
Martini, Giovanni Battista. *Storia della Musica.* 3v. Bologna, 1757–81. Repr.: Graz, 1967.
Mattheson, Johann. *Grundlage einer Ehren-Pforte.* Hamburg, 1740. Repr.: Berlin, 1910.
———. *Der vollkommene Capellmeister.* Hamburg, 1739. *Johann Mattheson's Der vollkommene Capellmeister.* Tr. by Ernest C. Harriss. Ann Arbor: UMI Research Pr., 1981.
Mendel, Arthur. "Evidence and Explanation." *Report of the Eighth Congress of the International Musicological Society,* New York 1961, vol. 1, pp. 3–18. Ed. by Jan LaRue. 2v. Kassel: Bärenreiter-Verlag, 1962.
Meyer, Ernst H. *English Chamber Music; From the Middle Ages to Purcell.* 2nd rev. ed. London: Lawrence & Wishart, 1982.
Mickelsen, William C. *Hugo Riemann's Theory of Harmony* [with tr. of] *History of Music Theory, Book III,* by Hugo Riemann. Lincoln: Univ. of Nebraska Pr., 1977. (See also Riemann.)
Music Theory Spectrum. Bloomington: Society for Music Theory (School of Music, Indiana Univ.), 1979– , v. 1– .
Narmour, Eugene. *Beyond Schenkerism: The Need for Alternatives in Musical Analysis.* Chicago: Univ. of Chicago Pr., 1977.
Nattiez, Jean-Jacques. *Fondements d'une sémiologie de la musique.* Paris: Union Générale d'éditions, 1976.

New Oxford History of Music. London: Oxford Univ. Pr., 1954– .

Oliver, Alfred. *The French Encyclopedists as Critics of Music.* New York: Columbia Univ. Pr., 1947.

Oxford History of Music. 6v. London, 1901–5; 7v., London, 1928–34.

Piston, Walter. *Harmony.* 4th ed. Rev. by Mark DeVoto. New York: Norton, 1978.

Rameau, Jean-Philippe. *Treatise on Harmony.* Tr. by Philip Gossett. New York: Dover, 1971.

Reese, Gustave. *Music in the Middle Ages.* New York: Norton, 1940.

———. *Music in the Renaissance.* 2nd ed. New York: Norton, 1959.

Riemann, Hugo. *History of Music Theory, Books I and II: Polyphonic Theory to the Sixteenth Century.* Tr. by Raymond Haggh. Lincoln: Univ. of Nebraska Pr., 1962. (Partial tr. of *Geschichte der Musiktheorie im IX.–XIX. Jahrhundert.* 2nd ed. Berlin, 1921. Repr.: Hildesheim, 1961.)

Rosenstiel, Leonie, ed. *Schirmer History of Music.* New York: Schirmer Books, 1982.

Rousseau, Jean-Jacques. *Dictionary of Music.* Tr. by William Waring. London, 1771. Repr. of 2nd, 1779 ed.: New York, AMS Pr., 1975.

Schenker, Heinrich. *Free Composition.* Tr. and ed. by Ernst Oster. 2v. New York: Longman, 1980.

Scholes, Percy. *The Great Dr. Burney.* 2v. London: Oxford Univ. Pr., 1948.

———. *The Life and Activities of Sir John Hawkins.* London: Oxford Univ. Pr., 1953.

Schrade, Leo. *Monteverdi: Creator of Modern Music.* New York: Norton, 1950.

Scruton, Roger. "The Semiology of Music [rev. of Nattiez, above]." *The Cambridge Review* 100 (June 2, 1978): 172–76.

Shirlaw, Matthew. *The Theory of Harmony.* 2nd ed. De Kalb, Ill.: Birchard Coar, 1955.

Subotnik, Rose Rosengard. "The Role of Ideology in the Study of Western Music." *The Journal of Musicology* 2 (1983): 1–12.

Thayer, Alexander. *Ludwig van Beethoven's Leben.* 3v. Berlin, 1866–79. Tr. and rev. by Elliott Forbes. Princeton, N.J.: Princeton Univ. Pr., 1964.

Tovey, Donald. *Essays in Musical Analysis.* 6v. London: Oxford Univ. Pr., 1935–39. Abridged ed.: 2v. London, 1981.

Treitler, Leo. "On Historical Criticism." *The Musical Quarterly* 53 (1967): 188–205.

———. " 'To Worship That Celestial Sound': Motives for Analysis." *The Journal of Musicology* 1 (1982): 153–70.

Tunstall, Patricia. "Structuralism and Musicology: An Overview." *Current Musicology,* no. 27 (1979): 51–64.

Winterfeld, Carl. *Johannes Gabrieli und sein Zeitalter.* 3v. Berlin, 1834. Repr.: Hildesheim, 1965.

Wiora, Walter, ed. *Die Ausbreitung der Historismus der Musik* [from symposia in 1966, 1967]. Studien zur Musikgeschichte des 19. Jahrhunderts, 14. Regensburg: G. Bosse, 1969.

———. *The Four Ages of Music.* Tr. by M. D. Herter Norton. New York: Norton, 1965.

Music

Music itself, that is, the musical score, is the most important primary source material for the musicologist, and preparing critical, or scholarly, editions has been a main activity since the middle of the nineteenth century. The collected works of individual composers, repertoires of music from various periods, editions of individual sources or groups of sources, and monuments of music reflecting a geographical or national orientation have been issued in considerable abundance. Editing music presents problems that differ according to the eras of music history, but the central issue is constant: how to provide an authoritative edition of a work that is based as much as possible on sources closest to the composer's original intention.

Music written before modern notation was generally codified in the early sixteenth century provides increasingly greater problems the further one goes back in time. Indeed, much music of the Middle Ages cannot be deciphered to the common satisfaction of all scholars, especially some Christian liturgical chant, monophonic trouvère and troubadour songs, and considerable polyphonic music as well. The main varieties and problems of polyphonic notation are discussed in Willi Apel, *The Notation of Polyphonic Music, 900–1600*. The *Liber Usualis* (prefatory matter) gives a brief introduction to Gregorian chant and its history and to the work of the monks of the abbey of St. Peter, Solesmes, France. These scholar-clerics led the movement to restore Gregorian chant to its original state and their efforts were acknowledged in Pope Pius X's *Motu proprio* of November 22, 1903, which ratified the revised versions of the melodies. Apel presents a comprehensive discussion of chant's history and problems in his *Gregorian Chant*, still the authoritative single-volume treatment in English. (He covers also Ambrosian and Old Roman chant.)

Deciphering ancient musical notations—Greek, Byzantine, and various neumatic notations that only suggest pitch or rhythm, or both—has received much scholarly attention. An illuminating discussion of one set of problems is given by Egon Wellesz (1885–1974) in *A History of Byzantine Music and Hymnography*. Wellesz's cracking of Byzantine chant notation is the basis for all modern studies of this branch of Christian chant, which is itself of vital importance to the understanding of early Christian music in all its aspects.

The manuscripts that are used to study Western and Eastern Christian chant are scattered over the whole of Europe and parts of the Mideast as well. The manuscripts themselves reflect not only the influence of Rome, but also local and regional dialects of liturgy and musical preference. Unscrambling these dialects is a principal problem, as is the method of transmission of chants from area to area and from generation to generation.

Authenticated musical holographs are rare for the period before 1500, the time when a system of music printing was first perfected in Italy. Copyists, working mainly in monastic scriptoria, compiled extensive anthologies of sacred and secular music, and a much smaller number of instrumental music anthologies. How such music was transmitted through copyists is a problem of great importance; Charles Hamm's proposal that scribes used "fascicle manuscripts" as sources for their copying is widely accepted, and the notion provides a useful means of tracking compositions through their appearances in a variety of manuscript sources. (See also chapter 3.)

On the other hand, extant autograph scores and those authoritatively prepared by copyists for the composers become increasingly more common after the middle of the seventeenth century. Thus, authoritative manuscript sources and printed music combine to provide the main source of information for scholars in succeeding eras. Nowadays, composers are often sensitive to the needs of history, and frequently are careful to preserve sketches, preliminary scores, final manuscript scores, printer's proofs, first issues, and any similar materials.

The scholar's task, whatever the era, is to identify the primary sources, evaluate their authenticity, collate the variety of manuscripts or prints that may exist, make decisions as to what will constitute a reliable musical (and literary) text, and finally to present the music in a form suitable for critical evaluation and study. Whereas the first critical editions that began to appear in the nineteenth century were sometimes exclusively concerned with an authoritative musical text, modern scholars typically supply critical and supplementary information, often of considerable dimensions. Such a critical apparatus aims to justify decisions, offer variant readings found in the sources, and place the music in its historical context, at least to some extent. One principle has remained clear: an editor is obliged to indicate when his or her own judgments and decisions have been exercised.

Yet another guiding principle has come more strongly to the fore: sources are more critically evaluated within a stricter philological methodology. Closer attention to source criticism during very recent years is often reflected in the greater breadth of information and interpretative writing in modern critical editions, and also in the reevaluations that are being made of quite well-known musical sources.

A wide range of useful comments on the problems and methods of scholarly editions may be found in two relatively brief essays by Walter Emery (1909–74), *Editions and Musicians,* and Robert Donington, *A Performer's Guide to Baroque Music.* Two important editions that incorporate rigorous methods of editing and source criticism are by Edward Lowinsky, *The Medici Codex,* and Allan Atlas, *The Cappella Giulia Chansonnier;* both deal with famous manuscript sources of Renaissance polyphony. In addition to editing the music itself, Lowinsky and Atlas develop theories for the provenances of the manuscripts, their relationships to other manuscript (their filiation), and they discuss the style of the compositions in the sources. Each scholar draws extensively on general historical documents of politics, economics, and social history. While some of their conclusions may have been challenged seriously or slightly, the intensity and detail of their research are praised widely.

Additional insight into detailed problems and methodology is gained by consulting almost any of the numerous scholarly editions published by university presses (for example, the University of Chicago Press's *Monuments of Renaissance Music*), by the American Institute of Musicology (within the series *Corpus Mensurabilis Musicae,* for Medieval and Renaissance music; *Corpus Scriptorum de Musica,* for literary works of music theory; *Corpus of Early Keyboard Music;* and *Renaissance Manuscript Studies*), and by commercial editions of Bach, Mozart, Schubert, Handel, etc.

The music sources for nineteenth-century composers are getting much more attention as that century recedes further from the present. A common misapprehension is that the familiar works of Giuseppe Verdi, to take but one handy example, are usually performed in editions intended by the composer, and are completely authoritative. A collected edition for Verdi is underway, and will reflect, in time, the true shape and details of the operas and other works.

The works of contemporary composers are, in a few instances, being edited in scholarly editions: Paul Hindemith, Sergei Prokofiev, and Arnold Schoenberg, for example. Such editions are identical in intention and method to the editions of old music and include, insofar as possible, the issuing of previously unpublished works.

The needs of scholarship have been rightly kept uppermost in the minds of those preparing authoritative editions. That is, authority of musical text has been preferred to editorial additions specifically designed to aid in performance. In slight contrast, the first important scholarly edition, the works of J. S. Bach, was begun (1851) in part to offer music for performance and, consequently, the scholarly apparatus is relatively insignificant. The several hundred scholarly editions since that time have, to a greater or lesser degree, also served as performing editions or as bases for such editions. Therein lies one of the greatest contributions of musicology: the impact that critical editions have had on modern concert life through revivals of old music, establishing standards of performance, more authentic performance styles, and expansion of the concert repertoire of the music of almost all eras.

Studies of composer's notes and sketches for musical compositions may be related directly, although rarely exclusively, to the preparation of scholarly editions. Through study of sketches made before or during the process of composing a piece, or both, scholars seek to learn about the creative processes and biography of a composer. (Because Beethoven left the first rich legacy of sketchbooks, he has received the most attention.) Scholars disagree about whether sketch studies do indeed illuminate the creative process and about the relationship that drafts or sketches may have to a completed composition. To oversimplify: some researchers profess to trace in a series of autograph sketches an initial musical idea through its refinement to its appearance in the finished work, thereby discerning a compositional process. Others argue against identifying a refining process that inevitably has headed the composer from choice to choice towards a higher aesthetic ideal and its achievement. The relevance of sketch studies to biography is perhaps more clear, in that sketches may assist in establishing a more accurate chronology of a composer's life and works.

In any event, the issue over the value of sketch studies is far from settled, and intense research and debate continue today. The following titles demonstrate both the methodology and results of sketch studies: Joseph Kerman, *Ludwig van Beethoven: Autograph Miscellany;* Alan Tyson, *The Authentic English Editions of Beethoven,* and *Beethoven Studies I,* and also two articles, "Sketches and Autographs," and "Steps to Publication—And Beyond." Douglas Johnson, himself an active student of Beethoven's sketches, has issued a caution to his colleagues about the meaning of such work; see his "Beethoven Scholars and Beethoven's Sketches."

Related Materials

The notion that documents other than music are appropriate to a scholarly edition of a composer's music is seen in the inclusion of diaries, letters, and other literary writings in some editions. In addition, iconographical and a variety of other sorts of documents are sometimes included; see, among many sources, Otto Erich Deutsch's *Schubert: A Documentary Biography*. The earliest edition of this book (1913) was a pathbreaker in scholarly methodology for music research: by examining an array of carefully selected documents, including iconographic ones, Deutsch (1883–1967) offered a clearer understanding of the man and his music. Other representative documentary biographies are Deutsch's later *Handel: A Documentary Biography* and *Mozart und seine Welt in Zeitgenössischen Bildern;* Hans T. David and Arthur Mendel's *The Bach Reader;* and H. C. Robbins Landon's two contributions, *Haydn: Chronicle and Works,* and *Beethoven: A Documentary Study.*

Archival research, especially for medieval and Renaissance scholars, is being pursued with increased vigor as scholars comb a great variety of documents for economic, political, social, and biographical detail. Correspondence, payment books, notaries' records, church registers, royal court records, and many similar sources help to fill in details of a composer's life, how the art of music was practiced in a given time, or how music functioned in a certain place. For example, Craig Wright, in "Dufay at Cambrai," provides through painstaking examination of mainly archival documents new evidence for details on this medieval composer's life and his relationship with contemporaries. The study is exemplary of the new emphasis on archival research.

Iconography

The study and use of musical iconography—paintings, drawings, sculptures, and the like—has greatly increased since the 1960s, although it has been present in the field of music research since the first histories of the eighteenth century. Iconography's importance lies in adding to our knowledge of old instruments, of performance practice through representations of ensembles and soloists, of music in its numerous social contexts, and of the details of the lives of composers, theorists, and others related somehow to music. Art historians have been of special aid to musicology colleagues as the methodologies have been developed.

The single modern methodological monograph for the field of music is Howard M. Brown and Joan Lascelle's *Musical Iconography;* it provides details on how to describe and catalog an iconographic item. In "The Iconology of Musicology" and "The Visual Arts as a Source for the Historian of Music" Emanuel Winternitz outlines areas for research and the cautions that must accompany the scholar as iconographic objects are examined, for example the "prettification" and artistic license that an artist may impose on his work. Winternitz's *Musical Instruments of the Western World* set a new standard for interweaving pictures and an interpretive commentary. *Musikgeschichte in Bildern*, begun under the joint editorship of Heinrich Besseler (1900–69) and Max Schneider (1875–1967), is the most ambitious publication project in musical iconography. It includes Western and non-Western music, and each volume contains extensive textual commentary to accompany the reproductions.

The foregoing bibliography is representative of the interest in musical iconography that has led to the founding (1971) of Répertoire international d'iconographie musicale, an internationally endorsed effort aimed at identifying iconographic items and properly describing, cataloging, and interpreting them. Equally symptomatic of scholars' interest is *Iconographie musicale,* a series of bilingual (French-English) volumes aimed at covering music from the Middle Ages to the present. One of the latest volumes—and one of the best—is Edmund Bowles's *Musical Performance in the Late Middle Ages.* Bowles relies heavily on miniatures in manuscripts to draw his own picture of performance practices and settings for music.

Apel, Willi. *Gregorian Chant.* 3rd ed. Bloomington: Indiana Univ. Pr., 1966.
———. *The Notation of Polyphonic Music, 900–1600.* 5th ed., rev. Medieval Academy of America, Publications, 38. Cambridge, Mass.: The Medieval Academy of America, 1961.
Atlas, Allan W. *The Capella Giulia Chansonnier: Rome, Biblioteca Apostolica Vaticana, C. G. XIII.27.* Musicological Studies, 27/1–2. 2v. Brooklyn: Institute of Mediaeval Music, 1975–76.
Besseler, Heinrich, and Max Schneider, eds. *Musikgeschichte in Bildern.* Leipzig: Deutscher Verlag für Musik, 1961– .
Bowles, Edmund. *La pratique musicale au Moyen-Age/Musical Performance in the Late Middle Ages.* In *Iconographie musicale.* Gênève-Paris: Editions Minkoff & Lattes, 1983.
Brown, Howard M., and Joan Lascelle. *Musical Iconography: A Manual for Cataloguing Musical Subjects in Western Art to 1800.* Cambridge, Mass.: Harvard Univ. Pr., 1972.
Corpus Mensurabilis Musicae. Rome and Dallas: American Institute of Musicology, 1951– .
Corpus of Early Keyboard Music. Rome: American Institute of Musicology, 1963– .

Corpus Scriptorum de Musica. Rome: American Institute of Musicology, 1956– .

David, Hans T., and Arthur Mendel, eds. *The Bach Reader: A Life of Johann Sebastian Bach in Letters and Documents.* Rev. ed. New York: Norton, 1966.

Deutsch, Otto Erich. *Handel: A Documentary Biography.* New York: Norton, 1955.

————. *Mozart und seine Welt in Zeitgenössischen Bildern.* Neue Ausgabe sämtlicher Werke, Ser. 10, Werkgruppe 32. Kassel: Bärenreiter-Verlag, 1961.

————. *Schubert: A Documentary Biography.* Tr. by Eric Blom. London: Dent, 1947. (Rev. and aug. translation of *Franz Schubert: Die Dokumente seines Lebens*, 1913.)

Donington, Robert. *A Performer's Guide to Baroque Music.* 2nd ed. London: Faber, 1978.

Emery, Walter. *Editions and Musicians. A Survey of the Duties of Practical Musicians & Editors towards the Classics.* Rev. London: Novello, 1958.

Hamm, Charles. "Manuscript Structure in the Dufay Era." *Acta musicologica* 24 (1962): 166–84.

Iconographie musicale. Geneva: Minkoff, 1973– .

Johnson, Douglas. "Beethoven Scholars and Beethoven's Sketches." *19th-Century Music* 2 (1978–79): 3–17.

Kerman, Joseph, ed. *Ludwig van Beethoven: Autograph Miscellany from circa 1786–1799: British Museum Additional Manuscript 29801, ff. 39–162 (The Kafka Sketchbook).* 2v. London: British Museum, 1970.

Landon, H. C. Robbins. *Beethoven: A Documentary Study.* New York: Macmillan, 1970.

————. *Haydn: Chronicle and Works.* 5v. Bloomington: Indiana Univ. Pr., 1976–81.

The Liber Usualis. Tournai, N.Y.: Desclée Co., 1963.

Lowinsky, Edward. *The Medici Codex of 1518.* 3v. Monuments of Renaissance Music, 3–5. Chicago: Univ. of Chicago Pr., 1968.

Monuments of Renaissance Music. Chicago: Univ. of Chicago Pr., 1964– .

Renaissance Manuscript Studies. n.p. (Rome?): American Institute of Musicology, 1975– .

Tyson, Alan. *The Authentic English Editions of Beethoven.* All Souls Studies, 1. London: Faber & Faber, 1963.

————. "Sketches and Autographs." "Steps to Publication—and Beyond." In *The Beethoven Reader*, pp. 443–58; 459–89. Ed. by Denis Arnold and Nigel Fortune. New York: Norton, 1971.

————, ed. *Beethoven Studies I.* New York: Norton, 1973.

Wellesz, Egon. *A History of Byzantine Music and Hymnography.* 2nd ed. Oxford: Oxford Univ. Pr., 1961.

Winternitz, Emanuel. "The Iconology of Musicology: Potentials and Pitfalls." In *Perspectives in Musicology*, pp. 80–90. Ed. by Barry Brook. New York: Norton, 1972.

————. *Musical Instruments and Their Symbolism in Western Art: Studies in Musical Iconography.* 2nd ed. New Haven: Yale Univ. Pr., 1979.

———. *Musical Instruments of the Western World*. London: Thames & Hudson, 1967.

———. "The Visual Arts as a Source for the Historian of Music." International Musicological Society, *Report of the Eighth Congress, New York, 1961*, vol. 1, pp. 109–20. Ed. by Jan LaRue. 2v. Kassel: Bärenreiter-Verlag, 1962.

Wright, Craig. "Dufay at Cambrai: Discoveries and Revisions." *The Journal of the American Musicological Society* 28 (1975): 175–229.

PERFORMANCE PRACTICE

Performance practice (or practices) is the term indicating study that leads to music performance in a style authentic to the period in which the music was composed, in a style that is closest to a composer's intention. The internal evidence of a score is combined with an era's other primary documents: theoretical writings, correspondence, histories, information on instruments, iconography, criticism, reviews of performances—anything that sheds light on how the music sounded. Pitch levels and tunings, articulation of musical phrases and motives, the timbres of voices and instruments—all are relevant to some degree to the work of modern scholars and performers. By combining evidence of all sorts, modern performances attempt to replicate, as far as possible and practicable, the sounds and performing styles of earlier times, recreating the achievements of the composers, and perhaps their ideals as well.

An issue met, but not fully resolved, is the extent to which performers should go in recreating musical styles of the past, including old vocal and instrumental techniques. For many—probably most—listeners, authentic styles best bridge the gap between them and music of another time. Authentically performed music may recall best the aesthetic and musical experience of times past. For others, discarding familiar but anachronistic performance idioms is jolting and disruptive, especially with well-known music of, say, the late eighteenth or nineteenth centuries. For example, the radically different sound of the fortepiano, used by Mozart, is a musical, or at least sonic, experience quite different from that of the modern grand piano. What is undeniable, however, is that the scholar's insistence on historical integrity in performance shapes what is heard presently in concert halls and, most especially, through recordings.

The problems that confront scholars in performance practice range from minutiae to fundamental issues, and in some instances resolutions of the problems may overturn commonly accepted views of and reactions to a great body of music. To take only one instance, the issue of how music from various periods, particularly the Baroque Era, was ornamented and improvised upon is a fundamental problem for scholars and performers. For scholars and performers alike, it is now increasingly essential to know with the greatest precision possible how to take a score from the seventeenth century and add music to it, how to supply—because the composer assumed a performer would be able to—ornaments of various kinds, scales, dissonant notes, and so forth. In most musical quarters of today, it is simply no longer acceptable to perform only the bare bones of a seventeenth-century score, such has been the impact of new scholarly research in performance practice during the last two or three decades.

In the broadest and most general sense, a great deal of the writing about music relates to performance practice, in that description and commentary illuminate how musicians should perform a score, which itself only graphically represents how the music should sound. Through their works on notation, discussions of compositional techniques, descriptions of the place of music in daily secular and religious life, and so on, the writers and commentators of the Middle Ages and Renaissance shed light on how music should sound, if sometimes only a small light. Especially has the more enigmatic nature of musical notation in the Middle Ages always presented problems in performance practice, not only with the pitches and rhythms, but with how a text should be placed under a vocal melody.

The essential problems of notating music—pitch, rhythm, and multi-voiced scores—were solved by the sixteenth century. Late in that century and especially at the beginning of the seventeenth century, composers began to exercise more control over the score and to add various markings intended to tell the performer how to perform the music. Markings such as *piano* and *forte* appeared and, more importantly, thorough-bass (continuo) symbols. These symbols, only numbers at first but later including other symbols, tell a keyboard player how to add the essential harmonies above a single bass line. Composers have steadily increased their score instructions to the point that a modern composition may present a very bewildering appearance. Even though the history of musical scores clearly shows more remote control by the composer, performance practice research is essential to authentic performance styles. And since music has no absolute standards for "soft," "loud," "fast," or "slow," students of performance practice provide historical guidance and a somewhat flexible range of standards.

In the end, no matter how intensely scholars study performance practice or how detailed the instructions of composers in their scores, the artistry of a performer is what brings the music to life. Scholarship places music of an era in its proper performing context, defines parameters of style, and describes detail; informed judgment and taste, "le bon goût" in eighteenth-century terms, make the music live.

The bibliographic notes that follow are highly selective of the literature on performance practices; there has been a surge of interest and publications since the 1960s that is little short of phenomenal. Musicologists, performers, and instrument makers contribute to the literature.

Robert Haas's *Aufführungspraxis der Musik* (1931) is the seminal book for modern scholarship in performance practice. Haas drew on all of the relevant sources to some degree—primary literary sources, scores, iconography, and his own considerable skills as a performer—and although many details of his book have subsequently been proved in error, he set for later researchers and performers a high standard in methodology and scope of learning.

The flood of studies in performance practice and the widespread interest in the problems by scholars, performers, and listeners began in the 1960s; an almost symbiotic relationship has continued apace between research and recordings—the public's appetite for authoritative performances appears to be insatiable. The principal bibliography aimed at controlling the literature is *Performance Practice,* by Mary Vinquist and Neal Zaslaw; a second edition is forthcoming. Although the first edition proved to be uneven in coverage, it did highlight the need for many research projects. Of equal importance in the area of research studies themselves is Robert Donington's *The Interpretation of Early Music,* the largest and most comprehensive statement since Haas's *Aufführungspraxis.* It set a new standard for comprehensiveness and detail of information, for example, on ornamentation in Baroque music. Donington, like Haas, is a performer who fully understands the technical problems of presenting music in concert and who attempts to reconcile the theory of performance practice with its very practical application. Donington's second major contribution, *A Performer's Guide to Baroque Music,* is less comprehensive, but equally essential to researchers and performers. His ideas on musical rhythm in the Baroque and Early Classic eras are sometimes at variance with those of Frederick Neumann. Neumann's *Ornamentation in Baroque and Post-Baroque Music* is a highly controversial summation of one scholar's lengthy research into how a musical score of that time represents the composer's intention, especially with respect to rhythm and ornamentation.

Representative other works concerned with music of other periods in music history are Howard M. Brown's *Embellishing Sixteenth-Century Music*, William S. Newman's *Performance Practices in Beethoven's Piano Sonatas*, and Paul and Eva Badura-Skoda's *Interpreting Mozart on the Keyboard*. *Readings in the History of Music in Performance*, by Carol MacClintock, is a remarkable anthology, carefully selected (and translated when necessary) from original sources to offer information as well as insight with regard to performance of music from the late Medieval Era to the middle of the nineteenth century.

As Albert Schweitzer managed to bring a vast public to the organ music of J. S. Bach, faulty though his understanding was, so Wanda Landowska established the harpsichord and its music in the first half of this century. Her vitality and dedication to harpsichord music, coupled with attractive eccentricities, led to widespread cultivation of both solo and chamber music that requires harpsichord. But, if Landowska reestablished the harpsichord as a chamber and solo instrument, it is Frank Hubbard who has reestablished understanding of harpsichord construction and who has proved, along with others, that instrument builders can contribute much to our understanding of performance practice.

Hubbard's book, *Three Centuries of Harpsichord Making*, reveals the old construction standards and practices, thereby defining more clearly the possibilities regarding performance techniques. Through actually building various types of harpsichords (and marketing them) Hubbard and his colleagues have helped validate performance practice theory in many repertories, vocal and instrumental.

In 1973 *Early Music* was begun and quickly established itself as the principal journal devoted to performance practice. Aside from the articles it prints, *Early Music* provides the most extensive current chronicle of events and publications related to performance practice.

Badura-Skoda, Eva, and Paul Badura-Skoda. *Interpreting Mozart on the Keyboard*. London: Barrie & Rockliff, 1962.
Bent, Ian, ed. *Source Materials and the Interpretation of Music: A Memorial Volume to Thurston Dart*. London: Stainer & Bell, 1981.
Brown, Howard M. *Embellishing Sixteenth-Century Music*. Early Music Series, 1. London: Oxford Univ. Pr., 1976.
————, and James McKinnon. "Performing Practice." *The New Grove*.
Donington, Robert. *The Interpretation of Early Music*. Rev. ed. New York: St. Martin's Pr., 1974.

————. *A Performer's Guide to Baroque Music.* 2nd ed. London: Faber, 1978.

Dreyfus, Laurence. "Early Music Defended against Its Devotees: A Theory of Historical Performance in the Twentieth Century." *The Musical Quarterly* 69 (1983): 297–322.

Early Music. London: Oxford Univ. Pr., v. 1– , 1973– .

Haas, Robert. *Aufführungspraxis der Musik.* Handbuch der Musikwissenschaft, 8. Wildpark-Potsdam: Akademische Verlagsgesellschaft Athenaion, 1931.

Hubbard, Frank. *Three Centuries of Harpsichord Making.* Cambridge, Mass.: Harvard Univ. Pr., 1965.

MacClintock, Carol, ed. *Readings in the History of Music in Performance.* Bloomington: Indiana Univ. Pr., 1979.

Neumann, Frederick. *Ornamentation in Baroque and Post-Baroque Music, with Special Emphasis on J. S. Bach.* Princeton: Princeton Univ. Pr., 1978.

Newman, William S. *Performance Practices in Beethoven's Piano Sonatas: An Introduction.* New York: Norton, 1971.

Strunk, Oliver. *Source Readings in Music History.* New York: Norton, 1950.

Vinquist, Mary, and Neal Zaslaw. *Performance Practice: A Bibliography.* New York: Norton, 1971. (Rev. ed. forthcoming.)

3

The Periods
of Music History

The origins of music are unknown, and will doubtless remain so. Men and women—primitive and civilized—have speculated, theorized, and postulated about how music came into being, and modern humanists and scientists have continued to wonder and investigate, but still only speculation is the result.

Modern thought and research into music's origins and early development were carried on mainly by ethnomusicologists. The earlier term for ethnomusicology, comparative musicology, reveals both the methodology and concept, or the bias. It was thought that by comparing so-called primitive music to the European fine art tradition the historical stages of development could be reconstructed; the notion was abandoned. A principal reason for rejecting the idea was that as "primitive music" became more familiar, scholars soon learned that "primitive" did not equate with "simple" or "nonstructured," as had been assumed. As Curt Sachs and others observed, societies—including primitive ones—are not static but are dynamic in their social and artistic structures, and that to work by analogy is dangerous and overly speculative in conclusions.

What does seem plausible to modern scholars is that vocal music preceded instrumental music, that human sound likely antedates the use of various objects to make the early sounds of music. But, even that argument cannot be resolved to the satisfaction of all scholars.

The areas of musicology and ethnomusicology have been united with respect to trying to determine the origins of music and they are, in turn, related to the work of anthropologists and cultural and

46

social historians as well. The research of modern linguistics into the evolution and structure of speech will doubtless impinge at some point on thinking about music's earliest history. Inflected speech and distress calls, for example, have at times been put forward as the earliest stages of music.

A humane and perceptive view of the problems surrounding the origins of music is offered by Curt Sachs in *The Wellsprings of Music*, a book that offers also a digest of the ethnomusicological thinking of one of the great musical scholars of modern times. Sachs was a leader in ethnomusicology as well as in scholarship in the history and theory of Western art music. His pioneering volume, *The Rise of Music in the Ancient World*, attempts to show the roots of Western music in the ancient civilizations of Asia, the Mideast, Greece, and Rome. He was the first to discuss the origins of music in such a systematic way, on a hemispheric basis. The breadth of Sachs's approach has led to detailed studies of various musics by a whole generation of scholars. Still another book by Sachs reflects the scope of his concerns: *The Commonwealth of Art*, a book that explicates further his development of what might be called a unified field theory for the arts. While factual error and misinterpretation have been found in some of Sachs's writings, the intellectual breadth and the sweep and grandeur of his ideas have rarely been matched in modern scholarship. That he is again being read and reconsidered is a tribute to his creative and fecund mind.

Musical scholarship is on firmer ground when dealing with the music of Antiquity, that is, music to about the middle of the fifth century A.D. For Jewish, Byzantine, Greek, and Roman music, and for the music of the early Christian Church, a multitude of literary documents and iconographical sources survives, helping to foster understanding of how music functioned, how the foundations of its modern theory were laid, and how music was seen in relationship to secular and religious life. For some musical traditions the music itself is also extant, but in notations that are imprecise by later standards, or not yet fully or even partially understood.

The obviously centuries-old tradition of Greek music from classical times must be reconstructed from little over a dozen fragments from various centuries, in comparison to the many surviving writings on the philosophy and theory of Greek music that include detailed descriptions of Greek musical notation. We know that Greek music was flourishing greatly by the fifth century B.C. and that by about 320 B.C. the standards and practices that had dominated the tradition were in decline, and had largely died by the late second century B.C. We know from the writings of Plato and Aristotle how music's role in society was viewed; from Alypios, the ancient Greek notation is revealed in great detail; from Pythagoras and Aristoxenus, how the science of acoustics and theories of scales began. Thus, modern scholars are confronted with a wealth of literary information but only the equivalent of about 1000 measures of music from a period covering many hundreds of years. How to deduce a history for Greek music from only literary sources is the central problem, and how in some way to recreate the sound of Greek music will endure as the central frustration.

Isobel Henderson's caution concerning Greek writings still stands: "With the notable exception of Aristoxenus, the purpose of Greek theorists was not to analyse the art of music, but to expound the independent science of harmonics; and ultimately the transmission of this harmonic science had no more to do with the history of musical art than the transmission of Greek astronomy or medicine." And both Henderson and Edward Lippman tend to be clearer than most scholars in Greek music in warning against placing inordinate confidence in a given theorist's explanations of musical theory.

The difficulties that confront today's scholar in Greek music are tackled by both musicologists and classicists. Of the latter group, Isobel Henderson, "Ancient Greek Music," and R. P. Winnington-Ingram, "Greece," both offer short histories, cogent summaries of Greek theory, notation, and the ethical properties ascribed to music, and challenging speculations and conclusions. The ever-useful *Source Readings in Music History,* by Oliver Strunk (1950), has recently been joined by Ruth H. Rowen's *Music through Sources and Documents* (1979); both include numerous translations from original Greek sources, whose reading is essential to more than a cursory understanding of the complexities faced by scholars.

Musical Thought in Ancient Greece, by Edward Lippman, provides the most extensive and penetrating survey of Greek harmony; of the role of ethics in theory and practice wherein Lippman clearly delineates the various and often contradictory aspects of a difficult subject; and of the philosophers' views of music. For Greek music, "harmony" has none of its modern implications of "chords" or "polyphony" or "functional harmony." Harmony signified acoustic theory, or tuning; how strings were stretched, divided, and plucked to produce notes of different pitch. Accounting for acoustic phenomena and arranging systems for explanation is a central theme throughout Greek theoretical sources; explicating the system is the scholar's role. The ethical properties of music relate to music's effects on will and emotion, its power to soothe and incite. How music should function within education and in daily life, and how it should be used by the church (i.e., religion) and state are the concern of Plato. In *The Republic,* he contends that "good" music is necessary and that "bad" music leads to society's decay, a notion that seems to have eternal validity; orgiastic music is specifically condemned (see Lippman).

The following two studies will lead the student to original sources and offer basic information: Thrasybulos Georgiades, *Greek Music, Verse, and Drama* and W. D. Anderson, *Ethos and Education in Greek Music,* which includes a comprehensive bibliography in addition to penetrating insights. E. Pöhlmann, *Denkmäler altgriechischer Musik,* provides the most exhaustive bibliography on Greek music and also transcribes all of the fragments into modern notation, except for a half-dozen only recently discovered. R. P. Winnington-Ingram, in the entry on "Greek Music" in *The Oxford Classical Dictionary,* gives a brief but excellent introduction to Greek music in all its aspects, including theater.

The Greek heritage unquestionably had significant impact on early Christian music. There is another tradition that is as inextricably linked to its origins and development in both the Western and Eastern (Byzantine) branches, namely, the Jewish tradition. Both musical and liturgical elements of the Jewish traditional religious ceremonies were adopted, modified, and incorporated into the early Christian church. Eric Werner, in *The Sacred Bridge,* sees also considerable penetration by Syrian and Northeast Mesopotamian music into early Christian music, as well as Greek influences on Jewish music and ritual. The title of his book reveals the importance he notes between Jewish traditions and the evolving Christian ones, a relationship that was maintained to some degree for the first millenium.

The relationship of Byzantine chant to Gregorian chant, although studied seriously since the middle of the nineteenth century, has been fully developed only since 1918, when Egon Wellesz successfully deciphered Byzantine musical notation. Since that date, philologists and musicologists have clarified the significant influence of Byzantine chant (in Greek) on early Christian chant (in Latin). As does Werner, Wellesz sees the synagogue as the prime source for both branches of Christian chant. Wellesz's *History of Byzantine Music and Hymnography* gives the reader a most comprehensive and detailed view and his *Eastern Elements in Western Chant* exposes the relationships between the two repertoires. Oliver Strunk's important contributions to Byzantine studies have been gathered in *Essays on Music in the Byzantine World;* contributions by Miloš Velimirović and others may be found in *Studies in Eastern Chant.*

Other notable essays on early church music include W. F. Jackson Knight, *St. Augustine's "De musica"* for that Church Father's important reflections on music, especially meter and rhythm; Carl H. Kraeling, "Music in the Bible"; and Werner's "The Music of Post-Biblical Judaism." These last two and other relevant short surveys of non-Western musical systems by a variety of scholars are found in *The New Oxford History of Music,* volume 1.

Boethius (ca. 480–ca. 524) is a major link between ancient and medieval speculation on music theory. His "De institutione musica" became "the most widespread theoretical treatise on music in the late Middle Ages and Renaissance" (Bower, "Boethius").

Anderson, Warren D. *Ethos and Education in Greek Music.* Cambridge: Harvard Univ. Pr., 1966.

Bower, Calvin M. "Boethius." *The New Grove.*

Georgiades, Thrasybulos. *Greek Music, Verse, and Drama.* New York: Merlin Pr., 1956.

Henderson, Isobel, and David Wulstan. "Introduction: Ancient Greece." In *Music from the Middle Ages to the Renaissance,* pp. 27–58. Ed. by F. W. Sternfeld. Praeger History of Western Music, 1. New York: Praeger, 1973.

Knight, W. F. Jackson. *St. Augustine's "De Musica:" A Synopsis.* London: Orthological Inst., 1949.

Kraeling, Carl H. "Music in the Bible." In *Ancient and Oriental Music,* pp. 283–312. Ed. by Egon Wellesz. *The New Oxford History of Music,* 1. London: Oxford Univ. Pr., 1957.

Lippman, Edward A. *Musical Thought in Ancient Greece.* New York: Columbia Univ. Pr., 1964.

Pöhlmann, E. *Denkmäler altgriechischer Musik.* Erlanger Beiträge zur Sprach- und Kunstwissenschaft, 31. Nüremberg, 1970.

Rowen, Ruth H. *Music through Sources and Documents.* Englewood Cliffs, N.J.: Prentice-Hall, 1979.

Sachs, Curt. *The Commonwealth of Art. Style in the Fine Arts, Music and the Dance.* New York: Norton, 1946.

————. *The Rise of Music in the Ancient World.* New York: Norton, 1943.

————. *The Wellsprings of Music: An Introduction to Ethnomusicology.* Ed. by Jaap Kunst. The Hague: Martinus Nijhoff, 1962.

Strunk, Oliver. *Essays on Music in the Byzantine World.* New York: Norton, 1977.

————. *Source Readings in Music History.* New York: Norton, 1950.

Velimirović, Milŏs. "Present Status of Research in Byzantine Music," *Acta musicologica* 43 (1971): 1–20.

———, ed. *Studies in Eastern Chant*. London: Oxford Univ. Pr., 1966– . (I, 1966; II, 1971.)

Weiss, Piero, and Richard Taruskin. *Music in the Western World: A History in Documents*. New York: Schirmer Books, 1984.

Wellesz, Egon. *Eastern Elements in Western Chant: Studies in the Early History of Ecclesiastical Music*. 2nd ed. Monumenta musicae byzantinae, Subsidia, v.2. Oxford: Byzantine Institute, 1967.

———. *A History of Byzantine Music and Hymnography*. 2nd ed. Oxford: Oxford Univ. Pr., 1961.

Werner, Eric. "The Music of Post-Biblical Judaism." In *Ancient and Oriental Music*, pp. 313–35. Ed. by Egon Wellesz. *The New Oxford History of Music*, 1. London: Oxford Univ. Pr., 1957.

———. *The Sacred Bridge. The Interdependence of Liturgy and Music in Synagogue and Church during the First Millenium*. New York: Columbia Univ. Pr., 1959.

Winnington-Ingram, R. P. "Greece. I: Ancient." *The New Grove*.

———. "Greek Music." *The Oxford Classical Dictionary*. 2nd ed. Oxford: Oxford Univ. Pr., 1970.

THE MIDDLE AGES

The greatest single body of music from the early Middle Ages is the collection of Christian liturgical melodies that has become known as plainchant. Gregorian chant is the largest and most important strain among the regional varieties (Coptic, Syrian, Gallican, Mozarabic, etc.) of plainchant. Legend ascribes to Pope Gregory (fifth-sixth centuries) a large role in the initial codification of the melodies, either as composer or as founder of the Schola Cantorum; scholarship has yet to determine precisely what influence he had, if any.

The earliest documents containing the melodies date from about the eighth century, and it is the business of musical scholars to trace the changes and transmission of the melodies over succeeding centuries, to determine how the melodies functioned as part of the liturgical celebrations and as musical compositions. The problems of musical mode, melodic structure, how melodies were preserved and transmitted in oral traditions and in manuscripts, how melodies were changed, how rhythm functioned and how it was modified, the relationship between music and text—these and other problems remain under very active scrutiny by contemporary scholars.

The principal manuscripts studied by scholars are available in facsimile in *Paléographie musicale* (see *The New Grove*). This monumental assemblage of sources derives from the work of the Benedictine monks of Solesmes, the scholars most responsible for restoring the melodies to their original forms and for clarifying the rhythm as well, following the many accretions and other changes over the centuries. The monks began their work after the middle of the nineteenth century and it continues today.

The authoritative survey in English is Willi Apel, *Gregorian Chant;* in German, Peter Wagner, *Einführung in die gregorianischen Melodien.* Neither scholar settled for all time—either through their own research or through critical analysis of the work of others—the central rhythmic question in Gregorian chant: whether a fixed relative mensural value can be applied to the notes, or whether free, unmeasured rhythm prevails. Those who advocate a free rhythm style of performance have generally dominated in the twentieth century, but there is beginning again a reconsideration of the position; see Lance Brunner, "The Performance of Plainchant," and Mary Berry, "The Restoration of the Chant." Dom Joseph Pothier's pivotal statement on the rhythmic freedom of Gregorian chant is *Les mélodies grégoriennes* (1880).

Helmut Hucke, in his "Toward a New Historical View of Gregorian Chant," gives a neat and concise review of the main scholarly studies in Gregorian chant. He touches on sources, transmission, liturgical codification, and theory. A principal concern is the relationship between Roman Gregorian chant and Frankish Gregorian chant, and the changes or retentions exercised by Frankish musicians, especially with regard to systemizing modes, use of neumatic notation, and actual musical practice.

Three sources that offer cogent introductions to the substance and problems of Gregorian chant are: Richard Crocker, *A History of Musical Style,* Richard Hoppin, *Medieval Music,* and Higini Anglès, writing in *The New Oxford History of Music,* II. Hoppin and Anglès also describe medieval liturgical drama and its liturgical and chant components. Two other studies that are revealing of the depth of modern scholarship in chant are Michel Huglo, *Les Tonaires,* and Richard Crocker, *The Early Medieval Sequence.* Huglo explores what are among the earliest and most basic chant manuscripts, and Crocker provides a challenging analysis and theory for a complicated species of chant in the Middle Ages. Both works are exerting influence on contemporary scholarship.

Development and refinement of the Roman liturgy—and other Western ones as well—was carried on for the entire Medieval Era, as was that of the chant used to present a great part of that liturgy. The structure of the liturgy is, therefore, of considerable interest and importance to scholars, and indeed is integral to serious study of plainchant. Hoppin nicely interweaves liturgical and musical developments in all of his discussions of chant.

It is no easy matter for scholars to find their way through the great body of surviving liturgical books that present the medieval liturgy; dialects of liturgy were widespread and the codexes that retain them are often great puzzles. Andrew Hughes's *Medieval Liturgical Manuscripts for Mass and Offices* offers, for the first time, a detailed guide, a roadmap, in effect, to their varying contents and structures. His work is a pioneering effort to clarify the confusion that has surrounded a huge body of sources.

Around the tenth century, polyphony begins to develop as an elaboration upon plainchant, and within little more than two hundred years results in the important body of sacred music known as Notre Dame polyphony. The famous cathedral in Paris was a home for cultivation of two-voice organum and its further development during the course of the thirteenth century into three- and four-voice polyphony. The central problem for polyphony—as for chant—is rhythm, in this case, rhythmic coincidence of voices. No single monograph summarizes scholarship in the field, but for information and discussion see Hoppin, *Medieval Music;* William Waite, *The Rhythm of Twelfth-Century Polyphony;* and Heinrich Husmann, "The Origin and Destination of the *Magnus liber organi.*"

Aside from the beauty and elegance of this music and the fineness of its integration into the liturgy, an essential contribution of the medieval composers and theorists was the creation of a fairly clear way of showing musical rhythm through the half-dozen rhythmic modes. The rhythmic modes codified a system of rhythmic patterns based on the shape and succession of note forms, a very important chapter in the early history of polyphonic musical notation. See Willi Apel, *The Notation of Polyphonic Music* and, for a briefer but more sharply focused exposition on rhythmic modes, Richard Hoppin's *Medieval Music.*

The thirteenth and fourteenth centuries saw the development of techniques of indicating musical rhythm in ever-increasing accuracy and detail, far outstripping the rhythmic modes in resources for rhythmic intricacy. Indeed, a most central aspect of all musical development then was clearer musical notation; through innovations in notation composers and theorists provided themselves with the means of writing for several voices at once, for writing complicated polyphonic works. Notational developments led inevitably to more artistic freedom for the composer and reached an apogee of technical complexity in the Middle Ages in the "mannered notation" of the last quarter of the fourteenth century, just before the Renaissance in music began to be felt.

Ursula Günther has introduced the term "ars subtilior" to distinguish the highly distinctive and intricate music of the late fourteenth century, and the phrase is finding acceptance among scholars. "Ars subtilior" derives from a theoretical treatise and, aside from a suitably authentic birth, it captures the notion of notation and music evolving into a more complex stage from the time of the Ars nova, around 1310. (See the two Günther citations in the bibliography.) It can be argued that highly refined and complex notational procedures reflect a high point of medieval musical (compositional) learning.

While the polyphonic development of sacred music was taking place, monophonic songs flourished as well. The first significant body of secular music from the Middle Ages is that of the troubadour and trouvère legacy, from the twelfth and thirteenth centuries. Although the poetic lyrics have become accessible and well-known to scholars and although the pitches of the melodies are decipherable, there is still no generally accepted single solution to the rhythmic interpretation of the tunes. The long-standing and vigorous dispute concerns whether the rhythm was free, that is, unmeasured, or whether rhythm was governed by the rhythmic modes. Stevens and Karp, in "Troubadours, Trouvères," outline both the history and the controversies. Van der Werf, in *The Chansons of the Troubadours*, is among the few recent full-length studies within this area. He draws on methodology proposed by Sachs in *The Wellsprings of Music* (see p. 47). See also Karp, "Interrelationships between Poetic and Music Form."

The pioneering study of medieval music for the twentieth century is by Gustave Reese, *Music in the Middle Ages*, published in 1940. Though woefully out-of-date in detail and bibliography, it nonetheless is still consulted as the single most comprehensive study of medieval music; a new edition was begun by Reese before his death in 1978 but it is being revised entirely and completed by another medievalist, Edward Roesner. Reese's study influenced a generation of scholars through his exacting and detailed approach, by which he sifted the then entire bibliography surrounding medieval music and offered both new thinking and summaries of studies; in effect, an example of critical methodology.

The most recent general history of the period is by Richard Hoppin, *Medieval Music*, which is of more modest dimensions than Reese but which reflects contemporary scholarship and the ideas of Hoppin himself. In addition to introducing the music of antiquity and its heritage and influences, Hoppin clearly exposes the repertoire and course of plainchant, the early development of secular music—as found especially in the songs of the troubadours and trouvères—and the intellectual and cultural life of the eras up to the beginning decades of the fifteenth century. Hoppins's approach is marked by an obvious enthusiasm for the music and its time. It is a landmark publication with respect to general histories of medieval music. Albert Seay's *Music in the Medieval World* is a briefer account; his viewpoints on music as learning are especially penetrating. Donald Grout, in *A History of Western Music*, provides a basic introduction although the space allotted is small. Ernest Sanders, writing in Sternfield's *Music from the Middle Ages to the Renaissance*, surveys "Polyphony and Secular Monophony: Ninth Century–c. 1300," and the history of English music to the middle of the sixteenth century. Curt Sachs, in *The Commonwealth of Art*, attempts to ally the fine arts and music, and represents one of the few efforts to do so. Johan Huizinga, in *The Waning of the Middle Ages*, offers to the students of music history (as indeed he does to all students of medieval life) a background in which to view music, and his work is widely referred to by musical medievalists. Huizinga's weaknesses in the details of music are far outweighed by the author's synthesis of medieval history.

The problems that confronted composers of the thirteenth through the fifteenth centuries—how to notate more precisely the rhythm and pitch of music, how to join the ancient theoretical writings with their own modern theory and artistic ideals; in other words, how to practice their craft and art—have, in turn, generated problems for modern scholars to solve. The history of musical notation, up to about 1500, is one of increasing explicitness and accuracy, but still it besets today's scholar with ambiguities. For example, *musica ficta*, the application of largely unwritten accidentals to a line of music, is understood more clearly but it remains at the center of music discussion of medieval musical style and its theory. Interpretation, judgment, and the application of principles and rules from various periods in the Middle Ages all relate to the scholar's perception of the problem and its resolution in specific instances in music. The most ambitious statement on *musica ficta* in relation to a certain repertory of music and a particular span of time is Andrew Hughes's *Manuscript Accidentals*.

Margaret Bent, "Musica recta," offers an equally challenging view on the problem as seen in fifteenth-century music.

Compositional intricacy reached heights in the later years of the fourteenth century that perhaps remained unmatched until the twentieth century. Rhythmic, melodic, and notational elements all were combined to create complex works, and especially was isorhythm a part of the phenomenon. Isorhythm is an organizing principle involving repetition of a rhythmic and melodic pattern; it may appear simply in one voice and provide structure, or it may be applied to all voices in complicated and obscure ways. The use of isorhythm—which is largely unperceived by the listener—is another of the ways composers sought to write for their colleagues, rather than for a larger audience (to use Nino Pirrotta's notion of scholasticism in music).

Tinctoris himself had noted the importance of English composers to the development of Late Medieval/Early Renaissance music during the fifteenth century. In recent decades of research the English influence has received much attention, notably Sylvia Kenney's *Walter Frye and the Contenance angloise*, and Frank Ll. Harrison, *Music in Medieval Britain*. David Fallows, in *Dufay*, sees the Council of Constance (1414–18) as an event during which the English musical style could have been on display for the Europeans, perhaps for Dufay himself, who was the consummate adapter and refiner of the English traits. Whatever the means of transmission, English music was the keystone for much of fifteenth-century innovation and development.

Medieval Music: The Sixth Liberal Art, by Andrew Hughes, is a comprehensive bibliography of studies in or relating to music. The citations themselves are of great usefulness, and Hughes's organization of the book itself reveals the interrelatedness of studies in medieval music, literature, linguistics, paleography, liturgics, and so forth.

Anglès, Higini. "Gregorian Chant." In *Early Medieval Music up to 1300*, pp. 92–127. Ed. by Dom Anselm Hughes. The New Oxford History of Music, 2. London: Oxford Univ. Pr., 1954.

Apel, Willi. *Gregorian Chant*. 3rd ed. Bloomington: Indiana Univ. Pr., 1966.

———. *The Notation of Polyphonic Music*. 5th ed. Cambridge, Mass.: Mediaeval Academy of America, 1961.

Bent, Margaret. "*Musica recta* and *musica ficta*." *Musica disciplina* 26 (1972): 73–100.

Berry, Mary. "The Restoration of the Chant and Seventy-Five Years of Recording." *Early Music* 7 (1979): 197–217.

Boethius, Ancius M. S. "*The Principles of Music*": *An Introduction and*

Translation, by Calvin M. Bower. New Haven, Conn.: Yale Univ. Pr., forthcoming.

Brunner, Lance. "The Performance of Plainchant: Some Preliminary Observations of the New Era." *Early Music* 10 (1982): 317–28.

Crocker, Richard. *The Early Medieval Sequence.* Berkeley: Univ. of California Pr., 1977.

———. *A History of Musical Style.* New York: McGraw-Hill, 1966.

Fallows, David. *Dufay.* London: Dent, 1982.

Grout, Donald. *A History of Western Music.* 3rd. ed. New York: Norton, 1982.

Günther, Ursula. "Das Ende der Ars nova." *Die Musikforschung* 16 (1963): 105–20.

———. "Zitate in französischen Liedsätzen der *Ars nova* und *Ars subtilior.*" *Musica disciplina* 26 (1972): 53–68.

Harrison, Frank Ll. *Music in Medieval Britain.* 4th ed. Buren: Fritz Knuf, 1980.

Hoppin, Richard. *Medieval Music.* New York: Norton, 1978.

Hucke, Helmut. "Toward a New Historical View of Gregorian Chant." *Journal of the American Musicological Society* 33 (1980): 437–67.

Hughes, Andrew. *Manuscript Accidentals: Ficta in Focus, 1350–1450.* Musicological Studies and Documents, 27. Dallas: American Institute of Musicology, 1972.

———. *Medieval Liturgical Manuscripts for Mass and Office.* Toronto: Univ. of Toronto Pr., 1982.

———. *Medieval Music: The Sixth Liberal Art.* 2nd ed. Toronto Medieval Bibliographies, 4. Toronto: Univ. of Toronto Pr., 1980.

Huglo, Michel. *Les Tonaires: inventaires, analyse, comparaison.* Publications de la Société française de musicologie, 3. sér., t. 2. Paris: Société française de musicologie, 1971.

Huizinga, Johan. *The Waning of the Middle Ages. A Study of the Forms of Life, Thought and Art in France and the Netherlands in the XIVth and XVth Centuries.* New York: St. Martin's Pr., 1949.

Husmann, Heinrich. "The Origin and Destination of the *Magnus liber organi.*" *The Musical Quarterly* 49 (1963): 311–30.

Karp, Theodore. "Interrelationships between Poetic and Musical Form in Trouvère Songs." In *A Musical Offering: Essays in Honor of Martin Bernstein.* Ed. by Edward Clinkscale and Claire Brook. New York: Pendragon Pr., 1977.

Kenney, Sylvia. *Walter Frye and the Contenance angloise.* New Haven: Yale Univ. Pr., 1964.

Pirrotta, Nino. "Medieval." *The New Grove.*

Pothier, Joseph. *Les mélodies grégoriennes.* Tournai: Impr. Liturgique de St. Jean l'évangeliste, Desclée Lefebvre, 1880.

Reese, Gustave. *Music in the Middle Ages.* New York: Norton, 1940.

Sachs, Curt. *The Commonwealth of Art: Style in the Fine Arts, Music and the Dance.* New York: Norton, 1943.

Sanders, Ernest. "Polyphony and Secular Monophony: Ninth Century–c. 1300." In *Music from the Middle Ages to the Renaissance*, pp. 89–143. Ed. by Frederick Sternfeld. Praeger History of Western Music, 1. New York: Praeger, 1973.

Seay, Albert. *Music in the Medieval World.* 2nd ed. Englewood Cliffs, N.J.: Prentice-Hall, 1975.

Sparks, Edgar. *Cantus Firmus in Mass and Motet, 1420–1530.* Berkeley and Los Angeles: Univ. of California Pr., 1963.

Stevens, John, and Theodore Karp. "Troubadours, Trouvères." *The New Grove.*

Van der Werf, Henrik. *The Chansons of the Troubadours.* Utrecht: A. Oosthoek's Uitgeversmaatschappi NV, 1972.

Wagner, Peter. *Einführung in die gregorianischen Melodien.* 3v. Leipzig: Breitkopf & Härtel, 1911–21. Repr., Hildesheim, 1962.

Waite, William. *The Rhythm of Twelfth-Century Polyphony.* New Haven: Yale Univ. Pr., 1954.

THE RENAISSANCE

Clearly, something new in music appears in the years bounding 1400. Scholars argue about the best ways of defining the opening of music's Renaissance, but there is more or less general agreement that key new elements—reflecting skills, attitudes, and wishes—show up in the music and may be traced to varying degrees in nonmusical documents. The fourteenth century had shown music as more fully embracing a secular setting (although not abandoning the ecclesiastical one); Pirrotta has characterized Machaut as reaching for a "small audience."

Many scholars have attempted to identify those elements that indicate surely how music responded to Italian humanism emanating from Florence. Emancipation of text and a growing belief that text may be *the* dominant element in music are often put forward as the signals that humanism is ascendent. Lessening of the Boethian dominance in music theory and its recodification by persons such as Johannes Tinctoris (late fifteenth century) and Franchino Gaffurio (early sixteenth century) is another tag indicating a "new music." Rediscovery of the ancient Greek sources and their promulgation is another indicator. Edward Lowinsky, in "Music in the Culture of the Renaissance," gives a good introductory view of the relationships among the new ideas that were taking place, music, and Renaissance culture.

The fourteenth century established secular music as the dominant branch, and that century saw composers begin to be more frequently identified and recognized as individuals. The fifteenth century confirmed and made permanent the place of secular music while renewing interest in music for the Church. And as Guillaume de Machaut stands out among fourteenth-century musicians, so do Guillaume Dufay and Gilles Binchois dominate the first three-quarters of the fifteenth century, and Johannes Ockeghem and (later) Josquin Desprez the latter half.

The sources for study of music written by composers of the fifteenth century are manuscripts—literary as well as musical—and for all the eras after 1500, printed documents as well as manuscripts. Scholars have always placed source study high on their agenda (cf. chapter 2) but today's researchers seek new ways of study and a broader range of documents for scrutiny. Allan Atlas, in his study of a Vatican Library manuscript containing songs of the fifteenth century, has helped reshape the way scholars look at problems of manuscript provenance and filiation, the study of relationships within a group of sources containing the same pieces. His adaptation of methodology from literary studies—principally the setting up of criteria that define "significant" and "insignificant" similarities and dissimilarities—is provoking others to reexamine their own methodology. Not all of his conclusions or adaptations are fully accepted, but his work has to be considered as pivotal in Renaissance manuscript studies. Some researchers question the grounds on which judgments about "significance" or "insignificance" are made; some question the absence of detail with respect to musical and literary variants in the songs he studies. None question, however, the new scope Atlas established for his inquiries: he exhaustively examined all related sources, and thus has provided a rationale for the manuscript's provenance and importance. Likewise, Leeman Perkins, applying similar investigative techniques, established the provenance and importance of an equally important source for fifteenth-century secular songs. Through collaborators and a wider interest in all aspects of a given source, still other scholars are marking new standards for source studies in fifteenth- and sixteenth-century music, prints and manuscripts. (See the studies by Boorman and Noblitt, on the first important printed collection of music, from 1501.)

As editions of manuscript and printed music are completed, scholars include them in their broader, interpretative studies. Which is to say that the scholars who study the history of music theory, musical style, music in society, and similar topics, increasingly find their tasks simultaneously easier and more challenging. Easier, because the music and music literature is more readily accessible; more challenging, because new relationships are established and new data are abundant.

Gustave Reese's *Music in the Renaissance* has had an influence on studies of the era that is difficult to overestimate. Few, if any, modern scholars of Renaissance music are untouched by his work. Having established an exhaustive methodology for his earlier study of medieval music, Reese applied it to the succeeding era, with measurably more success. Reese's comprehensiveness has only on occasion been matched by scholars writing on other topics: he carried out a survey of the bibliography—original and secondary sources—that has proved exemplary for students and colleagues. He confronted head-on a serious problem of historiography, whether to use a chronological, topical, or geographic frame on which to hang the story. By adopting a large geographic scheme with a chronological trapping, Reese succeeded in describing how musical processes were carried forward, and how the "central musical language" was developed and dispersed in Europe over two centuries. A major success of this scholar was to detail how musical style evolved with respect to time, locale, and composer. His work is largely descriptive of musical processes and heavily larded with fact and detail. The somewhat impersonal, uninvolved approach generated certain criticism, but the monumental effect remains intact, and *Music in the Renaissance* still is a central source for students and scholars.

Howard M. Brown's *Music in the Renaissance*, though much smaller and aimed mainly at students, is cast in a different posture: especially through evaluation of styles—as contrasted to relentless description—does he exemplify a newer trend that is increasingly devoted to judging the expressive quality of music. Brown, like others now in the field, is intrigued not only by the intricacy and technical skill of a composer, but by the expressive content of the music. He and others are reshaping the language used to write about the intellectual and emotional content of music, music of all eras.

Numerological symbolism in music fascinated Renaissance composers and theorists, as it has fascinated all intellectuals throughout history. Tracing and uncovering mathematical symbolism in music fascinates modern scholars as well. Mainly through careful study of musical scores and styles—and original sources on intellectual and metaphysical themes—have scholars learned about numerical infrastructures. Charles Warren's "Brunelleschi's Dome and Dufay's Motet" is intriguing as he reveals that the fifteenth-century composer, Guillaume Dufay, wanted "a sounding model of Brunelleschi's architecture," that Dufay sought an "architectural allegory." By establishing a direct relationship between the architectural marvel of the Renaissance—the dome of the cathedral in Florence—and a piece of music, Dufay's motet "Nuper rosarum flores," Warren confirms again that composers placed mathematics in compositions and that scholars may discover the mathematics. Or, somewhat more accurately, Warren reveals the mathematical basis for Dufay's composition, for his planning and execution of a motet. In contrast to Warren's work, Marcus van Crevel's analysis of Jacob Obrecht's "Missa Maria zart" seems troublesome and unconvincing to many scholars. Van Crevel attempts to provide a complex and dense arithmetic underpinning for Obrecht's large composition, and he has likely overstated the relationship of number to the music. See Carl Dahlhaus's comments on van Crevel's notions and also Willem Elders, *Studien zer Symbolik in der Musik der alten Niederländer,* both cited in the bibliography.

Obscure, hidden compositional elements in Renaissance music, especially that of the fifteenth century, may range from the "seen but not heard" (certain proportional rhythmic practices, certain kinds of canon) to the "not seen but audible" (for pitch modifications not actually written in the score). The high cultivation of cantus firmus technique—in which a borrowed melody undergirds the composition—may be seen as one aspect of "hidden elements." The use of "puzzle canons" is another. This procedure involves instructions, sometimes exceedingly cryptically stated, as to how a single melody may be used to provide multiple voices, even up to a full polyphonic composition.

Edward E. Lowinsky's *Secret Chromatic Art in the Netherlands Motet* pursues the thesis that "composers of that time [the Renaissance] intentionally developed a technique devised to hide the true extent to which they applied chromatic alterations [*musica ficta*] in their works. . . ." Lowinsky proposes that a double meaning for some music arises from the secret art: a composition could be performed in the open, nonsecret way by not using chromatic alteration. Or, if the full array of "secret" accidentals is used, a vastly different, sometimes shocking, musical sound results. He ties the process to a much broader aspect of intellectual life in the era: the deliberate intent of artists and writers to be recondite and learned, to layer works with meaning. Lowinsky's *Secret Chromatic Art* has been highly controversial from its first appearance, but its influence—positive or negative—has been considerable, particularly with regard to a fairly small number of pieces and their realization into sound.

Lowinsky's view that the Renaissance may be characterized as a "revolutionary" reaction to the Middle Ages is convincing in some respects, less so in others. A short criticism of his ideas is offered by Lewis Lockwood, "Renaissance," where the rather categorical and dogmatic quality of Lowinsky's "theses" is blunted by Lockwood's putting them in larger, more evolutionary contexts.

As composers in the thirteenth and fourteenth centuries brought music for three voices to a high art, so composers of the Renaissance expanded vocal sonority to four, five, and more voices. They began to expand the vocal pitch ranges, thereby achieving clearer separation of the parts as well as increasing the potentialities imbedded in imitative procedures. Through development of melodic imitation among voices, new structural possibilities were quickly realized. Thus, a new fluidity and nobility of melody in all singing voices gradually replaced dominating single or double lines.

As the boundaries of the original church modes were exceeded, composers and theorists were faced with problems and opportunities for tonal organization in music. Early on, there arose the difficulty of identifying the mode of a polyphonic work in which each voice might display the pitch characteristics of a different church mode. Renaissance theorists vary in their specificity about how to determine the controlling mode of a polyphonic work of the fifteenth and sixteenth centuries, and modern scholars have yet to agree fully on how to interpret and understand modal theory. In addition to modal identification, a second concern of theorists was the working out of various systems of tunings, a matter of central importance as instrumental music began its full development as an independent genre. Reordering of tonal resources towards only two modes—the major-minor system—was on its way during the Renaissance. It remained for Baroque composers to complete the development into the full equal temperament system, the system that was to control Western art music for 300 years, until the end of the nineteenth century. Understanding modal theory and emerging tonality is a principal concern of scholars.

Harold Powers, in "Mode," presents the most recent and comprehensive account. He offers a broad and detailed survey of historical thinking and how it was expressed by theorists in writings and by composers in music. By dwelling on the relationship between modality and counterpoint, a clear picture of development is drawn. Powers also assesses the contributions of the two preeminent sixteenth-century theorists: Heinrich Glarean and Gioseffo Zarlino (Friedrich Blume termed Zarlino's work the "Magna Carta of Renaissance music").

The way music behaves at cadences, particularly at strong internal and at final cadences, has been helpful in sorting out modal-tonal problems. The term "drive to the cadence" has been used to designate the tonal forces in voices that seem to press towards a resting point. Most important is how the fifth degree of the scale relates to the first; that is, the dominant-tonic relationship.

Edward E. Lowinsky, in *Tonality and Atonality in Sixteenth-Century Music*, provides persuasive—though, to some, limited—evidence of cadential chordal relationships and patterns in late fifteenth-century music that, for him, clearly show music arranged around a tonal center. While parts of Lowinsky's proposal concerning tonal aspects of Renaissance music have been accepted, his inventive term "floating tonality" and anachronistic use of "atonality" have not; nor has his "triadic tonality."

Most scholars retain, or try to, the terms of contemporary theorists in describing early music, in spite of linguistic and theoretical difficulties. Many find it disturbing to see Renaissance music analyzed in terms of (vertical) chord progressions, with all of their implicit tonal qualities; most prefer to describe sonorities in terms of vertical relationships among the voices, that is, intervallic structure. Used judiciously, though, modern terminology can be helpful in revealing aspects of the music without doing injustice to it; see, for example, Howard M. Brown's "The Genesis of a Style: The Parisian Chanson, 1500–1550."

In 1923 Knud Jeppesen published the Danish edition of *The Style of Palestrina and the Dissonance,* later issued in English in 1927. The volume created a new model for the study of Renaissance music (cf. chapter 2). The depth of his study of the works of one of the greatest of the Late Renaissance masters led to more or less similar analytic studies of earlier and contemporary composers, great and small. He identified Palestrina as the summation of an era that had as a musical aim the careful control of all aspects of vocal composition: melodic contour, dissonance, the interplay of voices, text setting, and so forth.

By exhaustively analyzing Palestrina's compositional technique, Jeppesen led the way to more careful and accurate views on, for example, Josquin Desprez, as the true master of the High Renaissance in the early sixteenth century, on Orlande de Lassus, as the more vigorous and emotional equal of Palestrina in the Late Renaissance, on the Italian madrigalists, whose compositions thereby stand in clearer relief from church music, and on a multitude of other composers and genres.

In his later years Jeppesen likewise afforded the potential for the same rethinking of secular music around 1500 with his monumental stylistic-bibliographic work, *La Frottola*. It is a summing up of decades of work with original sources.

Among the exemplary studies of a few notable composers or genres of the Renaissance are *Dufay*, by David Fallows; *Josquin Desprez*, by Helmut Osthoff together with *Josquin des Prez*, ed. by Edward E. Lowinsky; "Lassus" by James Haar together with *Orlando di Lasso* by Wolfgang Boetticher; *The Italian Madrigal*, by Alfred Einstein; *The Elizabethan Madrigal*, by Joseph Kerman; *The Music of William Byrd*, by Joseph Kerman, Philip Brett, and O. W. Neighbour; and Lawrence Bernstein's "Notes on the origin of the Parisian Chanson." Standard specialized works on music printing include Daniel Heartz's *Pierre Attaingnant* and Samuel Pogue's *Jacques Moderne*.

Music for instruments—as an independent genre—steadily rose in popularity during the Renaissance. It is a credit to contemporary scholarship that the role of instrumental music is beginning to be more fully investigated and understood today. Generally, the use of instrumental music is timed to advances in music printing and distribution, to the development of a fully imitative musical style, and to improvement and expansion of available instruments. Especially did keyboard instruments and plucked stringed instruments—particularly the lute—receive attention from composers, who gradually moved from intabulating preexisting music to offering newly composed pieces.

The history of instrumental music in the Renaissance has yet to be fully written. Howard M. Brown's *Instrumental Music Printed before 1600*, best reveals the extent to which Renaissance music, designed for instruments, derives from vocal sources. Willi Apel, in *The History of Keyboard Music to 1700*, describes an important and sizable portion of instrumental music in a thorough way.

Two intellectual and artistic currents in the Late Renaissance, roughly 1530–1620, lay some of the foundations for musical expression in early Baroque music: humanism and mannerism. Although both receive much attention and ink, the former seems more susceptible to modern scholarship's explanation.

A fundamental questioning of polyphony by theorists and other writers occurred in the mid-sixteenth century, largely as a result of the intense study of ancient Greek sources, newly available. A conscious effort was made to rededicate music to monodic song that would express texts ideally, in an appropriate melodic-rhythmic relationship.

In Italy, the effort led to Giovanni de Bardi's Camerata, a circle of intellectuals and composers; in France, Jean-Antoine de Baïf was the focal point with his Academie de Poésie et de Musique. Baïf's procedure was to found a supersecret society designed to foster the *vers mésurés à l'antique*, a new way of relating the measure of both poetry and music through quantification of the syllables in French rhyme. Since the secrecy was so successful, some of the written rationale of Baïf and the members of the Academie has been lost. Nonetheless, the influence of ancient writings through Baïf was significant.

Bardi and his colleagues—especially Vincenzo Galilei—appear to have sought to restore through monody what they thought to be the high artistic principles and procedures of Greek music, in opposition to the prevailing contrapuntal styles of the period. Affective expression of text was the prime objective.

Both of these Late Renaissance developments are important as scholars trace musical styles of a mature era, the Late Renaissance, as they articulate with the newer styles of an emerging era, the Baroque. D. P. Walker's articles on Baïf and on humanism in the Renaissance remain central statements: his notions that Renaissance humanists universally held a belief in "the historical truth of most of the effects of ancient music" and that humanists influenced directly the prevalence of monody in the seventeenth century remain valid. Scholars' understanding of Bardi, the Camerata, and emerging Baroque music has been immensely aided by the work of Claude Palisca, in a series of studies, notably the documents and texts in *Girolamo Mei: Letters on Ancient and Modern Music to Vincenzo Galilei and Giovanni Bardi*, and by "The 'Camerata Fiorentina': A Reappraisal."

The Age of Mannerism is sometimes proposed as an alternate for the Late Renaissance, and in sister disciplines—notably art history—the proposal has gained ground. "Mannerism" derives from the Italian *maniera* (*manierismo*), and it remains a most elusive word to define with precision—or with common assent, for that matter. (*The New Grove* gives neither word an entry.) Mannerism may denote good style, effective style, expressive style, odd style, refined style, individual style, or stylized. No single comprehensive definition emerges from the original sources, from the music, or from the efforts of scholars.

Until recent decades, Carlo Gesualdo was given as the textbook illustration of a mannerist composer of the Renaissance, on the basis of his unusual and striking use of harmonies in some madrigals. Glenn Watkins's *Gesualdo* accurately assesses all of Gesualdo's music and he offers an important viewpoint on Mannerism, including its relationship to the Counter-Reformation. Maria Rika Maniates's *Mannerism in Italian Music and Culture, 1530–1630* is by far the most ambitious study of the topic. She states her "basic hypothesis— every aspect of musical development between renaissance and baroque styles gains in precision if we posit the viability of an Age of Mannerism." Music, music theory, examination of thought and styles in sister arts, and trends in scholarship, lead her to that basic hypothesis. Indicative of this new and more widespread interest in Mannerism is the congress on the topic that was held in Rome in 1973; the proceedings were published in *Studi musicali*. Especially valuable are the contributions by Lowinsky, Lewis Lockwood, and James Haar; terminological considerations and historical contexts for terms and music are primary issues.

The traditional polyphonic styles of the Late Renaissance (exemplified by Palestrina and Lassus, among others) became known as the *prima prattica;* the newer, evolving style as the *seconda prattica.* These terms were used in the seventeenth century as composers clearly discriminated between the styles. (The next section in this book expands on the styles.) In addition to the viewpoints of Watkins, Reese, and Maniates, two other scholars provide summaries of the traits of the diverging compositional practices. Alfred Einstein's *The Italian Madrigal* traces through the madrigal the emerging seconda prattica; Jerome Roche's *The Madrigal* is considerably less detailed but useful. In *The Elizabethan Madrigal,* Joseph Kerman views that tradition in relation to both the Italian influence and the native contributions of the English composers; the study ranks with Einstein's in thoroughness and perception.

Those who study Renaissance music regularly confront problems such as expanded polyphony, modality, systems of music theory, emerging instrumental music, Mannerism, the effects on music by the Reformation and Counter-Reformation, among many topics. The discovery of new repertoires of music and intensive documentary research in archives are major present-day components of research in Renaissance music.

Apel, Willi. *The History of Keyboard Music to 1700.* Tr. and ed. by Hans Tischler. Bloomington: Indiana Univ. Pr., 1972.
Atlas, Allan. *The Capella Guilia Chansonnier: Rome, Biblioteca Apostolica Vaticana, C. G. XIII.27.* Musicological Studies, 27/1–2. 2v. Brooklyn: Institute of Mediaeval Music, 1975–76.
"Atti del Congresso internazionale sul Tema 'Manierismo' in arte e musica—

Roma, Accademia Nazionale di Santa Cecilia, 18–23 ottobre 1973." *Studi musicali* 3 (1974): 1–397. (See especially Edward L. Lowinsky, "The Problems of Mannerism in Music: An Attempt at a Definition"; Lewis Lockwood, "On 'Mannerism' and 'Renaissance' as Terms and Concepts in Music History"; James Haar, "Self-consciousness about Style, Form, and Genre in 16th–century Music."

Bent, Margaret. "*Resfacta* and *Cantare super librum.*" *Journal of the American Musicological Society* 36 (1983): 371–91.

Bernstein, Lawrence F. "Notes on the Origin of the Parisian Chanson." *Journal of Musicology* 1 (1982): 275–326.

Boetticher, Wolfgang. *Orlando di Lasso und seine Zeit.* Kassel: Bärenreiter-Verlag, 1958.

Boorman, Stanley. "The 'First' Edition of the *Odhecaton A.*" *Journal of the American Musicological Society* 30 (1977): 183–207.

Brett, Philip. *The Songs, Services and Anthems of William Byrd.* The Music of William Byrd, 2. Berkeley: Univ. of California Pr. (in preparation).

Brown, Howard M. "The Genesis of a Style: The Parisian Chanson, 1500–1550." In *Chanson and Madrigal, 1480–1530,* pp. 1–50. Ed. by James Haar. Cambridge: Harvard Univ. Pr., 1961.

————. *Instrumental Music Printed before 1600: A Bibliography.* Cambridge: Harvard Univ. Pr., 1965.

————. *Music in the Renaissance.* Englewood Cliffs, N.J.: Prentice-Hall, 1976.

Crevel, Marcus van. "Introduction." In Jacob Obrecht, *Opera omnia, editio altera,* vol. 7, pp. vii–clxiv. Amsterdam: Vereniging voor Nederlandse Muziekgeschiedenis, 1964.

Dahlhaus, Carl. "Zu Marcus van Crevels neuer Obrecht Ausgabe." *Die Musikforschung* 20 (1967): 425–30.

Einstein, Alfred. *The Italian Madrigal.* Princeton: Princeton Univ. Pr., 1949. 3v. Repr., with additions, 1971.

Elders, Willem. *Studien zur Symbolik in der Musik der alten Niederländer.* Bilthoven: A. B. Creyghton, 1968.

Fallows, David. *Dufay.* London: Dent, 1982.

Gaffurio, Franchino. *Practica musicae.* Milan, 1496. Repr.: Westmead, 1967. (Tr. of 2nd ed. (1497) by Irwin Young, Madison, Wisc., 1969; and by Clement Miller, Dallas, 1968.)

Glarean, Heinrich. *Dodecachordon.* Basle, 1547. Repr.: New York, 1967. (Tr. by Clement Miller, n.p. (Rome?), 1965.)

Haar, James. "Lassus." *The New Grove.*

Heartz, Daniel. *Pierre Attaingnant: Royal Printer of Music.* Berkeley: Univ. of California Pr., 1969.

Jacquot, Jean, ed. *La luth et sa musique [Colloque]: Neuilly-sur-Seine, 10–14 septembre 1957. Colloques internationaux du Centre national de la recherche scientifique,* 511. 2nd ed. Paris: Editions du Centre national de la recherche scientifique, 1976.

Jeppesen, Knud. *La Frottola.* 3v. Aarhus: Universitetsforlaget i Aarhus, 1968–70.

————. *The Style of Palestrina and the Dissonance.* 2nd ed. Tr. by Edward J. Dent. London: Oxford Univ. Pr., 1946.

Kerman, Joseph. *The Elizabethan Madrigal.* Studies and Documents, 4. New York: American Musicological Society, 1962.

———. *The Masses and Motets of William Byrd.* The Music of William Byrd, 1. Berkeley: Univ. of California Pr., 1980.

Lockwood, Lewis. "Renaissance." *The New Grove.*

Lowinsky, Edward E., ed. *Josquin des Prez. Proceedings of the International Josquin Festival . . . 21–25 June 1971.* 2v. (v.2: recordings) New York: Oxford Univ. Pr., 1976.

———. "Music in the Culture of the Renaissance." *Journal of the History of Ideas* 15 (1954): 509–53.

———. *Secret Chromatic Art in the Netherlands Motet.* Tr. by Carl Buchman. Columbia University Studies in Musicology, 6. New York: Columbia Univ. Pr., 1946.

———. "Secret Chromatic Art Re-examined." In *Perspectives in Musicology,* pp. 91–135. Ed. by Barry S. Brook et al. New York: Norton, 1972.

———. *Tonality and Atonality in Sixteenth-Century Music.* Berkeley: Univ. of California Pr., 1961.

Maniates, Maria Rika. *Mannerism in Italian Music and Culture, 1530–1630.* Chapel Hill: Univ. of North Carolina Pr., 1979.

Neighbour, Oliver W. *The Consort and Keyboard Music of William Byrd.* The Music of William Byrd, 3. Berkeley: Univ. of California Pr., 1978.

Noblitt, Thomas. "Textual Criticism of Selected Works Published by Petrucci." In *Formen und Problem der Ueberlieferung mehrstimmiger Musik im Zeitalter Josquin.* Wolfenbüttel: Herzog August Bibliothek, 1981.

Osthoff, Helmut. *Josquin Desprez.* 2v. Tutzing: Hans Schneider, 1962–65.

Palisca, Claude. "The 'Camerata Fiorentina': A Reappraisal." *Studi musicali* 1 (1972): 203–36.

———. *Girolamo Mei: Letters on Ancient and Modern Music to Vincenzo Galilei and Giovanni Bardi: a Study with Annotated Text.* Rome: American Institute of Musicology, 1960.

Perkins, Leeman, and Howard Garey. *The Mellon Chansonnier.* 2v. New Haven: Yale Univ. Pr., 1979.

Pirrotta, Nino. "Medieval." *The New Grove.*

Pogue, Samuel. *Jacques Moderne, Lyons Music Printer of the Sixteenth Century.* Geneva: Librairie Droz, 1969.

Powers, Harold. "Mode." *The New Grove.*

Reese, Gustave. *Music in the Renaissance.* 2nd ed. New York: Norton, 1959.

Roche, Jerome. *The Madrigal.* New York: Scribner's, 1972.

Tinctoris, Johannes. *Liber de arte contrapuncti.* Tr. by Albert Seay as *The Art of Counterpoint.* n.p.: American Institute of Musicology, 1961. (Consult *The New Grove,* "Tinctoris," for other titles and translations.)

Walker, D. P. "The Aims of Baïf's *Académie de Poësie et de Musique.*" *Musica Disciplina* 1 (1946): 91–100. (Formerly *Journal of Renaissance and Baroque Music.*)

———. "Musical Humanism in the 16th and Early 17th Centuries." *Music Review* 2 (1941): 1–13; 3 (1942): 55–71.

Warren, Charles. "Brunelleschi's Dome and Dufay's Motet." *The Musical Quarterly* 59 (1973): 92–105.

Watkins, Glenn. *Gesualdo: The Man and His Music.* Chapel Hill: Univ. of North Carolina Pr., 1973.

Zarlino, Gioseffo. *L'istitutioni harmoniche.* Venice, 1562. Repr.: Ridge-wood, N.J., 1966. (Partly tr. by Claude Palisca and Guy Marco as *The Art of Counterpoint,* New Haven, 1968. Consult *The New Grove,* "Zarlino," for other titles and translations.

THE BAROQUE ERA

Baroque, as a term for roughly 150–plus years of music history that ends about 1750, likely covers even a greater variety of styles and musical concepts than does Renaissance, for the preceding era. The term has not always been widely accepted even though it was applied to music shortly after the middle of the eighteenth century. Claude Palisca discusses the word's etymology and usage in music in both *Baroque Music* and "Baroque," as does Friedrich Blume, *Renaissance and Baroque Music.* Two writers outside musicology whose ideas have helped shape our definition of baroqueness are René Wellek, particularly in "The Concept of Baroque in Literary Scholarship" and J. H. Mueller, in "Baroque—Is It Datum, Hypothesis, or Tautology?" *Baroque,* in some of its earlier connotations, may indicate "odd" music, ornate music, overblown music, or music of a certain emotional character. Palisca is especially helpful in tracing the earliest and succeeding usages of the word.

The styles of Baroque music range from the late madrigals of the sixteenth century through the origins and full development of opera, from simple, controlled monody to the "Art of Fugue" by J. S. Bach, from embryonic to full-grown literature for organ and harpsichord, and from relatively simple polychoral motets to, say, Handel's *Messiah.* And in musical thought, the range is from the ideas of the Camerata (see Palisca, "The 'Camerata fiorentina' ") through René Descartes to Johann Mattheson, from the Camerata's attempts to restore ancient musical principles to Mattheson's full-flowered doctrine of musical affections (see Lenneberg).

Manfred Bukofzer's *Music in the Baroque Era* (1947) fundamentally reshaped the modern scholar's view of the period and the musical forces that dominated it. It was the first history of Baroque music in the English language, as Bukofzer noted in the opening sentence, and aimed at using musical style to define the era's "inner unity." Confidence in the ability of scholars to define the "inner unity" of the Baroque has waned somewhat as more and more details are found.

Bukofzer's approach was strict, even rigid, and today aspects of his declaration on the processes of musicology might be vigorously challenged: "Those writers to whom the description of music is no more than a matter of elegant variation in judiciously chosen adjectives may be shocked to learn that the word 'beautiful' does not appear in this book." Thus, he stakes out style criticism as the single most important method of relating the history of Baroque music, and uses the metaphor of disassembling an engine to describe how it works. By relying on what the music itself says, along with commentators on music from the period, Bukofzer made somewhat easier the problems of marking off the adjacent Renaissance and Classic eras from the Baroque. And by studying the theorists and other writers he influenced future scholars towards critical approaches to the sociology of music and towards performance practices.

Claude Palisca, a true music historian of ideas, has condensed his ideas on styles, theory, and music in society into a short history of the era, *Baroque Music*. Although it is a brief introduction to the period, it is by far the best recent contribution. *Baroque Music* is complemented by Palisca's newer article "Baroque" in *The New Grove*.

Prima and *seconda prattica* were mentioned in the preceding section on the Renaissance. These two styles are perhaps the clearest signs of the break between Renaissance and Baroque compositional ideals. Palestrina was recognized as the grand old master of the first, the polyphonic choral style, in which melodic structure, dissonance, and rhythmic flow were carefully controlled. The inevitable search for innovation and expressive impact led Monteverdi, among many others, towards a clear break with inherited traditions and to paving the way towards the rich sacred and secular, vocal and instrumental styles of the seventeenth and eighteenth centuries. One event in the bifurcation is detailed by Claude Palisca, "The Artusi-Monteverdi Controversy." Palisca's account of the challenge between new and old styles—between Artusi, the antiquarian, and Monteverdi, the modernist—is based on historical documents on the controversy, stylistic elements in music, and on intellectual conceptualization of the importance of the controversy. That is, Palisca puts the controversy within the history of ideas.

Opera—with some degree of justification, but grossly oversimplified—may be said to have been invented and first presented in Florence in either 1597, when Peri's *Dafne* was presented (the music does not survive except for fragments) or on October 6, 1600, when the same composer's *Euridice* was performed. Opera's roots in the sixteenth century and its course in succeeding centuries have consistently fascinated scholars, at least in part because the genre combines theater, music, dance, spectacle, and the best and worst of human emotions into a particularly satisfying experience. The appeal of music drama is not solely a part of Western art music; it may be seen, for instance, in Chinese opera and Japanese Kabuki theater. The history of opera through the Baroque Era is one of original simplicity and modesty of music toward complexity and (sometimes) outlandish exuberance in music, story, and production.

For scholars and students, Donald Grout offers the most comprehensive modern synthesis in *A Short History of Opera* (two-volume edition, 1947; rev. ed., 1965). Although Grout masterfully covers existing bibliography and adds insight to our understanding of dramatic and musical changes over the early history of opera, he did not provide genuinely new ideas and details until his work on late Baroque opera: *Alessandro Scarlatti: An Introduction to His Operas*. Before this book, knowledge of this master's operas was based on scholars' pitifully small real acquaintance with the music. Grout's sizable contribution has been to illuminate opera both before and after Scarlatti's career in the decades surrounding 1700. By studying Scarlatti, Grout throws more clearly into relief the Venetian, Roman, French, and Viennese traditions, and, as well, the monumental early seventeenth-century achievements of Claudio Monteverdi.

Tracing the history of opera is to see development of writing for the voice change from simple recitative to florid aria, from simple choral to elaborate ensemble composition. Comprehending the nature of the changes involves understanding how composers and dramatists worked together to insure dramatic impact through words and music. What begins as dramatic monody in early opera evolves into a new style of recitative in the first half of the seventeenth century. Monody itself follows its own shorter-lived course. As scholars have explored more literature and as details of performance and intention have been found, a new understanding of the development of secular vocal music and opera has emerged. Palisca, in *Baroque Music*, gives a brief but perceptive account of recitative in early opera. Nigel Fortune has documented in significant detail the history of monody, with its implications for vocal music in the later seventeenth century; see his three citations in the bibliography.

The impetus for operas has many parts—intellectual, musical, and theatrical—and the multiplicity of the forces that led to Baroque opera comprises an important part of Robert Donington's *The Rise of Opera*. Neoplatonism, humanism, the pastoral drama—these and other early manifestations of operatic intent are seen more clearly and discussed at greater length than heretofore in histories of Baroque opera up to the end of the seventeenth century. Especially does Donington examine in new detail the poetic and dramatic content of seventeenth-century opera; the French contribution of synthesizing music and dance into operatic spectacle, which had implications for the future of all opera, is emphasized. In addition, the implications of Italian monody for opera are freshly evaluated, particularly from the viewpoint of the performer.

Howard E. Smither, in *The Oratorio in the Baroque Era*, reaches back well into the sixteenth century for those seeds that ultimately flowered in the great works of Handel. Through careful research on people, places, styles, and the function of oratorios—and on texts used by composers—his two-volume study provides for the first time a panoramic view of this important genre of musical composition. Without undue emphasis, he also describes for the oratorio the vestiges of *prima prattica* and the rising *seconda prattica* during the early seventeenth century. Smither's comprehensive work is complemented by the essential book on the single most important composer of oratorios, Handel: Winton Dean's *Handel's Dramatic Oratorios and Masques.*

Smither, as others, encounters semantic difficulties in deciding what *oratorio* means, or when a work is an oratorio. The criticism of terminology, while important to conceptualizing and generalizing about such an important genre, fails to detract from the importance of his contributions.

Instrumental music, in all its facets, must rank with opera as a great contribution of Baroque composers. The roots for the astounding development of nonvocal music may lie in the Renaissance—with persons such as William Byrd, among others—but cultivation and expansion belong to the seventeenth century. Harpsichord and organ music, the solo and ensemble concerto, the sonata, and the sinfonia are Baroque achievements; the intellectual and emotional success of the developments paved the way for the consummate work of late eighteenth-century composers such as Mozart and Haydn. Boyden's study on the violin and Newman's on the sonata broke new ground in showing, in great detail, how both major and minor composers rapidly adopted new styles and concepts in their instrumental writing. And although they—and others—confirm that Italy led in this development, newer studies are uncovering important works and composers in other countries, particularly in the Late Baroque and Early Classic eras.

William S. Newman's *The Sonata in the Baroque Era* purposefully adopts a semantic approach, wherein "sonata" is treated within its historical context. Newman's work may be seen as sharing certain methodologies with Smither in that both have pioneered in examining numerous original sources, in identifying works, in establishing chronologies, and in clarifying the stylistic processes that composers used in writing music to about the middle of the eighteenth century.

As modern surveys that incorporate new research, Newman and Smither's studies are companions to major contributions such as David Boyden's *The History of Violin Playing from Its Origins to 1761*, and Willi Apel's *The History of Keyboard Music to 1700*. Each of these scholars, in individual ways, has contributed towards the now common recognition that the end of the Baroque Era is woven in a most complex way with the musical styles that came to be called Classic, and that matured most clearly in the late works of Haydn and Mozart.

Since about 1960, performers and audiences have increasingly been fascinated by Baroque music, as have been amateurs. What was perceived to be perhaps just a fad has evolved into a "growth industry." It may be safe to conjecture that part of the attraction of Baroque music is its tradition of improvisation and ornamentation. Performers increasingly turn to seventeenth- and eighteenth-century music and scholars are rapidly providing the needed information on how to perform the scores in an authentic fashion. F. T. Arnold's *The Art of Accompaniment from a Thorough-Bass* has remained as the best compendium of original writings devoted to instructing keyboard players how to provide a full keyboard sonority from a single bass line. One of the most important of the late Baroque treatises on thorough-bass playing has been translated by George Buelow, *Thorough-Bass Accompaniment according to Johann David Heinichen*, which describes not only the role of the keyboardist, but also comments on composition, musical rhetoric and the doctrine of the affections, and demonstrates ornamentation, how the performer is to elaborate on melodies in the scores. Of no less importance is the light shed by Johann Joachim Quantz. Edward Reilly's published translation of Quantz's *On Playing the Flute* opened to scholars and performers a rich source for all of the essential aspects of performance styles in Baroque music (see pp. 41–44).

Equal to Quantz's *Versuch* in contemporary and modern importance is Carl Philipp Emanuel Bach's *Essay on the True Art of Playing Keyboard Instruments.* Bach and Quantz, among others, help bridge the transitional period from Baroque to Early Classic. Bach looks backward to some degree by the extent of his comments on thoroughbass; he looks to his own time particularly with respect to ornamentation. The reader of Bach must keep in mind that he wrote some of the most elegant and dramatic music to be composed in the *empfindsamer* style, forsaking the stylistic achievements of his father. Quantz and Bach are probably the two principal sources regarded as Bibles for performance practices of the Rococo or Early Classic years.

Among the growing number of books now available to scholars and performers that aid in authentic performance of Baroque music are Robert Donington's various studies (see pp. 40, 44–45) and the most recent large contribution, Victor Rangel-Ribeiro's *Baroque Music: A Practical Guide for the Performer.* He acknowledges—gratefully, and from the viewpoint of a performer—the work of scholars and proceeds to prescribe specifics that vocal and instrumental performers of today should consider. His ideas owe much to the work of Donington, Neumann, Thurston Dart, and others, but the freshness of presentation is rare among such guides.

In the same vein as Donington—but often in opposition with respect to many details—is Frederick Neumann; his *Ornamentation in Baroque and Post-Baroque Music, with Special Emphasis on J. S. Bach* is a summing-up of long study of Baroque music and theory. His ideas are convincing to many, challenged by others. How trills, appoggiaturas, turns, and other ornaments are to be applied to the great range of French, German, and Italian music is a central concern and Neumann seeks to resolve the many problems through examination of scores and the writings of theorists. Some scholars perceive in Neumann's discussion a too dogmatic and rigid approach to a type of music that has as an essential element freedom and plasticity of expression. Controversy over ornamentation will continue, and it simply represents the ongoing attempt to get to the heart of performance problems in Baroque music.

Tonal harmony became dominant during the course of the Baroque Era; it is yet another of those musical phenomena that can reasonably be seen as an achievement of Baroque composers, who sought not only innovation but also a functional organizing means for forms in music. Functional harmony was, of course, nascent during the sixteenth century, but only after about 1600 did rapid progress set in that was to evolve into the system of keys with the two modes of major and minor.

In the Baroque, music shows increasingly an organization built on keys, chords, chromaticism, and enrichment through nonharmonic tones; that is, dissonance. As noted in chapter 1, Rameau may be seen as the main theoretical spokesman for harmony as it had matured up to 1722. The richness of the harmonic vocabulary developed by composers needed explication and a theoretical basis; Rameau provided it in his *Traité de l'harmonie*. A central contribution of Rameau is the notion of functional harmony which describes relationships between chords and a tonal center. As composers clarified tonal centers in their music, the large-scale forms of Baroque music became possible.

The articles by Carl Dahlhaus in *The New Grove*—"Harmony" and "Tonality"—give clear historical information as well as contemporaneous and modern bibliography.

The towering figures of Johann Sebastian Bach and George Fredric Handel have been the focal points of much research. Bukofzer hit upon pithy and accurate appellations in describing Bach's music as a "fusion of national styles" and Handel's as "coordination of national styles." The details of styles and new information have generally tended to support the epigrammatic phrases, and Bukofzer's generalizations can still be read with profit (see his *Music in the Baroque Era*).

Since World War II, scholarship in the music of J. S. Bach has been revolutionized. The extent of the revolution is seen in a series of bibliographic essays by Walter Blankenburg in *Acta musicologica* in which he summarizes what scholars have been doing since the early 1950s. New scientific approaches to the study of sources, archival research, and documentary discoveries have clarified the chronology of Bach's compositions, have led to more reliable editions of his music, and have deepened our understanding of his musical values. Whatever remained of the Schweitzerian view of Bach as pious mystic has been removed and in its place is a more rational appreciation of his genius and subtlety in abstract musical thought.

The relationship of rhetoric to music is discussed by Baroque theorists to a degree unparalleled in any other era. Among modern scholars who study musical rhetoric, few have matched the revelations of Ursula Kirkendale in "The Source for Bach's *Musical Offering: The Institutio oratorio* of Quintilian." Her methods of scholarship "are based on the fact that music, instrumental as well as vocal, was not an abstract pattern of sounds, but possessed content and conveyed meaning. Once the text has provided the clue for our understanding of musical formulations in the vocal repertoire, the same formulations can easily be recognized when they occur in instrumental music, with the same or similar meaning." Kirkendale's view of "The Musical Offering" is that Bach carefully and deliberately created a musical work based on ancient principles of rhetoric, and that the music can be—must be—seen in that light. If true—and there is high probability—then Bach is again confirmed as not only great artist but great intellectual.

Robert Marshall has made a notable contribution to Bach research in *The Compositional Process of J. S. Bach: A Study of the Autograph Scores of the Vocal Works.* Marshall's method of studying Bach's alterations and changes in the autographs evokes in detail and approach the sketch studies currently underway in Beethoven research.

Rococo is often used to describe the elements of lightness and playfulness that began to appear in music about 1720–30 in reaction to the grandeur and monumentality of mature Baroque music. Melodic simplicity, slower harmonic rhythm, and reconsideration of formal organization, some of the elements in the developing "galant" style, attracted composers who sensed the end of the Baroque and who laid the ground for the late eighteenth-century classicism of Mozart, Haydn, and Beethoven.

Warren Kirkendale, in *Fugue and Fugato in Rococo and Classical Chamber Music,* traces these polyphonic traits from the early decades of the eighteenth century through Haydn. He illuminates particularly the waning of the Baroque (the Rococo years) noting that it is "less of a prologue to the classical era than an epilogue to the baroque"; he eschews "pre-classical."

Delicate sensibility and the aims of fine expressive content mark the *galant* style of the middle of the eighteenth century. The sensitive *galant* style shifted so that in the 1760s the *Sturm und Drang* of literature became evident in music: musical tumult, unusual juxtapositions of harmony and rhythm, drama, and so forth. The trend was, however, short-lived: the Viennese classicists were to establish a new standard in musical language. The next section outlines thought about their music in the late eighteenth century through the early decades of the nineteenth.

Apel, Willi. *The History of Keyboard Music to 1700.* Tr. and rev. by Hans Tischler. Bloomington: Indiana Univ. Pr., 1972.
Arnold, Denis. *Monteverdi.* Rev. ed. London: Dent, 1975.

————, and Nigel Fortune, eds. *The Monteverdi Companion.* New York: Norton, 1968.

Arnold, Frank T. *The Art of Accompaniment from a Thorough-Bass.* London: Oxford, 1931. Repr. London, 1961.

Bach, Carl Philipp Emanuel. *Essay on the True Art of Playing Keyboard Instruments.* Tr. by William J. Mitchell. New York: Norton, 1949.

Blankenburg, Walter. "Die Bachforschung seit etwa 1965: Ergebnisse—Probleme—Aufgaben." *Acta musicologica* 50 (1978): 93–154; 54 (1982): 162–207; 55 (1983): 1–58.

————. "Zwölf Jahre Bachforschung." *Acta musicologica* 37 (1965): 95–158.

Blume, Friedrich. *Protestant Church Music.* New York: Norton, 1974. (Revised and augmented translation of *Geschichte der evangelischen Kirchenmusik.* 2nd ed. Kassel: Bärenreiter-Verlag, 1965.)

————. *Renaissance and Baroque Music.* Tr. by M. D. Herter Norton. New York: Norton, 1967.

Boyden, David D. *The History of Violin Playing from Its Origins to 1761.* London: Oxford Univ. Pr., 1965.

Buelow, George J. *Thorough-Bass Accompaniment according to Johann David Heinichen.* Berkeley and Los Angeles: Univ. of California Pr., 1966.

Bukofzer, Manfred. *Music in the Baroque Era.* New York: Norton, 1947.

Cannon, Beekman C. *Johann Mattheson, Spectator in Music.* New Haven: Yale Univ. Pr., 1947.

Dahlhaus, Carl. "Harmony"; "Tonality." *The New Grove.*

Dean, Winton. *Handel's Dramatic Oratorios and Masques.* London: Oxford Univ. Pr., 1959.

Descartes, René. *Compendium musicae.* Paris, 1611. Tr. by Walker Robert. Rome: American Institute of Musicology, 1961.

Donington, Robert. *The Rise of Opera.* London and Boston: Faber & Faber, 1981.

Fortune, Nigel. "Italian Secular Monody from 1600 to 1635: An Introductory Survey." *The Musical Quarterly* 39 (1953): 171–95.

————. "Monody." *The New Grove.*

————. "Solo Song and Cantata." In *The Age of Humanism, 1540–1630,* pp. 125–217. Ed. by Gerald Abraham. The New Oxford History of Music, 4. London: Oxford Univ. Pr., 1968.

Geiringer, Karl. *Johann Sebastian Bach: The Culmination of an Era.* New York: Oxford Univ. Pr., 1966.

Grout, Donald J. *Alessandro Scarlatti: An Introduction to His Operas.* Berkeley and Los Angeles: Univ. of California Pr., 1979.

————. *A Short History of Opera.* 2nd ed. 2v. New York: Columbia Univ. Pr., 1965.

Harris, Ellen. *Handel and the Pastoral Tradition.* New York: Oxford Univ. Pr., 1980.

Hutchings, Arthur. *The Baroque Concerto.* 3rd ed. London: Faber, 1973.

Kirkendale, Ursula. *Antonio Caldara: Sein Leben und seine venezianisch-römischen Oratorien.* Wiener musikwissenschaftliche Beiträge, 6. Graz: Hermann Böhlaus, 1966.

————. "The Source for Bach's *Musical Offering:* The *Institutio oratorio* of

Quintilian." *Journal of the American Musicological Society* 33 (1980): 88–141.

Kirkendale, Warren. *Fugue and Fugato in Rococo and Classical Chamber Music.* 2nd ed. Tr. by Margaret Bent. Durham: Duke Univ. Pr., 1979.

Lang, Paul Henry. *George Fridric Handel.* New York: Norton, 1966.

Lenneberg, Hans. "Johann Mattheson on Affect and Rhetoric in Music." *Journal of Music Theory* 2 (1950): 47–84, 193–236.

Lester, Joel. "Major-Minor Concepts and Modal Theory in Germany: 1592–1680." *Journal of the American Musicological Society* 30 (1977): 208–57.

Marshall, Robert. *The Compositional Process of J. S. Bach: A Study of the Autograph Scores of the Vocal Works.* 2v. Princeton: Princeton Univ. Pr., 1972.

Mueller, J. H. "Baroque—Is It Datum, Hypothesis, or Tautology?" *Journal of Aesthetics and Art Criticism* 12 (1953–54): 421–37.

Neumann, Fredrick. *Ornamentation in Baroque and Post-Baroque Music, with Special Emphasis on J. S. Bach.* Princeton: Princeton Univ. Pr., 1978.

Newman, William S. *The Sonata in the Baroque Era.* 4th ed. New York: Norton, 1983.

Palisca, Claude. "The Artusi-Monteverdi Controversy." In *The Monteverdi Companion,* pp. 133–66. Ed. by Denis Arnold and Nigel Fortune. London: Faber & Faber, 1968.

———. "Baroque." *The New Grove.*

———. *Baroque Music.* 2nd ed. Englewood Cliffs, N.J.: Prentice-Hall, 1981.

———. "The 'Camerata Fiorentina': A Reappraisal." *Studi musicali* 1 (1972): 203–36.

Quantz, Johann Joachim. *On Playing the Flute.* Tr. by Edward R. Reilly. New York: Free Pr., 1966.

Rangel-Ribeiro, Victor. *Baroque Music. A Practical Guide for the Performer.* New York: Schirmer Books, 1981.

Reilly, Edward R. *Quantz and His Versuch.* Studies and Documents, 5. New York: American Musicological Society, 1971.

Smither, Howard E. "The Baroque Oratorio: A Report on Research since 1945." *Acta musicologica* 48 (1976): 50–76.

———. *The Oratorio in the Baroque Era.* 2v. Chapel Hill: Univ. of North Carolina Pr., 1977.

Wellek, René. "The Concept of Baroque in Literary Scholarship." *Journal of Aesthetics and Art Criticism* 5 (1946): 77–106. Reprinted with "Postscript-1962" in his *Concepts of Criticism.* New Haven: Yale Univ. Pr., 1963.

THE CLASSIC ERA

Stylistic and chronological definition of a Classic Era in music is exceedingly troublesome. It is clear that "rococo," "galant," and "empfindsam" qualities appear in music after about 1720 and that the stylistic elements shape composition until the 1760s and 1770s;

but it is also clear that Baroque grandeur did not disappear entirely, as witnessed most dramatically by Bach and Handel. Although Mattheson and Quantz, in many ways, railed against some aspects of Baroque practices, they still codified much of Baroque style, while foretelling and advising on future developments. What is clear—and acceptable to about everyone—is that there finally emerged a Viennese Classical style that derived most of all from the works of Haydn, joined by Mozart and by Beethoven, especially in his earlier works. But, Beethoven presents very special problems for the categorizing historian: is he Classic or Romantic? Strong elements of both forces appear in his music, and he will provide, for present purposes, the best transition from this section to the Romantic Era.

A simple example of the variety of opinion about the validity of a Classic Era is the absence of a separate article on the period in the *Harvard Dictionary of Music* (Renaissance and Baroque are discussed as eras). The serious problem of periodizing the eighteenth century is documented in the record of a colloquium held during the 1967 Congress of the International Musicological Society in Ljubljana, "Critical Years in European Musical History: 1740–1760." The panelists, while agreeing on certain stylistic and cultural events that marked changes around 1720–60, found it difficult to assess fully the importance of various movements by composers towards clarity, simplicity, and elegance in music, or to evaluate all of the implications found in theoretical writings of the earlier eighteenth century.

Daniel Heartz, one of the panelists at Ljubljana, treats not only the idea of a Classic Era in his article in *The New Grove*, but also classicism in music generally. His statements on earlier manifestations of classicism, and on neo- and romantic classicism, provide a needed perspective on the whole issue and they throw more light on the achievements of the Viennese Classicists.

Mozart, Haydn, and Beethoven dominate their times as few musicians have dominated any other period in the history of music. They were acknowledged as great, lionized to varying degrees, and they created styles that are at the same time related but highly individual, even idiosyncratic; Beethoven, of course, expanded the common language they shared to provide both spiritual and technical bases for Romantic music, especially as it grew in the late nineteenth century.

Scholars vary in their attempts to grapple with music of the late eighteenth century. Charles Rosen, in *The Classical Style: Haydn, Mozart, Beethoven,* emphatically asserts the value of genius in examining an age: "There is a belief, which I do not share, that the greatest artists make their effect only when seen against a background of the mediocrity that surrounded them. . . ." Naturally he does not entirely dismiss contemporaries; especially does the relationship between the music of Gluck and Mozart receive attention.

Rosen's book centers on the achievements of the three composers in symphony, opera, chamber music (especially the string quartet), and piano music. The approach is through musical and aesthetic meaning, form, cultural setting and function, and a personal reaction to the music. The usual scholar's trappings—necessary for documentation of dates, places, people, bibliography—are absent; in their place are the fervor of personal conviction and penetrating observations on how the classical style originated, developed, and matured. Since *sonata* received most attention in the Classic Era (as a work entitled "Sonata" and as the word indicating something about musical form), Rosen dwells at length on how *sonata* was used and what it meant at various times, always returning to his conviction that form, to have any meaning, must be heard and not only seen.

William S. Newman's *The Sonata in the Classic Era* merges with his earlier volume on the sonata during the Baroque Era. The encyclopedic approach is antipodal to Rosen's in that Newman illuminates not only the three Classic Era masters, but the hundreds of others who, in his view, contributed to the Classical style, to the musical life of the time, and to disseminating music in the new era of popular music. He can, through looking at essentially all of the relevant music, aim at providing a rationale for his statement that "the high-Classic style represents, above all, the peak at which the ideal and most purposeful coordination of Classic style traits obtained." How that coordination came about occupies most of the book. Newman's breadth is not unlike that of Gustave Reese's treatment of the Renaissance Era: few composers, ideas, or influences are left untouched; little bibliography escapes their notice and evaluation.

Although Rosen and Newman have much in common, the choice of language to discuss music is widely different. Rosen reacts directly to the emotional impact he finds; Newman prefers a cooler, more objective set of modifiers. Therein lies a principal difference between two extremely important books on music in this period, even though, for instance, their analyses of form may more or less agree in some cases.

Sonata has had a variety of meanings and Newman traces them in his series of books. Not until the nineteenth century, however, did the phrase "sonata form" come into common use; the concept has remained as a pedagogic means to teach analysis and composition.

Newman, in "Style and Form," chapter 6 of *The Sonata in the Classic Era,* provides for the first time a full historical context for the late eighteenth-century treatment of the sonata. Through painstaking detail with regard to musical motive and phrase, key structure and theme, and harmonic schemes, he describes the evolution of the sonata from galant style to the final monumental piano sonatas of Beethoven.

Rosen's second book, *Sonata Forms,* stays close to the music itself and ranges across almost the entire gamut of music in which sonata forms (Rosen's plural) had impact. His approach to the music is not unlike that of the composer in the eighteenth century. The Classic Era composer identified a new public, the music lover; Rosen, as performer and commentator, aims to bridge the gap between the academy and the listener.

Eugene Wolf, in his "Classic Period," acknowledges that Rosen "includes numerous interesting analytical views on eighteenth-century formal structure," but he finds Rosen short in presenting "a *history* of such structure." In the same article Wolf identifies several problems in present-day research in the era; one derives from the sheer abundance of music and its typical format of parts rather than scores. Another is the lack of certain standards and methods of scholarship that are accepted in studies of earlier music. And another is the lack of a "true history of eighteenth-century theory."

Contributing towards an understanding of eighteenth-century music theory has been a principal interest of Leonard Ratner. In particular, he seeks to understand the principles that governed composers in the Classic style and his orientation derives from theoretical writings of the period. Ratner's most recent publication is *Classic Music: Expression, Form, and Style.* In this important book Ratner suggests that Classic style may have more connection to preceding generations of composers than to the Romantic style that was to follow. His extensive discussions under "Expression" and "Rhetoric" draw heavily on theoretical sources and stylistic elements he sees in the scores themselves.

The new public for music—as opposed to the traditional audiences of church and court—was a product of those political, intellectual, economic, and artistic forces that spurred both the Enlightenment and revolution. The musical amateur, dilettante, lover, and student provided a market that had been unknown until the middle years of the eighteenth century; that public was to grow forevermore. Paul Henry Lang, in *Music in Western Civilization*, has captured best the environment and spirit of both Rococo and Classic years; his setting of music within the arts and literature has remained the standard for several decades. Lang discusses the immediate influence of Johann Joachim Winckelmann's *History of the Art of Antiquity*, the beginnings of modern classical archaeology, and the influence of Hellenistic ideas. In addition, Lang ranges through the nature of rational and classical influences on the eighteenth-century spirit.

Jean-Jacques Rousseau's philosophical pronouncements, theories, and writings had much more effect on eighteenth-century music than did his compositions, charming and moving though some of them may be. While advocating "naturalness," "simplicity," and "a return to nature" (to use clichés applied to him), Rousseau provided for contemporaries a rationale for at least some of the qualities found in Classic music. In the long run, Rousseau had the most effect on the Romantic movement in his assertion about feelings dominating reason.

Peter Le Huray and James Day have edited a comprehensive collection of readings on *Music and Aesthetics in the Eighteenth and Early-Nineteenth Centuries;* selections from Rousseau are included. Their introduction to the anthology (pp. 1–16) succinctly narrates the history of musical aesthetics in the time span of 1719–1848, and the collection "is designed to illustrate some of the main aesthetic issues that were so hotly and continuously debated during the eighteenth and early-nineteenth centuries." Le Huray and Day include passages from the eighteenth-century histories of Hawkins and Burney; for comment on the music historiography of the eighteenth century and additional bibliography, see chapter 2.

The universality of humanity—as expressed and longed for by Rousseau and those of similar persuasion—was an ideal sought and pondered. In music, this universality may perhaps have been achieved to some degree: a common musical style existed at the end of the eighteenth century that had not been seen before. This style—found in the symphony, string quartet, the concerto—allowed composers such as Haydn and Mozart to share a common idiom while at the same time it gave them the widest range of personal expression. This universal language contained folk elements—song, dance, myth—that gave an immediate appeal to the new public, who could pay for and happily attend concert and opera. Widest dissemination was the result.

Opera in the Classic Era departed from Baroque ideals in both musical expression and in story. The heroic-mythic librettos of Pietro

Metastasio, so popular in the early eighteenth century, gradually declined in favor as antiroyalist, democratic, revolutionary notions came to the fore; even so, Metastasian librettos continued right through the life of Mozart. Michael Robinson, in *The New Grove*, notes a new revisionist attitude currently among some modern scholars, i.e., a less negative appreciation of Metastasio's librettos.

Mankind becomes opera's main theme, one that was to lead to works such as Mozart's *The Marriage of Figaro* and Beethoven's *Fidelio*. Mozart's operas represent Classic idiom and ideals as no other; his facility and ease in writing *opera seria* and *opera buffa* are unmatched. Although it was first published in 1913, Edward J. Dent's *Mozart's Operas* has yet to be surpassed as a study that consistently offers perceptive comment on the interrelation of music and drama in the composer's works.

The success of the operatic reforms of Gluck may be measured by the fact that the repertoire of today's opera houses begins with his works that introduced drastic changes in stereotypical Baroque opera, notably *Alceste* and *Orfeo ed Euridice*, and the two on the Iphigenia theme. Assessing the reasons for the continued artistic success of these operas provides scholars with a key to music of the Classic Era: balance, form, and a new lyricism in music are recombined with drama that restores emotional intensity to the theater.

The view of Haydn as something of a "failed" composer of operas has changed in recent decades. A new appreciation of the numerous operas he wrote and produced for the Court of Esterháza has emerged, aided immensely by Dénes Bartha's *Haydn als Opernkapellmeister*. H. C. Robbins Landon's article in *The New Oxford History of Music* provides details about musical elements, librettos, and the high artistry and success that Haydn enjoyed as a composer of operas. The new image of Haydn's operas is being enhanced with modern productions in Europe and America.

In the early 1960s, H. C. Robbins Landon began his intensive study of Haydn's life and works and the ensuing decades have seen dozens of works edited and published, Haydn's life and times newly revealed through archival research, and Landon's monumental five-volume biography completed, *Haydn: Chronicle and Works*. In some respects, Landon's pursuit of historical detail—biographical, cultural, economic—has set a new standard for biographical studies.

Beethoven serves to end this section on Classic music and to introduce the Romantic Era. He represents at one and the same time a continuation of the Viennese Classical style and the essential elements of Romanticism, including a fully Romantic personage and mode of living. The dramatic, pathetic, and heroic aspects of his life have attracted and kept the attention of performers, audiences, and scholars as few others in the history of music.

Both Rosen (*The Classical Style*) and Newman (*The Sonata in the Classic Era*) trace the stylistic development and expansion that Beethoven as Classic composer applied to his own music, the transmutation of his heritage into a personal style. Neither author sees easy ways to link Beethoven securely to succeeding decades. Rosen is unequivocal: "A discontinuity of style between Beethoven and the generation that followed is an inescapable hypothesis for understanding the musical language of the nineteenth century."

Beethoven is the first composer to have left a sizable number of sketches for his compositions; early on after his death, they attracted the attention of scholars, and today much research concentrates on interpreting their meaning in relationship to his compositional practice and finished works. (Chapter 2, pp. 37, 39–41, presents sketch studies, with pertinent bibliography.)

Related to studies of Beethoven's sketches is Janet Levy's *Beethoven's Compositional Choices; The Two Versions of Opus 18, No. 1, First Movement*. In this instance, Beethoven wrote a first complete version and then, later, a revised complete version; Levy chooses to examine in detail the differences between the two, i.e., Beethoven's compositional choices, since he considered the later version to be authoritative. Her method shows considerable originality. She does not restrict her discussion to description or to constructing a typology of Beethoven's revisions. Rather, she invokes theory "about such fundamental matters as the nature of coherence in musical relationships, the creation of articulation, anacrustic versus nonanacrustic functions, additive versus cumulative structure." Levy's book inaugurates Studies in the Criticism and Theory of Music, edited by Leonard Meyer, himself a shaper of current analytic-critical methodology.

The force and peculiarities of Beethoven's personality, the mystery of the woman whom he addressed as the "Immortal Beloved," his relation with his nephew, and the innumerable idiosyncrasies he had—all this has fascinated music-lovers and scholars since his death. Editha and Richard Sterba published *Beethoven and His Nephew* in 1954; they provided a psychoanalytic probing of the relationship between the two men. Maynard Solomon is the most prominent among contemporary scholars who have thought seriously about Beethoven's psychological makeup and its reflection in his music. Solomon's *Beethoven* is cast as a critical biography in the sense of an evaluation of the events of Beethoven's life, the circumstances surrounding the compositions, and his psychological frame of mind and reference. It is yet another piece of critical evaluation that is at the center of contemporary Beethoven studies.

The Classic Era fully established popular audiences as well as consumers of music on a very large scale. The thousands of pieces of chamber music, vocal music, and keyboard music were disseminated widely; opera and oratorio were immensely successful in theaters and concert halls. How the music was performed, listened to, and gained acceptance is of concern to the scholar. Vital questions for the era— in addition to the ideas already presented—involve clarifying the history of the transition from harpsichord to fortepiano, the details of performance practices, the transition from patronage to more of a free market system for composers, and the unlocking of still more documents and archives for music.

Abert, Hermann. *W. A. Mozart, neuearbeitete und erweiterte Ausgabe Otto Jahns Mozart.* 7th ed. 2v. Leipzig: Breitkopf & Härtel, 1955–56. (Engl. tr. by Traute Marshall in preparation. See also Jahn, Otto, p. 32.)

Bartha, Denés, and László Somfai, eds. *Haydn als Opernkapellmeister: die Haydn-Dokumente der Esterhazy-Opernsammlung.* Budapest: Verlag der Ungarischen Akademie der Wissenschaften, 1960.

Blume, Friedrich. *Classic and Romantic Music.* Tr. by M. D. Herter Norton. New York: Norton, 1970.

Brook, Barry. *La symphonie française dans la seconde motíe de XVIIIe siècle.* 3v. Publications de l'Institut de musicologie de l'Université de Paris, 3. Paris: Institut de musicologie de l'Université de Paris, 1962.

Churgin, Bathia. "G. B. Sammartini and the Symphony." *The Musical Times* 106 (1975): 26–29.

"Critical Years in European Musical History: 1740–1760." (Symposium) International Musicological Society, *Report of the Tenth Congress, Ljubljana 1967,* v. 1, pp. 159–93. Ed. by Dragotin Cvetko. 2v. Kassel: Bärenreiter-Verlag, 1970.

Dent, Edward J. *Mozart's Operas.* 2nd ed. London: Oxford Univ. Pr., 1960.

Einstein, Alfred. *Mozart: His Character, His Work.* Tr. by Arthur Mendel and Nathan Broder. New York: Oxford Univ. Pr., 1972 (1945).

Heartz, Daniel. "Classical." *The New Grove.*

———. "From Garrick to Gluck: The Reform of Theatre and Opera in the Mid-Eighteenth Century." *Proceedings of the Royal Musical Association* 94 (1967–68): 111–27.

Kerman, Joseph. *The Beethoven Quartets.* New York: Knopf, 1967.

Kirkendale, Warren. *Fugue and Fugato in Rococo and Classical Chamber Music.* 2nd ed. Tr. by Margaret Bent. Durham: Duke Univ. Pr., 1979.

————. "New Roads to Old Ideas in Beethoven's *Missa Solemnis*," *The Musical Quarterly* 61 (1970): 665–701. Reprinted in Paul Henry Lang, ed., *The Creative World of Beethoven*. (Originally published as "Beethovens Missa Solemnis und die rhetorische Tradition," in *Beethoven Symposium Wien 1970*, pp. 121–58. Wien: Böhlau, 1971.)

Landon, H. C. Robbins. *Essays on the Viennese Classical Style: Gluck, Haydn, Mozart, Beethoven*. New York: Macmillan, 1970.

————. *Haydn, A Documentary Biography*. New York: Rizzoli, 1981.

————. *Haydn: Chronicle and Works*. 5v. Bloomington: Indiana Univ. Pr., 1976–80.

————. "The Operas of Haydn." In *The Age of Enlightenment*, pp. 172–99. Ed. by Egon Wellesz and Frederick Sternfeld. The New Oxford History of Music, 7. London: Oxford Univ. Pr., 1973.

————, and Donald Mitchell, eds. *The Mozart Companion*. London: Rockliff, 1956.

Lang, Paul Henry, ed. *The Creative World of Beethoven*. New York: Norton, 1971. (Essays from *The Musical Quarterly*)

————, ed. *The Creative World of Mozart*. New York: Norton, 1963. (Essays from *The Musical Quarterly*)

————. *Music in Western Civilization*. New York: Norton, 1941. (Especially ch. 13, "The Classic Era," pp. 618–74, and ch. 15, "The Confluence of Classicism and Romanticism," pp. 734–800.)

Le Huray, Peter, and James Day, eds. *Music and Aesthetics in the Eighteenth and Early-Nineteenth Centuries*. New York: Cambridge Univ. Pr., 1981.

Levy, Janet. *Beethoven's Compositional Choices: The Two Versions of Opus 18, No. 1, First Movement*. (Studies in the Criticism and Theory of Music, 1.) Philadelphia: Univ. of Pennsylvania Pr., 1982.

Newman, William S. *The Sonata in the Classic Era*. 3rd ed. New York: Norton, 1983.

Pauly, Reinhard. *Music in the Classic Period*. 2nd ed. Englewood Cliffs, N.J.: Prentice-Hall, 1973.

Ratner, Leonard. *Classic Music: Expression, Form, and Style*. New York: Schirmer Books, 1980.

Robinson, Michael F. "Metastasio, Pietro." *The New Grove*.

Rosen, Charles. *The Classical Style: Haydn, Mozart, and Beethoven*. New York: Viking, 1973.

————. *Sonata Forms*. New York: Norton, 1980.

Solomon, Maynard. *Beethoven*. New York: Schirmer Books, 1977.

————. "Beethoven and His Nephew: A Reappraisal." In *Beethoven Studies* 2, pp. 138–52. Ed. by Alan Tyson. New York: Oxford Univ. Pr., 1977.

Sterba, Editha, and Richard Sterba. *Beethoven and His Nephew*. Tr. by Willard R. Trask. New York: Pantheon, 1954.

Wolf, Eugene. "Classic Period." *The Journal of Musicology* 1 (1982): 50–53.

THE ROMANTIC ERA

The nature of Romanticism attracted contemporaneous comment as few other cultural or artistic forces had done before. Writer after writer—from Goethe to E. T. A. Hoffmann to Jean Paul—sought to explain it, to characterize it, to define it, to contribute to it through fiction and pamphlet. Goethe wrote about Romanticism in an old-fashioned, dispassionate way. Others, particularly Hoffmann, relied on hyperbolic, metaphoric, and symbolic descriptions that conjured up passion, heroic concepts, rapture, mystery, and the like. Literary and musical journals were founded and filled with explanations, book and music reviews, and declarations about Romanticism.

The German *Sturm und Drang* of the 1770s and 80s is best viewed as a reaction to the German *Aufklärung*, the German Enlightenment. Many scholars trace the seeds of the Romantic movement to that time, especially because of the romantic qualities of extreme emotion, the concern with pathos, and a preoccupation with ecstasy, love, and death, as in Goethe's *Werther*, for example. The Classicism promulgated in Gotthold Lessing's *Laoköon* (1776)—his view that uncrossable boundaries exist between painting and poetry—was to fall under the onslaught of Romantic fervor. The literary leader of the onslaught was E. T. A. Hoffmann.

It should be remembered that Hoffmann (1776–1822) was only barely junior to Beethoven (1770–1827). Yet he was the major spokesman for early Romanticism and the leading pamphleteer for the cause that sometimes championed Beethoven as one of its own but also at times rejected him. Among the best of the earliest writings on the Romantic spirit as well as one that lauds Beethoven and claims him for Romanticism, is Hoffmann's "Beethoven's Instrumental Music" (1813), an amalgam of two pieces he had written a little earlier, in 1810 and 1813.

Anyone interested in capturing at the outset something of the flavor of a movement that held the nineteenth century in thrall could do much worse than to begin by reading Hoffmann on Beethoven, Jean Paul on Romantic poetry, and Robert Schumann's music criticism. Translations from the writings (including letters) of all three appear in Strunk and in Rowen, as do selections from other composers and critics such as Mendelssohn, Liszt, Wagner, and Berlioz.

Leon Plantinga has best shown the brilliance of Robert Schumann's writings in *Schumann as Critic*. Schumann—with a small coterie of participants—founded the *Neue Zeitschrift für Musik* in 1834 (and it continues today, much changed, but still a testament to the founder's vision). Plantinga remarks at the outset that "Its most characteristic features—vigorous idealism, partisanship, and often, irreverent impetuosity—result from Schumann's involvement in live contemporary issues in music, and it was the purpose of the NZfM to make these issues clear." The journal and its editor were to embody, in many ways, all of the characteristics of the movement, including raising of standards in music and in criticism, making known the important heritage of the past—especially that of J. S. Bach, whom many regarded reverentially within a Romantic context—and establishing what might be called the ground rules for Romanticism, establishing the credo. As well, there is a sense of history in the writings of Schumann and other Romantic composers: they sought to see themselves as another force within broad music history and to document their own activities and achievements, through the journals, memoirs, polemical tracts, and position papers that they issued by the gross.

The *Neue Zeitschrift für Musik* is only one of many sources modern scholars use for documentation and for insight, with respect to nineteenth-century studies. There is presently considerable interest in a broad range of journalistic sources from the nineteenth century, when musical biography, autobiography, journalism, and pamphleteering became firmly established.

The Romantic Era was the century par excellence for the musician-writer, for the critic, and for the music journalist, all of whom sought to explain music as the greatest of the arts and to take positions on issues in the arts, to evaluate, to promulgate. The Romantic musician as a person of many parts may be best illustrated by Wagner, who considered himself a musician, poet, critic, statesman—and more.

In general, it is owing to the preoccupation with the ties between music and literature that Romantic composers saw in song the potential for expression of sentiment and feeling. Beethoven is credited with the first song cycle, *An die ferne Geliebte* (1816), but it was the Romantic composers who created the great legacy of lieder and *mélodies*. Specifically, Schubert gave it the greatest importance as a genre, in the song cycles and in the independent settings, all using poetry of the time. Musical balance between voice and piano, participants in the effort to reveal the emotion of the text in music, was the aim of composers from Schubert through Schumann, Brahms, Hugo Wolf, to Henri Duparc and Debussy. Eric Sams's volumes on the songs of Hugo Wolf and Robert Schumann remain standard introductions, along with, for example, Frits Noske on the French *mélodie*.

R. Murray Schafer brings a composer's view to *E. T. A. Hoffmann and Music*, an anthology that alternates between translations from

Hoffmann's German and Schafer's commentary. Taken as a whole, this modest volume clearly establishes the thesis held by Hoffmann and his contemporaries, that music was the supreme vehicle for Romanticism, and that instrumental music was highest in the pantheon of sounds. Instrumental music could express the inexpressible, the ineffable, the indescribable, the unutterable.

Any concept of a Romantic Era has to account for these literary influences, for the cult of genius and heroic figures, for the new and forceful nationalistic movements in music, for composers as disparate in time, place, and spirit as Schumann, Chopin, Liszt, Wagner, Bruckner, Brahms, and Tschaikovsky, as well as Gustave Mahler and Richard Strauss.

Carl Dahlhaus has expanded on the old notion that the second half of the nineteenth century reflects "neo-Romanticism," in that the general forces begun in the earlier half of the century were still at work in music while the other arts had moved to Expressionism, Naturalism, and Impressionism. The usefulness of "neo-Romanticism" is considerable: it allows a clearer separation for Wagner and Liszt, Brahms and Bruckner. Alfred Einstein (*Music in the Romantic Era*) proposed "hyper-Romanticism" to characterize the end of neo-Romanticism as seen in, for example, the works of Scriabin. Dahlhaus's "Neo-Romanticism" (the first essay in *Between Romanticism and Modernism*) is a clear, albeit brief, outline of the various stages of Romanticism throughout the century. He comments on nineteenth-century Positivism, which gained strength in the later years of the century.

Friedrich Blume's summary of the era in *Classic and Romantic Music* is steeped in literary references, the psychology of the age, and in penetrating stylistic observations about the music of the Romantic composers. His tracing of the elements that evolved into a "Classic-Romantic" style is perhaps the clearest available to students. The most serious fault with Blume's account is his absorption with German Romanticism, to the neglect of France, Italy, and England.

Like most surveyors of the period (including John Warrack, "Romantic," *The New Grove*), Blume has trouble ending the Romantic Era. The 1890s saw Verdi's last efforts (*Otello* and *Falstaff*) but only the beginning great successes of Gustave Mahler (d. 1911) and Richard Strauss (d. 1949).

Literature, philosophical movements, and artistic life provide the panorama against which Jacques Barzun portrays *Berlioz and the Romantic Century*. While details on musical style are deficient, the richness of Barzun's familiarity with nineteenth-century Romanticism far outweighs the deficiencies. The two volumes on Berlioz are close kin to Paul Henry Lang's discussions on the Romantic Era in *Music in Western Civilization*. Together, Barzun and Lang give substance to many of those aspects of Romanticism that are difficult to discuss without lapsing into nonsense.

The concepts of absolute music and program music are talked about repeatedly by composers and writers of the nineteenth century. The notion that music is devoid of extramusical associations was rejected time and again by Romantic composers, as indeed it had been rejected in earlier times but with less finality than in the nineteenth century. Character pieces—whether works such as Schumann's *Scenes from Childhood* for piano or Liszt's *Faust Symphony* or Richard Strauss's *Thus Spake Zarathustra*—sought to express either a feeling or mood or an entire story.

Berlioz was a leader in symphonic program music: his *Symphonie fantastique* (1830) provided the impetus for the widest range of experimentation by composers in the nineteenth century as they also wrote pieces carrying some sort of story or specific allusion. Barzun has a stimulating discussion of program music in the first volume of *Berlioz and the Romantic Century*. His chapter entitled "Program Music and the Unicorn" places programmatic music of the century into a context of poetry, literature, and philosophy. Berlioz functions as catalyst for Barzun in another chapter, "The Century of Romanticism," in which Barzun emphasizes the idea of Wagner as realist—played against Romanticism and Debussy's "allusive" music.

Wagner and Verdi have dominated discussions of nineteenth-century opera for decades, to the detriment of our understanding of the course of opera in the Romantic Era. As a part of the new interest in all music of that century, clarifications of their contributions are being made along with intense study of the music of other composers. There is a true renewal of scholarly interest in, for example, Rossini and Verdi. New editions of both are in progress that apply all of the means and methods of scholarly methodology: comparison of sources, sketches, archival research, editions that reveal the composer's full intentions, insofar as is possible. The exhaustive three-volume study by Julian Budden, *The Operas of Verdi*, not only has portrayed Verdi and his music more fully than before, but sets him within the context of the history of opera, thereby reevaluating not only Verdi's achievements but those of Wagner and numerous others.

The other principal, Wagner, has likely had more ink spilled about him than anyone but Shakespeare, partly because he wrote so much prose himself. By laying out ideas on music and implementing them in his composition, Wagner has served as lightning rod for just about all future comment on music of the era, especially opera. Curt von Westernhagen, in *Wagner*, has complemented—through updating and some new material—but by no means superseded the classic four-volume study by Ernest Newman, *The Life of Richard Wagner*. Another important critique of the composer's achievements is Dahlhaus's study of the Wagnerian music drama, now available in English.

In 1970, the International Musicological Society held a colloquium on nineteenth-century music; the printed record is available as "Papers of the Colloque at Saint-Germain-en-Laye. . ." in *Acta musicologica*. The range of topics is representative of the burgeoning interest at that time in nineteenth-century music: virtuosity, the compositional process, Tschaikovsky, instrumentation, and historiography. While some of the information is dated, the overall scope of discussion reflects most of the problems still faced by scholars today with regard to methodology, interpretation, theories of value, and historical orientation.

Studien zur Musikgeschichte des 19. Jahrhunderts began in 1965; some sixty volumes have been published through 1981. It is a series of the greatest importance in all areas: composer studies, bibliography, philosophy, music theory, etc. Many of the volumes are collections of studies by a number of scholars—sometimes from a symposium—on specific topics or issues. A few of the more important are cited in the bibliography; see the titles under Dahlhaus and Vogel. Simply to indicate the scope of the series, the following volume is noted: Robert Gunther, *Musikkulturen Asiens, Afrikas und Ozeaniens im 19. Jahrhundert* (vol. 31, 1973). More relevant to present purposes—and revealing of current research interests as well as a changing scope for scholarship—is *Studien zur Trivialmusik*, edited by Carl Dahlhaus. Nineteenth-century salon and similar "light" music and musical *Kitsch* are treated seriously by the contributors.

19th-Century Music began in 1977, and the journal has rapidly become a main forum for the widest variety of articles, reviews, commentary, and editorializing. As *Early Music* is serving as the principal periodical for discussions relating to performance practices and other studies relating to music through the Baroque Era, so is *19th-Century Music* asserting prominence for articles relevant to its era. Especially frequent in the journal are discussions of problems relating to sources, composers' compositional sketches, theory as explanation of music, and critical analysis. The flavor and substance of *19th-Century Music* is captured in Joseph Kerman's "Viewpoint," provoked by Siegfried Levarie's article in the same issue: "Key Relations in Verdi's *Un Ballo in Maschera*" (cited under Kerman in the bibliography).

The foundations of musicology in the Romantic Era and the resulting methodologies, including analysis, are discussed in chapters 1 and 2. In the present section, it bears mentioning that Einstein (*Music in the Romantic Era*) and Lang (*Music in Western Civilization*) both include sections entitled "Musicology" and both relate currents of thought in the era as influencing the movement towards sound scholarly investigations. Of more recent vintage are two surveys—one on analysis, one more generally on theory—of nineteenth-century thought. Ian Bent, "Analytical Thinking in the First Half of the Nineteenth Century," begins his survey with a retrospective look at some theoretical statements from the last half of the eighteenth century and notes their implications and meanings as he describes changes in the first half of the nineteenth century. Martin Vogel has edited a substantial set of contributions in *Beiträge zur Musiktheorie des 19. Jahrhunderts*; here the coverage is mainly on the last half of the century.

Tonality reaches its boundaries in musical composition at the end of the century, and new compositional theories assert themselves. "The Breakdown of Traditional Tonality" (Eric Salzman's term) is the milestone that marks the end of the Romantic and the beginning of the Modern Era. Debussy will serve as connector in the next section.

Abraham, Gerald. *Slavonic and Romantic Music. Essays and Studies.* New York: St. Martin's Press, 1968.

Barzun, Jacques. *Berlioz and the Romantic Century.* 3rd ed. 2v. New York: Columbia Univ. Pr., 1969.

———. "The Meaning of Meaning in Music: Berlioz Once More." *The Musical Quarterly* 66 (1980): 1–20.

Bent, Ian. "Analytical Thinking in the First Half of the Nineteenth Century." In *Modern Musical Scholarship*, pp. 151–66. Ed. by Edward Olleson. Boston: Oriel Pr., 1980.

Blume, Friedrich. *Classic and Romantic Music. A Comprehensive Survey.* Tr. by M. D. Herter Norton. New York: Norton, 1970.

Budden, Julian. *The Operas of Verdi.* 3v. New York: Oxford Univ. Pr., 1973–81.

Cook, Deryck. *Vindications: Essays on Romantic Music.* New York: Cambridge Univ. Pr., 1982.

Dahlhaus, Carl. *Between Romanticism and Modernism. Four Studies in Mu-*

sic of the Later Nineteenth Century. Tr. by Mary Whittall. California Studies in 19th-Century Music. Berkeley: Univ. of California Pr., 1980. (The first essay, "Neo-Romanticism," appears also in *19th-Century Music* 3 (1970–80): 97–105.)

———, ed. *Das Drama Richard Wagners als musikalisches Kunstwerk.* Studien zur Musikgeschichte des 19. Jahrhunderts, 23. Regensburg: Gustav Bosse Verlag, 1970.

———. *Die Musik des 19. Jahrhunderts.* Neues Handbuch der Musikwissenschaft, 6. Wiesbaden: Akademische Verlagsgesellschaft Athenaion, 1980.

———. *Richard Wagner's Music Dramas.* Tr. by Mary Whittall. New York: Cambridge Univ. Pr., 1979.

———, ed. *Studien zur Trivialmusik des 19. Jahrhunderts.* Studien zur Musikgeschichte des 19. Jahrhunderts, 8. Regensburg: Gustav Bosse Verlag, 1967.

Donakowski, Conrad L. *A Muse for the Masses. Ritual and Music in an Age of Democratic Revolution, 1770–1870.* Chicago: Univ. of Chicago Pr., 1972.

Einstein, Alfred. *Music in the Romantic Era.* New York: Norton, 1947.

Hoffmann, E. T. A. "Beethoven's Instrumental Music" (with the letter of response from Beethoven). Tr. by Oliver Strunk. In Strunk, *Source Readings in Music History.*

Kerman, Joseph. *Opera as Drama.* New York: Knopf, 1956.

———. "Viewpoint." *19th-Century Music* 2 (1978–79): 186–91. (Response to Siegfried Levarie, "Key Relations in Verdi's *Un Ballo in Maschera,*" pp. 143–47.)

Lang, Paul Henry. *Music in Western Civilization.* New York: Norton, 1940. (Ch. 16, "Romanticism"; 17, "From Romanticism to Realism"; 18, "Counter Currents," pp. 801–915.)

Longyear, Rey M. *Nineteenth-Century Romanticism in Music.* 2nd ed. Englewood Cliffs, N.J.: Prentice-Hall, 1973.

Lovejoy, Arthur O. "On the Discriminations of Romanticisms." In *Essays in the History of Ideas,* pp. 228–53. Ed. by Lovejoy. Baltimore: Johns Hopkins Pr., 1948. Repr.: 1978.

Newman, Ernest. *The Life of Richard Wagner.* 4v. New York: Knopf, 1933–47.

Newman, William S. *The Sonata since Beethoven.* 3rd ed. New York: Norton, 1983.

19th-Century Music. vol. 1– . Berkeley: Univ. of California Pr., 1977– .

Noske, Frits. *French Song from Berlioz to Duparc.* 2nd rev. ed. Tr. by Rita Benton. New York: Dover, 1970.

"Papers of the Colloque at Saint-Germain-en-Laye (September 1970): Studies on 19th-Century Music." *Acta musicologica* 63 (1971): 112–283.

Plantinga, Leon B. *Schumann as Critic.* Yale Studies in the History of Music, 4. New Haven: Yale Univ. Pr., 1967.

Primmer, Brian. "Unity and Ensemble: Contrasting Ideals in Romantic Music." *19th-Century Music* 6 (1982): 97–140.

Rowen, Ruth H. *Music through Sources and Documents.* Englewood Cliffs, N.J.: Prentice-Hall, 1979.

Salmen, Walter, ed. *Beiträge zur Geschichte des Musikanschauung um 19.*

Jahrhundert. Studien zur Musikgeschichte des 19. Jahrhunderts, 1. Regensburg: Gustav Bosse Verlag, 1965.

Salzman, Eric. *Twentieth-Century Music: An Introduction*. 2nd ed. Englewood Cliffs, N.J.: Prentice-Hall, 1974.

Sams, Eric. *The Songs of Hugo Wolf*. London: Methuen, 1961.

―――. *The Songs of Robert Schumann*. 2nd ed. London: Methuen, 1975.

Schafer, R. Murray. *E. T. A. Hoffmann and Music*. Toronto: Univ. of Toronto Pr., 1975.

Strunk, Oliver, ed. *Source Readings in Music History*. New York: Norton, 1950.

Studien zur Musikgeschichte des 19. Jahrhunderts. Regensburg: Bosse, 1965–.

Vogel, Martin, ed. *Beiträge zur Musiktheorie des 19. Jahrhunderts*. Studien zur Musikgeschichte des 19. Jahrhunderts, 4. Regensburg: Gustav Bosse Verlag, 1966.

Warrack, John. "Romantic." *The New Grove*.

Weber, William. *Music and the Middle Class*. New York: Holmes & Meier, 1975.

Westernhagen, Curt von. *Wagner: A Biography*. Tr. by Mary Whittall. 2v. New York: Cambridge Univ. Pr., 1979.

THE TWENTIETH CENTURY

The ultimate boundaries of tonality began to be reached in Wagner's *Tristan and Isolde* (1865): chromatic harmony, with its evasive potential, reached a high point in this work. That evasive quality seen in *Tristan* has sometimes been labeled "incipient atonality" because of the lack of final resolution within a tonality. Although composers of the later part of the nineteenth century—particularly Brahms—certainly held on to tonality as a most important structural element, experiments that were to lead to desertion of tonality were carried on with considerable vigor.

Claude Debussy (1862–1918) is often noted as the composer in whom the seeds of twentieth-century music are most clearly evident. The harmonic, rhythmic, and formal elements in the orchestral work *Afternoon of a Faun* and in the opera *Pélleas and Mélisande* were controversial at the time of their writing; in retrospect, today's scholars and theorists see many implications for the musical languages that followed Debussy. Particularly insightful and sympathetic accounts of Debussy's important historical position are given by William Austin, *Music in the Twentieth Century,* and Eric Salzman, *Twentieth-Century Music* (the former is a musicologist, the latter, a composer). They, as others, see in the last works—especially the *Etudes* for piano—musical styles and thought that were to have great impact on younger composers. The idea of Debussy as colorist in music, while true, has been enlarged and made more accurate by evaluations that emphasize his revolutionary break with the traditional concepts of consonance and dissonance.

The years around 1910 saw first performances of many of the radical musical compositions that were to confirm the departure from old paths and set the stage for the future. Igor Stravinsky's *The Rite of Spring* (1913), Arnold Schoenberg's *Pierrot Lunaire* (1912), Béla Bartók's *Allegro Barbaro* (1910), and—in America—Charles Ives's *Concord Sonata* (1915), among many works that might be cited, are representative of the need composers felt to reject much of the past and to offer new artistic directions for the future.

In the first decade of the twentieth century Arnold Schoenberg began developing compositional methods that were to result in strictly atonal and serial (twelve-tone) music. Some of his motivation may be seen as deriving from the rebellious, violent, and energetic expressionistic movement that dominated all fields of art. The traditional hierarchy of degrees of consonance and dissonance was abandoned, along with the highly chromatic harmony that had even attracted Schoenberg in his earlier days (e.g., *Verklärte Nacht*, 1899). Schoenberg and others found that some organizational means had to replace tonality, and his search led him to develop the tone-row technique.

Tone-row technique is a means of ordering pitches, not tonal relationships, and in the ensuing years since Schoenberg's codification in the 1920s, the expanded serial technique has grown to include ordering of rhythm, dynamics, instrumentation, expressive markings—all the elements of composition. Indeed, much of the course of twentieth-century music is towards total control of the compositional—and performance—elements.

The standard book on Schoenberg's achievements with respect to serial technique (and on his two main disciples also) is George Perle's *Serial Music and Atonality: An Introduction to the Music of Schoenberg, Berg, and Webern*. Allen Forte, *The Structure of Atonal Music*, takes Schoenberg's "George Lieder" (1908) as a departure for a systematic elucidation of atonal principles being developed by the composer in those songs. Forte notes that serial music is not his topic, but rather atonal music: "It is the intention of the present work to provide a general theoretical framework, with reference to which the processes underlying atonal music may be systematically described."

Atonal, serial, and numerous other systems have been discussed in the journal *Perspectives of New Music,* one of the most important "new music" journals since its inception in 1962. *Perspectives* has been a principal forum for new proposals for analytic systems and processes, position and historical statements by composers, and papers on the role of computers in music composition and analysis. (The three volumes cited under Boretz in the bibliography are compilations of articles that first appeared in *Perspectives of New Music.*)

Serial technique has been applied to highly varying degrees by composers since Schoenberg, from extreme rigidity to partial application. There can be little doubt that twentieth-century composers have been more innovative and resourceful in constructing and contriving new "systems" than ever before in the history of music. New technology—including electric and electronic instruments, sound synthesizers, computers—along with swift communication within the musical world have tended to create a sense of confusion about artistic and musical aims for both general audiences and often for professional musicians as well.

The composer-as-essayist (apologist, polemicist, narrator), prevalent in the nineteenth century, has continued unabated in the twentieth. Arnold Schoenberg, Aaron Copland, Paul Hindemith, Milton Babbitt, Leonard Bernstein, Roger Sessions, Igor Stravinsky, Carlos Chavez, and many, many others have published explanations of their own music and that of others, have attempted to explain what they conceive to be the meaning of music, and have published theoretical tracts and volumes. László Somfai surveys some of the pitfalls and attractions of composers' explanations in "Self-Analysis by Twentieth-Century Composers." His call for critical reception by readers of composers' own analyses is tempered by his belief that self-analysis can be extremely helpful, even essential when dealing with complex twentieth-century scores.

Benjamin Boretz comments on the polemical quality often evidenced in writings on new musical theory of the twentieth century in the preface to *Perspectives on Contemporary Music Theory.* Noting that much of the writing is indeed exhortatory, Boretz goes on to state that, even so, the variety and vitality of the essays on new theory are simply reflections of the same qualities in new music.

Unmatched by any other era is the degree to which compositional and theoretical systems are analyzed and explicated by composers, composer-theorists, and theorists. The extraordinary complexity of a great deal of twentieth-century music, the immediate audience appeal that is usually missing, and the newness of the theory that may lie behind the compositions—all have seemed to require prose explanations, brief or lengthy. The interested reader can sample these writings in many anthologies, two of which are Elliott Schwartz and Barney Childs, *Contemporary Composers on Contemporary Music*, and Gilbert Chase, *The American Composer Speaks: A Historical Anthology, 1770–1965*. The former contains Milton Babbitt's "Who Cares If You Listen," remarkable for its particular sense of an individual's artistic integrity. Among the latest and most provocative compilations is Gregory Battcock's anthology of statements by avant-garde composers, *Breaking the Sound Barrier*.

Selected writings of Arnold Schoenberg have been gathered in *Style and Idea* (1975), edited by Leonard Stein. (In 1950 Schoenberg had published a modest collection of fifteen essays under the same title.) The composer's intellectual influence on the twentieth century is enormous, as is widely acknowledged: through not only the development of serial technique for musical composition but also through writing and teaching, Schoenberg transmitted an artistic credo that has reinforced the artistic independence of countless composers. Although Schoenberg is regarded as a revolutionist, with good reason, he had an accurate and respectful view of music history, and both his teaching and writing confirm that he had a firm grasp of the significance and implications of his new ideas.

There is a "traditionalist" group of composers in the twentieth century whose members range from Ralph Vaughan Williams to Ottorino Respighi to Dmitri Shostakovich and Sergei Prokofiev to Gian Carlo Menotti and Benjamin Britten, among others. Such composers have tended to depend less on superrationalistic systems of composition and musical experimentation than on further development of older concepts of music and its aesthetics.

John Cage—through his music but especially through personality and writings—has had an enormous impact on the avant-garde in the United States and abroad, ever since he first attracted sizable public notice in the early 1950s. Since those years, Cage has been involved—to a greater or lesser degree—in aleatoric (chance) music, electronic and tape music, antirational music, minimalism, musical "happenings" of the 1960s, futurism, indeterminacy, silence as music, noise as music, natural sounds, and recorded manipulated natural sounds (*musique concrète*). If there can be said to be an internationally acknowledged guru of the avant-garde, it is surely Cage. His book *Silence* (opinions, essays, poems, jottings, musings) best represents in prose Cage's basic philosophy that barriers between art and life must be removed. Hence, he mixes the mundane events of life (e.g., listening to the radio, the sounds of food mixers) into his compositions and concerts. Sensationalism is an important element of twentieth-century music, especially given modern communication systems.

Musical notation, including Cage's, has undergone radical revision during the course of the twentieth century. An early manifestation of the changes to come was Schoenberg's very modest innovation of a special symbol to indicate "Sprechstimme," something halfway between speaking and singing of pitches. The notational revolution has moved so far that in many instances each new piece may well be a new encounter with a unique form of musical notation. Conventional staff notation has generally given way to complex arrangements of new symbols, to graphic or nonrepresentational notation. In the 1960s there began to appear "scores" that bore no resemblance to notes or staves, but were pictures intended to inspire music from performers.

The notational departures of the 1960s and 70s are far too complex even to survey briefly. Among the best guides are Geoffrey Chew, "Notation" (*The New Grove*); Kurt Stone, *Music Notation in the Twentieth Century;* and Erhard Karkoschka, *Notation in New Music.*

The barriers between audiences and composers of the later twentieth century are considerable: concert halls and opera houses are, by and large, museums devoted to music before 1900, notwithstanding the fact that a number of pieces by Stravinsky, Bartók, Shostakovich, and others have entered the general repertoire. In spite of audiences' refusal to turn in great numbers towards their music, composers continue to experiment and to compose, no matter that the listeners are unreceptive. Charles Ives recognized the difficulty when he termed some of his own works "ear-cleaning music"—music that is hard at first hearing, but pays with repeated listening. It will remain for audiences and scholars of the coming century to determine which pieces will survive the test of time.

Eric Salzman sees the present age of the avant-garde as growing out of the age of modern music, a period now ending. The avant-garde is a transition to something else: "Any kind of statement is possible."

Austin, William W. *Music in the Twentieth Century; From Debussy through Stravinsky.* New York: Norton, 1966.
Babbitt, Milton. "Contemporary Music Composition and Music Theory as

Contemporary Intellectual History." In *Perspectives in Musicology*, pp. 151–84. Ed. by Barry S. Brook et al. New York: Norton, 1972.

Battcock, Gregory, ed. *Breaking the Sound Barrier: A Critical Anthology of the New Music*. New York: Dutton, 1981.

Boretz, Benjamin, and Edward T. Cone, eds. *Perspectives on American Composers*. New York: Norton, 1971.

————, eds. *Perspectives on Contemporary Music Theory*. New York: Norton, 1972. (Essays from *Perspectives of New Music*.)

————, eds. *Perspectives on Schoenberg and Stravinsky*. Princeton: Princeton Univ. Pr., 1968. (Essays from *Perspectives of New Music*.)

Brindle, Reginald S. *The New Music. The Avant-Garde since 1945*. New York: Oxford Univ. Pr., 1975.

Cage, John. *Silence; Lectures and Writings*. Middletown, Conn.: Wesleyan Univ. Pr., 1961.

Chase, Gilbert. *The American Composer Speaks: A Historical Anthology, 1770–1965*. Baton Rouge: Louisiana State Univ. Pr., 1966.

Chew, Geoffrey. "Notation." *The New Grove*.

Forte, Allen. *The Structure of Atonal Music*. New Haven, Conn.: Yale Univ. Pr., 1977.

Griffiths, Paul. *Modern Music: The Avant-Garde since 1945*. London: Dent, 1981.

Hamm, Charles. *Music in the New World*. New York: Norton, 1983. (Especially ch. 15, "The Search for a National Identity"; ch. 18, "The Second Wave and Its Impact on American Composition"; and ch. 19, "The American Avant-Garde."

Hays, William, ed. *Twentieth-Century Views of Music History*. New York: Scribner's, 1972. (See especially Eric Salzman, "The Revolution in Music," pp. 455–71; the article originally appeared in *New American Review*, no. 6 (1969): 76–96.

Hitchcock, H. Wiley. *Music in the United States: A Historical Introduction*. 2nd ed. Englewood Cliffs, N.J.: Prentice-Hall, 1974. (Especially ch. 7, "Charles E. Ives"; ch. 8, "The 1920's"; ch. 9, "The 1930's and Early 1940's"; and ch. 10, "After World War II."

Karkoschka, Erhard. *Notation in New Music. A Critical Guide to Interpretation and Realization*. Tr. by Ruth Koenig. New York: Praeger, 1972.

Mellers, Wilfrid. *Music in a New Found Land. Themes and Developments in the History of American Music*. London: Barrie & Rockliff, 1964.

Meyer, Leonard. *Music, The Arts and Ideas: Patterns and Predictions in Twentieth-Century Culture*. Chicago: Univ. of Chicago Pr., 1967.

Neighbour, O. W. "Schoenberg, Arnold." *The New Grove*.

Perle, George. *The Operas of Alban Berg*. Vol. 1, *Wozzeck*. Berkeley: Univ. of California Pr., 1981; vol. 2, *Lulu*; 1984.

————. *Serial Music and Atonality: An Introduction to the Music of Schoenberg, Berg, and Webern*. 5th ed., rev. Berkeley: Univ. of California Pr., 1981.

Perspectives of New Music. Princeton: Princeton Univ. Pr., v. 1– . 1962– .

Salzman, Eric. *Twentieth-Century Music: An Introduction*. 2nd ed. Englewood Cliffs, N.J.: Prentice-Hall, 1974.

Schoenberg, Arnold. *Style and Idea. Selected Writings of Arnold Schoenberg*. Ed. by Leonard Stein; tr. by Leo Black. London: Faber & Faber, 1975.

Schwartz, Elliott, and Barney Childs, ed. *Contemporary Composers on Contemporary Music.* New York: Holt, Rinehart & Winston, 1967.

Schwartz, Elliott. *Electronic Music: A Listener's Guide.* New York: Praeger Publishers, 1973.

Slonimsky, Nicolas. *Music since 1900.* 4th ed. New York: Scribner's, 1971.

Somfai, László. "Self-Analysis by Twentieth-Century Composers." In *Modern Musical Scholarship*, pp. 167–79. Ed. by Edward Olleson. Boston: Oriel Pr., 1980.

Stone, Kurt. *Music Notation in the Twentieth Century.* New York: Norton, 1980.

Wittlich, Gary, ed. *Aspects of Twentieth-Century Music.* Englewood Cliffs, N.J.: Prentice-Hall, 1975.

AMERICAN MUSIC

The treatment of American musical history is one of the more curious aspects of humanistic musical research; only since the 1950s have studies in American music begun to achieve full respectability among musicologists. The dominance of imported musical traditions—often seen in less artistically distinguished music of the late eighteenth and early nineteenth centuries—along with scholars' tendency to disparage, on aesthetic grounds, the salon and sentimental music of the nineteenth century, somehow combined to lead American scholars away from serious consideration of their own musical heritage.

A notable exception among early twentieth-century scholars was Oscar G. Sonneck (1873–1928). His monumental efforts, especially as chief of the Music Division of the Library of Congress, provided considerable bibliographical and historical documentation of American music history for all succeeding scholars. For an appreciation of Sonneck's work, see H. Wiley Hitchcock's *After 100 years.* Present-day distinguished scholars such as Gilbert Chase, Irving Lowens, H. Wiley Hitchcock, Richard Crawford, and Charles Hamm, are representative of the genuine quickening interest and substantial scholarly achievement in American music history.

America's Music, by Gilbert Chase, has continued since 1955 as a basic general history that ranges from the Colonial Era to the present; it is properly regarded as the first scholarly, comprehensive treatment of American music. Chase synthesized the more restrictive research of others while adding an important new breadth to the study of American music. His view of American music is comprehensive and reflects a philosophy he has restated in many forums: the entire range of music must be studied irrespective of any modern value judgments that modern scholars may wish to apply to parts of the heritage. Light and popular music, sentimental church music, folk music, ephemeral salon music, musical comedy—all must warrant the attention of scholars and all should be placed within the general and unique fabric of American history. Chase's reiteration of this view, supported by others at times in theory but too rarely in practice, nonetheless had a beneficial effect in persuading American musicologists to consider their own musical tradition as a fruitful area of research. (For further comment, see chapter 2.)

H. Wiley Hitchcock, founder of the Institute for Studies in American Music (Brooklyn College), has developed an extremely useful distinction between what he terms the vernacular and cultivated traditions in America during the nineteenth century. He recognizes, as have others, that "classical music" and "popular music" do not satisfactorily identify types of American music and that the terms also carry inappropriate connotations as well. Rather than "classical," he substitutes "cultivated music" to characterize fine-art music, typically of the European art music tradition; and "vernacular music" to typify the several other varieties of music (excluding folk music). Hitchcock suggests two periods of the cultivated tradition, 1820–1865, 1865–1920, and one of the vernacular tradition, 1820–1920. Songs, music for the piano, sacred music, and other similar genres fall within the cultivated tradition; minstrelsy, band music, gospel music, etc., within the vernacular tradition. Hitchcock, like Chase, avoids value judgments that falsely restrict the music selected for study and comment. By extensively interweaving American political, economic, and social history, Hitchcock provides an even broader view of American music than Chase had. (The forthcoming third edition of Chase's history is awaited with considerable interest: it will carry the subtitle, *A Cultural Interpretation.*) Hitchcock's careful selectivity in choosing works and composers provides a proper balance between cultural and musical history, and the history is accurately assessed as responding to the pleas of older scholars—such as Sonneck and Chase—to put aside aesthetic value as *the* criterion for discussing American music up to about 1900. After the turn of the century, the American contribution can be viewed and compared in its international contexts, as, for instance, Hitchcock does with the music of Charles Ives.

Music in the New World, by Charles Hamm, aims at examining all of the various musics found in America. He opens with an essay on

Native American music before turning to the imported European styles, and he ranges through vernacular music, written and orally transmitted music, jazz, popular song, rock, country and western music, and contemporary music. Hamm believes that "A large part of the history of American music is a history of 'contaminated' music; much of the energy characterizing such genres as jazz, country-western, and the various stages of American popular song results from the stimulation of this 'contamination'." One of the most useful aspects of *Music in the New World* is that it is closely keyed to *New World Records* (of which more below), thus linking Hamm's observations to available recorded performances.

Hamm's is the latest comprehensive history of American music and, by a generous margin, the largest as well. His slightly earlier book, *Yesterdays: Popular Song in America*, is the first extensive discussion of a genre of music that originated in America and that now dominates world popular music. Considered together or separately, the two studies represent a major achievement in scholarship in American music history. The work of Hamm specifically exhibits a distinct effort to create a model for studies in American music history.

The Bicentennial Celebration in 1976 gave important new impetus to studies in American music. One of the principal musical results of that observance was *New World Records, Recorded Anthology of American Music*, issued by a company founded specifically to organize and release the recordings. The anthology covers all genres that appear in the 200 years of America's history and has done more than any other single project to bring the heritage to new life. Indeed, the project tends to defeat Joseph Kerman's declaration that certain early American composers "would defy all efforts at resuscitation. Man, they are dead." (See Kerman, "A Profile. . . ," p. 13.)

Jazz as a subject for serious scholarly study has begun to come to the fore. Its tangled history, its improvisatory nature, the great varieties of style, all combine to make writing its history difficult. Frank Tirro's *Jazz: A History* is the latest general study; part of its considerable value lies in being keyed to the *Smithsonian Collection of Classic Jazz*. Gunther Schuller's *Early Jazz; Its Roots and Musical Development* is the first part of a planned multivolume history. André Hodeir's *Jazz, Its Evolution and Essence* was one of the first serious studies.

The role of black Americans has received extensive attention since about 1960, not only with regard to jazz and blues, but also in serious music, performance, and all aspects of musical life. Eileen

Southern's *The Music of Black Americans* and her *Readings in Black American Music* are the first major full-length introductions prepared by a trained musicologist.

The modern techniques of oral historians are being used to document the history of American music. Vivian Perlis has developed a number of specific projects at Yale University under the program called "Oral History, American Music." Contemporary composers and performers, American- and foreign-born, who have had careers in the United States, have been interviewed for their biographies and, most importantly, for their views on music in general with emphasis, however, on their own music. *Charles Ives Remembered: An Oral History* was Perlis's first major publication resulting from the activities of the center. Although some reservations are generally made concerning the reliability of recollections of which oral history in large part consists, the importance of the technique in documenting contemporary composers and events is unquestioned.

American Music. Urbana: Univ. of Illinois Pr. and Sonneck Soc., v. 1– . 1983– .

Austin, William W. *Music in the Twentieth Century; from Debussy through Stravinsky.* New York: Norton, 1966.

————. *"Susanna," "Jeanie," and "The Old Folks at Home": The Songs of Stephen C. Foster from His Time to Ours.* New York: Macmillan, 1975.

Boretz, Benjamin and Edward T. Cone, eds. *Perspectives on American Composers.* New York: Norton, 1971. (Articles reprinted from *Perspectives of New Music.*)

Chase, Gilbert. *The American Composer Speaks: A Historical Anthology, 1770–1965.* Baton Rouge: Louisiana State Univ. Pr., 1966.

————. *America's Music.* 2nd ed. New York: McGraw-Hill, 1966. (3rd ed., forthcoming: *America's Music: A Cultural Interpretation.*)

Crawford, Richard. *American Studies and American Musicology: A Point of View and a Case in Point.* Monographs in American Music, 4. Brooklyn: Inst. for Studies in American Music, 1975.

————. *Andrew Law: American Psalmodist.* Evanston, Ill.: Northwestern Univ. Pr., 1968.

Epstein, Dena. *Sinful Tunes and Spirituals. Black Folk Music to the Civil War.* Urbana: Univ. of Illinois Pr., 1977.

Hamm, Charles. *Music in the New World.* New York: Norton, 1983.

————. *Yesterdays: Popular Song in America.* New York: Norton, 1982.

Hitchcock, H. Wiley. *After 100 Years: The Editorial Side of Sonneck.* Washington, D.C.: Library of Congress, 1974.

————. *Music in the United States: A Historical Introduction.* Englewood Cliffs, N.J.: Prentice-Hall, 1974.

Hodeir, André. *Jazz, Its Evolution and Essence.* New York: Grove Pr., 1956.

Lowens, Irving. *Music and Musicians in Early America.* New York: Norton, 1964.

————. *Music in America and American Music: Two Views of the Scene.* Monographs in American Music, 8. Brooklyn: Inst. for Studies in American Music, 1978.

Perlis, Vivian. *Charles Ives Remembered: An Oral History.* New Haven, Conn.: Yale Univ. Pr., 1974.

Rockwell, John. *All American Music. Composition in the Late Twentieth Century.* New York: Knopf, 1983.

Rosenstiel, Léonie. "The New World." In *Schirmer History of Music*, pp. 837–946. Ed. by Rosenstiel. New York: Schirmer Books, 1982.

Schuller, Gunther. *Early Jazz; Its Roots and Musical Development.* New York: Oxford Univ. Pr., 1968.

Southern, Eileen. *The Music of Black Americans: A History.* 2nd ed. New York: Norton, 1983.

————. *Readings in Black American Music.* 2nd ed. New York: Norton, 1983.

Stevenson, Robert. *Protestant Church Music in America.* New York: Norton, 1966.

Tirro, Frank. *Jazz. A History.* New York: Norton, 1977.

PART II

REFERENCE WORKS

Dictionaries and Encyclopedias

GENERAL

Arnold, Denis, gen. ed. *The New Oxford Companion to Music.* New York: Oxford Univ. Pr., 1983. 2v.

The New Oxford Companion to Music is the successor to a respected reference source begun by Percy Scholes in 1938; it replaces the one-volume work last edited by John Owen Ward. The *Companion* covers individuals, instruments, the musical notations of the world, theory, and the history of music. The approach is global, although Western music receives most attention. The volumes reflect growing interest in iconography through generous use of illustrations. The range of information is from short definitions of musical terms to multicolumn treatment of major individuals, periods of music history, and other large topics; only brief bibliographies are given. The *Companion* is both a dictionary and an initial source for information leading to further inquiry.

Cooper, Martin, ed. *The Concise Encyclopedia of Music and Musicians.* New York: Hawthorn Books, 1958. 516p.

In his encyclopedia, Cooper stresses Western music as a fine art during the past 400 years. The length of the entries varies from one-line identifications to several pages of explication; but in general, the emphasis is on breadth rather than depth. Musicians, instruments, technical terms, foreign expressions, specific compositions, organizations and playing groups, and the history of music all furnish subject matter for the encyclopedia. Several plates are included, and line drawings and musical examples are occasionally provided. A bibliography and a pronouncing glossary are found at the front of the volume.

Jablonski, Edward. *The Encyclopedia of American Music.* Garden City, N.Y.: Doubleday, 1981. 629p.

This work is divided into seven chronological eras from 1620 to the date of publication. Within each section entries are arranged alphabetically. Entries include artists and performers, musical terms, associations, and publications. Each section is preceded by an essay that discusses the significant musical trends and personalities of that particular period. There are "see" but not "see also" references. The index is to name only.

Kennedy, Michael. *The Concise Oxford Dictionary of Music: Based on the Original Publication by Percy Scholes*. New York: Oxford Univ. Pr., 1980. 724p.

This is a major revision of the *Concise Dictionary*, which first appeared in 1952. Brief articles describe major composers and performers, music genres, and individual compositions. Lists of compositions are provided for prominent composers along with biographical and critical evaluations. Pronunciation is not indicated. There are separate name and subject indexes.

Die Musik in Geschichte und Gegenwart. Allgemeine Enzyklopädie der Musik. Unter Mitarbeit zahlreicher Musikforscher des In- und Auslandes. Kassel: Bärenreiter, 1949–79. 16v.

An international encyclopedia with contributors from many countries. The articles tend to be comprehensive and cover most topics in music, including theory, notation, and biographies of composers. German forms of the headings are employed. The work is lavishly illustrated and has excellent bibliographies. *M.G.G.*, with *The New Grove Dictionary*, provides the scholarly standards in the field of musical research.

The Piano in Concert. Comp. by George Kebler. Metuchen, N.J.: Scarecrow, 1982. 2v.; 1431p.

This work reproduces piano programs from approximately 2000 international artists. Major emphasis is on the nineteenth and twentieth centuries. Over 14,000 programs are listed chronologically under artist. Short biographical sketches are also provided. The index provides access both to name of pianist and to name of piano composition.

Roche, Jerome. *Dictionary of Early Music: From the Troubadours to Monteverdi*. London: Faber Music, 1981. 208p.

A compact dictionary with entries for composers, instruments, technical terms, and musical forms, this work covers the Middle Ages, Renaissance, and early Baroque periods. Included are some 700 entries devoted to composers, roughly half the number known to have been active during this period. Some of the criteria for inclusion of a composer were whether the composer's music has been recorded or reproduced in publications, acknowledgment in basic works of music history, and those who are currently the focus of scholarly research that could lead to performance or publication of their musical works. The amount of biographical information given was determined solely by the amount of material available for each composer.

Attempts were made to include every instrument from the medieval and Renaissance periods that can be heard in musical performances today. Only descriptions of the instruments are provided, as the history and ancestry of many instruments are controversial. Also included are entries for technical terms, musical forms, musical theorists and writers of the period, major music publishers of the Renaissance, and principal manuscripts and printed sources of music.

Sadie, Stanley, ed. *The New Grove Dictionary of Music and Musicians*. 6th ed. London: Macmillan, 1980. 20v.

The New Grove Dictionary represents a major revision of the fifth edition of Sir George Grove's dictionary, published in 1954. It remains the most comprehensive reference work in the field of music. For the first time since Grove published the first edition in 1879, the present volumes do not represent a revision of the original work but have been completely rewritten. As much as ninety-seven percent of the text of the sixth edition is completely new material, while the remaining three percent, which is based on information from previous editions, has been revised and expanded. A major change is the use of current research techniques for gathering data rather than basing much of the content on the opinion of the editor. This practice has served to broaden the scope of the new dictionary's coverage immensely. In addition, the articles were commissioned from a broad group of 2300 international scholars of music, one-third of which were American.

Some 22,500 entries appear citing composers, instruments, instrument makers, performers, musical forms and genres, music theory and composition, terminology, and many more. Entries are arranged alphabetically and range in coverage from the ancient to the modern period. The set provides 7500 cross-references and over 3000 illustrations in the form of portraits, instruments, family trees, maps, tables, diagrams, and more. Over half the entries, which vary greatly in length, deal with the lives of composers. They include lists of musical works as well as extensive bibliographies. Criteria for the selection of composers were based in part on historical significance and critical judgment of their works. Topics new to the sixth edition of Grove's dictionary are ethnomusicology, aesthetics, psychology, iconography, and computers, to name a few. Jazz, non-Western, and folk music also receive greater attention than in previous editions.

The new dictionary contains several bibliographies that cover specialized topics, such as musical genres of early periods. Other reference articles appear in *The New Grove Dictionary*, which also presents bibliographic information and deals with such subjects as "Dictionaries," "Periodicals," and "Private Collections." Another special feature is a separate ethnomusicological index to all entries dealing with non-Western and folk music. Details concerning organization of the dictionary appear in the introduction to volume 1. For convenience, a brief usage guide begins each volume of the set. The intent of the original dictionary of Sir George Grove is retained, in that *The New Grove Dictionary* continues to serve the general reader as well as the music expert.

A number of books are being derived from this massive effort of scholars: *The New Grove Dictionary of Musical Instruments, The New Grove Dictionary of Music in the United States,* and *The New Grove Composer Biography Series;* some have already been released. All of these titles, though based on the research in *The New Grove,* are being expanded and updated.

Thompson, Oscar, ed. *The International Cyclopedia of Music and Musicians.* 10th ed. New York: Dodd, 1975. 2511p.
Biographical entries ranging in length from a sentence to several pages make up the bulk of this work. Articles for composers, musicians, singers, conductors, teachers, and music publishers from the United States and Europe are included. The volume also explains musical terms and has entries

for organizations, institutions, music festivals, individual compositions, and musical instruments. A few portraits are included.

Vinton, John, ed. *Dictionary of Contemporary Music*. New York: Dutton, 1974. 834p.

Vinton's dictionary embraces four major areas in contemporary Western concert music: (1) biography, (2) surveys of technical and special subjects, (3) national surveys, and (4) terms. Normally, the beginning date for the contemporary period is 1880, although there are a few exceptions. Likewise, some general articles on non-Western and nonconcert (e.g., folk, jazz) music are included. The articles are not merely technically descriptive, but emphasize what are the new and different developments of the twentieth century. The biographical entries cover primarily composers and contain information on education and employment as well as a list of principal compositions and writings. Cross-references and bibliographic citations are supplied when important. Occasional graphic illustrations add to the value of the work.

Westrup, J. A., and F. Ll. Harrison. *The New College Encyclopedia of Music*. Rev. by Conrad Wilson. New York: Norton, 1976. 608p.

This one-volume encyclopedia contains entries for musicians, instruments, operas and other works, orchestras, and terms of various types, including many in foreign languages. Bibliographies are appended to some of the longer entries; and illustrations in the form of photographs and musical examples are abundant. A pronunciation key for over 1500 words is included at the beginning of the volume.

BIOGRAPHY, INTERNATIONAL

Cohen, Aaron. *International Encyclopedia of Women Composers*. New York: R. R. Bowker, 1981. 597p.

Entries for nearly 5000 women composers are listed alphabetically by name in this work. Although composers from all ages are included, nearly two-thirds of the composers listed are living. Entries include a biography, a list of compositions, publications, and a bibliography. Photographs of composers are arranged alphabetically in a separate section. The appendix lists composers by country and century.

Cohen-Stratyner, Barbara Naomi. *Biographical Dictionary of Dance*. New York: Schirmer Books, 1982. 970p.

Over 2900 men and women associated with dance since 1500 are described in brief entries; most individuals are from the nineteenth and twentieth centuries. Attention is limited to Europe and the Americas. A typical entry includes dates, training, dance career, critical evaluation, and (for modern performers) works choreographed, concert or theater works, films, and television appearances. There are no indexes, nor are "see" or "see also" references used.

Holmes, John L. *Conductors on Record*. Westport, Conn.: Greenwood, 1982. 734p.

This volume, in dictionary form, provides short biographical sketches of more than 1500 conductors. The scope is international, and both living and deceased conductors are included. Besides biographical information including dates, education, and careers, the entries also provide critical analyses. Recordings and recording companies are provided for each entry, but not date, record number, or record title if it is not identical to the title of the work recorded.

International Who's Who in Music and Musician's Directory. 9th ed. Ed. by Adrian Gaster. Cambridge, England: Melrose Pr., 1935– . 960p.

The ninth edition of this biographical dictionary provides short sketches of 10,000 living musicians and other individuals associated with serious music. More than 2000 new entries have been added to the previous edition. Information for each entry includes place and date of birth, music specialty, education, career, and recordings. Entries often also include citations to thirty other standard reference works. Appendixes include lists of orchestras, organizations, competitions and awards, music libraries, and conservatories.

Osborne, Charles, ed. *The Dictionary of Composers.* New York: Taplinger, 1978. 380p.

About 175 composers are treated in this biographical dictionary. The essays, by twenty-six British musicologists, are original, although the choice of the composers is decidedly conventional. The entries themselves range from skeletal sketches to essays. A profusion of illustrations accompany the text, making up approximately one-fifth of the book. For most of these composers only their well-known works are discussed. This volume is for the amateur who wants to know something about the most important composers but who does not want to get bogged down in details.

Performing Arts Biography Master Index. Ed. by Barbara McNeil and Miranda C. Herbert. 2nd ed. Detroit; Gale, 1982. 701p.

Replacing and updating *Theatre, Film and Television Biographies Master Index* (Gale, 1979), the book includes persons having some connection with theater, film, television, popular music, classical music, dance and other performing arts. The names are arranged alphabetically followed by years of birth and death when appropriate, as well as codes for the sources used. A key to the latter providing full bibliographic information is located in the front of the index. A list of the sources used, arranged by author, follows the key.

Schonberg, Harold C. *The Lives of the Great Composers.* Rev. ed. New York: Norton. 653p.

The evolution of musical composition from Monteverdi to Schoenberg is provided in this work. There are chapters on some individual composers, on the comparisons of contemporaries, and some individual times and places in musical development. There is a bibliography for each chapter. It is illustrated and indexed.

Slonimsky, Nicolas, revisor. *Baker's Biographical Dictionary of Musicians.* 6th ed. New York: Schirmer Books, 1978. 1955p.

This work includes entries for composers, musicians, patrons of music, and music publishers. The biographies are arranged alphabetically, and each entry includes date of birth and death, information on where and under whom the musician studied, a summary of his or her professional career, and a list of the musician's works. Alternative spellings of names are cross-referenced.

BIOGRAPHY, NATIONAL

Anderson, Ruth E. *Contemporary American Composers: A Biographical Dictionary.* 2nd ed. Boston: G. K. Hall, 1982. 578p.

This work contains an alphabetical listing of American composers born after 1869. Composers who have written only several compositions or who write exclusively popular music, rock, jazz, folk, or teaching pieces are not included. Also, composers who failed to respond to the author's questionnaire are excluded. Much of the information supplied in the entries was obtained by use of the questionnaire, with very little verification of the contents attempted. For the second edition of this volume, the separate listing of women composers has been deleted and the addendum combined with the text. Entries list date and place of birth, education, musical background, titles and positions, compositions completed, and addresses.

ASCAP Biographical Dictionary. Comp. by the Jacques Cattell Press. New York: R. R. Bowker, 1980. 589p.

Biographies of the 8200 living and deceased official members of the American Society of Composers, Authors and Publishers (ASCAP) are found in this work. Biographical entries for each ASCAP member are arranged alphabetically and contain the person's given and professional name, date and place of birth and death, educational background, the year he or she became an ASCAP member, career highlights, collaborations, and major works. A list of the 7000 publisher members of ASCAP is also included.

Canadian Music Library Association. *A Bio-Bibliographical Finding List of Canadian Musicians and Those Who Have Contributed to Music in Canada.* Ottawa: Canadian Library Assn., 1960–61. 53p.

Over 2000 musicians have been listed in this book, which provides brief identifications and serves as a combined index to over 100 biographical dictionaries and survey articles, as well as to 25 monographs on music and musicians. Each entry optimally includes the full name, birth and death dates with place of birth, the musical occupation(s), and abbreviations for sources in which information may be found.

Claghorn, Charles Eugene. *Biographical Dictionary of American Music.* West Nyack, N.Y.: Parker, 1973. 491p.

Claghorn's work encompasses composers, hymnists, librettists, lyricists, musicians, singers, and teachers who have been active in American music from the seventeenth century to the present. Included are both individuals and groups who were either born in America or who have lived here for a significant amount of time. Entries are brief, giving birth and death dates, education, information on type of musical proficiency or vocation, and names of key contributions and musical colleagues. Black musicians are so indicated in order to emphasize their cultural contribution.

MacMillan, Keith, and John Beckwith, eds. *Contemporary Canadian Composers.* Toronto: Oxford Univ. Pr., 1975. 248p.
This work provides sketches for over 140 Canadian composers who have made their major musical contributions since 1920. Popular and commercial music composers are omitted, and composers of jazz, church, and band music are sparsely represented. The sketches concentrate on training, careers, and contributions and frequently attempt some critical assessment. Appended to each sketch is a list of musical works arranged by genre and a list of publications by and about the composer. A few photographs are included.

Simon, George T. *The Best of the Music Makers.* Garden City, N.Y.: Doubleday, 1979. 635p.
The "music makers" in this title include some of the more popular performers of the past fifty years. The book consists of 282 biographies, with each containing between 500 and 1300 words on individuals and groups. Performers from many fields of popular music are included. Many of the biographies were written by Simon; others were contributed. Photographs of the performers supplement each article.

Southern, Eileen. *Biographical Dictionary of Afro-American and African Musicians.* Greenwood Encyclopedia of Black Music, v.2. Westport, Conn.: Greenwood, 1982. 478p.
All forms of music are represented in this dictionary of over 1500 musicians, living or dead. Selection was based on the influence and/or contribution made by the individual or group. The entries are listed alphabetically by professional names, with cross-references from alternate names. Entries discuss careers, representative compositions or performances, and sometimes contain evaluative comments. Bibliographies and discographies are included. There are lists of musicians by period of birth, place of birth, and by occupation in the appendix. Indexed.

BIOGRAPHY, JAZZ, POPULAR, AND FOLK MUSICIANS

Case, Brian, and Stan Britt. *The Illustrated Encyclopedia of Jazz.* New York: Harmony Books, 1978. 224p.
This colorful encyclopedia of jazz consists of entries on the musicians, groups, or schools that are well known for contributions to the world of jazz. Entries are arranged alphabetically, contain biographical data, and follow the careers of the jazz artist and other musicians who had an influence on the artist. Each entry includes the titles of songs for which the musician was most famous and a list of the artist's recordings. An index, consisting almost entirely of names, is found at the end of the volume.

Feather, Leonard G. *The Encyclopedia of Jazz in the Seventies.* New York: Horizon Pr., 1976. 393p.

This volume represents an examination of the ten-year period since the compilation of *The Encyclopedia of Jazz in the Sixties,* which covered events through mid-1966. It includes biographies of jazz musicians who became prominent during the 1970s as well as brief notations of those musicians whose biographies appeared in previous volumes of *The Encyclopedia of Jazz* series. This latest edition follows exactly the same format and provides the same features and types of information as its predecessor.

————. *The Encyclopedia of Jazz in the Sixties.* New York: Horizon Pr., 1966. 312p.

This work primarily consists of biographical sketches of the major personalities in American jazz music during the 1960s. Information for the entries was obtained directly from the musicians and their associates. Criteria for listing a jazz artist included participation in at least one musical recording and demonstration of significant new contributions to the field of jazz in the 1960s. Entries include such information as given and nicknames, date and place of birth and death, instruments played, education, career highlights, contributions to the jazz movement, addresses, major recordings, and more. Black and white photographs of many jazz musicians listed appear throughout the text. Several articles on various aspects of the jazz movement are also included. Other features include listings of popularity poll tabulations from the 1960s, major jazz recording companies and their addresses, important and critically acclaimed jazz recordings, and a bibliography.

Logan, Nick, and Bob Woffinden. *The Illustrated Encyclopedia of Rock.* New York: Harmony, 1977. 255p.

This volume combines color photography and biographies of rock artists and groups to tell the story of "rock n' roll." The biographies are arranged alphabetically and include entries for those rock artists who have become legendary performers or those who have remained popular through the years. The authors have also included some artists from other areas of music who may have influenced rock musicians. Each entry contains biographical information on the rock artists, tells of their influences, lists major hits, and gives a complete list of recordings. An index is also included in the volume.

MUSICAL INSTRUMENTS

Marcuse, Sibyl. *Musical Instruments: A Comprehensive Dictionary.* Garden City, N.Y.: Doubleday, 1964. 608p.

This dictionary provides concise definitions for musical instruments from all over the world. Derivations of words as well as translations from and to other languages are frequently provided. A bibliography at the end provides full information for works cited in abbreviated fashion after many of the entries. Examples of instruments cited are the ab-a-fu, a Philippine Jew's harp, the clapet, a clapper, the lute, the regal, a small organ, and the zurla, a

Yugoslavian shawm. Occasional photographs enrich the text. Based on Sach's *Real-Lexikon.*

TERMS

Apel, Willi. *Harvard Dictionary of Music.* 2nd ed. Cambridge, Mass.: Belknap Pr. of Harvard Univ. Pr., 1969. 935p.

Apel's book is designed to provide information on all musical topics and is addressed to the lay-person as well as the scholar. In some cases the articles have been divided into two paragraphs, one of which treats the subject from the present-day approach and the other from that of the historian. It is strong on bibliography, but omits biography. It has articles on "Societies," "Orchestras," and "Publishers." A fully revised, new edition is forthcoming (1984–85), edited by Don Randel.

Fink, Robert, and Robert Ricci. *The Language of Twentieth-Century Music: A Dictionary of Terms.* New York: Schirmer Books, 1975. 125p.

This dictionary is addressed both to the professional person and to the interested layperson. It defines some traditional terms, especially those that have taken on new meanings, but devotes most of its space to defining terms, practices, and instruments that originated from such contemporary musical forms as rock, electronic music, jazz, and twelve-tone music. Many terms from associated disciplines are also included. Musical examples are abundant. An appendix provides a topical listing of the terms included. The volume concludes with a classified bibliography.

Gold, Robert S. *A Jazz Lexicon.* New York: Knopf, 1964. 363p.

Gold provides not only definitions for the words in his lexicon, but also attempts to provide sociological background and roots for them. He traces the origins of jazz slang and provides numerous quotations to illustrate their evolutions in meaning. Examples of words discussed are "boxed," "drag," "hung-up," "moldy fig," "shootin' the agate," and "zonked." A bibliography is included after the definitions.

Polyglot Dictionary of Musical Terms. Budapest: Akadémiai Kiadó, 1978. 798p.

Providing an alphabetical listing of specialized musical terms in seven languages (German, English, French, Italian, Spanish, Hungarian, and Russian), this volume is more correctly a glossary rather than a dictionary, as definitions of musical terms are generally not given. It is intended to serve as the precursor of a larger, more comprehensive dictionary of musical terms to be presented in some eighteen to twenty languages. This work represents the first effort to compile a dictionary of music beyond a bilingual format and is the result of a cooperative effort between an international group of scholars.

The dictionary is arranged in one international alphabet of key-words, with precedence given to German as the basic language. Those terms that originated in the context of another of the representative languages is listed in that language. Any term that originated in a language not represented in the volume is given as a German key-word. Entries are arranged according to the standard order of the twenty-six letters of the Roman alphabet. Due to differences of the Cyrillic alphabet, all Russian key-word terms are placed in a separate section. All key-word entries list their equivalents in the six other representative languages.

Grammatical indications are provided for all key-words, but pronunciation, accent, and syllabication are not provided. Differences between British and American spelling and terminology are indicated. Cross-references are provided for all terms except key-words. Introductory remarks, extensive usage guides, and other useful material are given in all seven languages. A section of diagrams, illustrating some of the musical terms, especially the instruments, concludes the volume.

OPERA AND THEATER MUSIC

Gammond, Peter. *The Illustrated Encyclopedia of Recorded Opera.* New York: Harmony Books, 1979. 256p.

The encyclopedia was intended to serve as a survey of recorded opera accessible to most record buyers and to show what is available. Entries are arranged by composers and provide information on the composers, number of acts, librettists, dates of first performances in major cities, synopses, notes, and lists of recordings for works. Biographies of 100 opera singers of the postwar period are found along with black and white illustrations or photographs of composers, singers, or scenes from operas. This work concludes with indexes to operas, composers and librettists, and singers.

Jacobs, Arthur, and Stanley Sadie. *Opera: A Modern Guide.* Newton Abbot, Devon, England: David & Charles, 1971. 492p.

Jacobs and Sadie have dealt with almost seventy operas by more than thirty composers, linking each discussion with commentary. The arrangement is roughly chronological, with the entries each providing a general introduction, an act-by-act plot synopsis, and a musical analysis. Musical examples are plentiful. A bibliography is appended.

Johnson, H. Earle. *Operas on American Subjects.* New York: Coleman-Ross, 1964. 125p.

Johnson's work provides information on operas about North and South America written by some 275 composers of international provenance. The volume is introduced by a lengthy essay tracing themes and history. For the entries themselves, each composer's dates are noted; there follows information, in varying detail, about the composer's operas. The fullest entries note where and when the opera was first performed, the number of acts, the setting, a brief plot synopsis, and critical comments on the composition and its production. A thematic index lists titles under such subjects as Spanish America, the Civil War, Christopher Columbus, and urban North America. An alphabetical index of titles, a general index, and a bibliography are also included.

Loewenberg, Alfred, comp. *Annals of Opera 1597–1940*. 3rd ed. Ed. and corrected by Harold Rosenthal. Totowa, N.J.: Rowman & Littlefield, 1979 (©1978). 1756p.

This work contains factual information about several thousand operas. It is arranged chronologically according to the date of the first performance. The notes give the composer, the author of the text, place of first performance, number of acts, title, and information on later performances, translations, and textual changes. Indexes of operas, composers, and librettists as well as a general index listing other persons, subjects, and places are included.

Martin, George. *The Opera Companion: A Guide for the Casual Operagoer.* New York: Dodd, Mead, 1961. 751p.

An illustrated guide for understanding and enjoyment of opera. Discusses the parts of the opera, voices as artistic and mechanical instruments, the orchestra, ballet in opera, and opera history. The appendixes contain: a list of operas in the text with details such as librettist, composer, theater, and place and date of first performance; basic Italian for operagoers; and synopses of twenty-seven modern operas. Contains a glossary.

————. *The Opera Companion to Twentieth Century Opera*. New York: Dodd, Mead, 1979. 653p.

Martin's work is written as a guide for those who appreciate opera but have had little musical education. He provides information about operas, personalities, and opera companies that have most recently influenced the art form in this century. The main section of this work consists of synopses of seventy-eight operas chosen for their numerous recordings, popularity, and frequent performances. Another section contains seven essays on opera and its personalities. Statistics for the world's great opera houses make up the third section. Martin also provides a bibliography and index to the work.

May, Robin. *A Companion to the Opera*. New York: Hippocrene Books, 1977. 364p.

Divided into six distinct parts, this work has sections on select composers, singers, conductors, producers, and librettists. Preceding the alphabetical listing of short biographies in each of these sections is a discussion of legendary people and events within each of these fields. The last section is a guide to operatic countries, centers, and theaters of the world. The appendixes provide alphabetical listings of operatic terms and operatic roles, and a bibliography. This work is indexed by both operas and people.

Northouse, Cameron. *Twentieth Century Opera in England and the United States*. Boston: G. K. Hall, 1976. 400p.

Three parts make up this guide to modern operas. The first lists, in chronological order, first performances of operas in the twentieth century. For each of these works the composer and the title are given, with the date, place, and conductor of its premiere. The second section gives similar information on operas for which complete performance information is lacking; it is arranged by composer. In the appendix, operas from the first two parts are listed again if they have been published or if they are based on literary works. An index connects this appendix to the first two sections and provides access to the work.

Rosenthal, Harold, and John Warrack. *Concise Oxford Dictionary of Opera.* London: Oxford Univ. Pr., 1964; 2nd ed., 1979. 446p.

This work includes entries on singers, composers, cities, specific operas, particular arias, literary allusions, characters, institutions and companies, festivals, and technical terms. The editors have concentrated on delineating major themes and contributions rather than on providing comprehensive lists and analyses. One finds, for example, entries for Alessandro Scarlatti, leitmotif, Don Giovanni, New York City Center for Music and Drama, Beecham Opera Company, Faust, Leningrad, Poland, and Adelina Patti. A bibliography is included at the beginning of the book.

The Simon and Schuster Book of the Opera: A Complete Reference Guide— 1597 to the Present. New York: Simon & Schuster, 1979. 512p.

This beautifully illustrated volume serves as a chronological record of 800 operas performed in Europe and the United States from 1597 to the present. These operas were chosen on the basis of their popularity, quality, and historical significance and are arranged by the dates of the first performances. Each entry consists of the name of the opera, composer, first performance, first performance in the United States and United Kingdom, original cast members (when noteworthy), and a synopsis. For some operas further notes may be given on the performers and performances. The color illustrations of composers, sets, performances, opera houses, and floor plans add value to this work. The volume is well-indexed with an index to operas and an index to composers, librettists, and literary sources.

MUSIC INDUSTRY

Music Industry Directory. 7th ed. Chicago: Marquis Professional Publications, 1983. 678p.

Formerly known as *The Musician's Guide*, this directory was published irregularly in six editions from 1954 to 1980. The seventh edition brings with it a new title and publisher, but the contents and format have generally remained unchanged. Basic information is provided concerning such areas of music as organizations and councils, education, competitions and awards, libraries, publications, performance, trade and industry, and the music profession. Typical entries provide addresses and the names of contact persons for the various institutions along with some descriptive information. Concluding the volume is a general index and a music publishers index.

Rachlin, Harvey. *The Encyclopedia of the Music Business.* New York: Harper & Row, 1981. 524p.

In dictionary format, Rachlin provides more than 450 brief entries on all aspects of contemporary popular music production, including production, marketing, promotion, and distribution. The work also defines the jargon of commercial music. Appendixes provide lists of songs that have won Grammys or Oscars.

MUSICAL THEMES
AND DEVICES

Barlow, Harold, and Sam Morgenstern. *A Dictionary of Musical Themes.* New York: Crown, 1948. 656p.

Designed for both the professional in music and for the layperson, this dictionary provides two approaches to over 10,000 musical themes from important symphonies, concertos, sonatas, chamber music pieces, and other concert music. The first part of the volume contains a single line of upper-staff notation for each major theme of each important work of a composer. Composers are arranged in alphabetic order. The section enables someone who remembers the name of a composition but not its theme to identify the latter. The second part of the work is a notation index. The person who remembers a theme and who can transpose it to notations in the key of C, can then identify the title and composer of the work. A title index is included.

Morgenstern, Sam, and Harold Barlow, comps. *A Dictionary of Opera and Song Themes.* New York: Crown, 1950. 549p.

This work is primarily a compendium of one line of upper-staff notations of the main themes of operas, cantatas, oratorios, lieder, art songs, and miscellaneous vocal pieces. Words as well as notes are provided. Arrangement is alphabetical by composer and then by the title of the work. In order to provide a single volume work, Morgenstern and Barlow have normally included only American and European compositions that are likely to be of interest to the contemporary layperson or musician. Popular tunes are included only if they have gained a semiclassical status. Appended to the volume is a notation index as well as an index to songs and first lines.

Read, Gardner. *Thesaurus of Orchestral Devices.* New York: Greenwood, 1969. 631p.

This work provides a guide to the varied sound effects that may be achieved by symphonic orchestras. Read has sought out various colorful, sonorous devices in over 1000 compositions and provides citations to them. The work is first divided into parts for various groups of instruments, such as woodwinds, percussion, and harp, and then into techniques, such as flutter-tonguing, tremolandi, and glissandi. Various instrumental and technique subdivisions further refine these categories. The citations to orchestral examples are given next. Thus, under "percussion" following the subheading "thin stick," one finds a citation to measure 34, page 49 of Stravinsky's *Histoire du Soldat.* The work is introduced by three chapters on nomenclature of instruments, comparative ranges, and the evolution of the modern symphony orchestra. At the end are lists of publishers, composers, and works as well as indexes of abbreviations, notation, numerals, nomenclature, and terminology.

MUSICAL FILM

Green, Stanley. *Encyclopedia of the Musical Film.* New York: Oxford Univ. Pr., 1981. 344p.
This encyclopedia provides up-to-date information on the musical film produced in the United States and Britain. Entries are arranged alphabetically and can be found on the most prominent persons, songs, and productions of musical film. The entries on personalities include a list of films and best-known works of an actor, actress, producer, director, composer, musician, or lyricist. Production entries include all songs and performers from the film. Green's work also includes Motion Picture Academy award nominations and recipients, an index of title changes, a general bibliography, and discography.

Hirschhorn, Clive. *The Hollywood Musical.* New York: Crown, 1981. 456p.
A heavily illustrated chronology of American-made film musicals from their beginning in 1927 to the 1980s. The entries are essays that include a plot synopsis, remarks on the production, cast, composers, directors, and lists of the songs included. Side panels on some pages list awards for musical film and top money-making films for each year. The appendixes list "fringe," miscellaneous pop, and important documentary musicals. Indexes are provided for film, song, and music titles; performers; composers; lyricists, and other creative personnel.

Histories and Chronologies

HISTORIES

Bordman, Gerald. *American Musical Theatre: A Chronicle.* New York: Oxford Univ. Pr., 1978. 749p.
In eleven descriptive chapters this work moves season by season, show by show, to cover the American musical from 1866 to 1970. While a prologue covers the genre from its origins to 1866, an epilogue scrutinizes the 1965–70 period. With critical comments from reviews incorporated into the text, other information listed after the titles of musicals includes opening dates, theaters, plot synopses, and performers' names with the characters portrayed. Separate indexes for shows and sources, songs, and people provide further access. Name entries are listed alphabetically in an appendix.

New Oxford History of Music. London: Oxford Univ. Pr., 1954– .
The *New Oxford History of Music* was published as a replacement for the *Oxford History of Music* issued at the beginning of the century. The present volumes represent a complete reworking of the material, and many additions to the scope of the work have been made. The eight volumes published to date deal with ancient and oriental music, early medieval music, *ars nova* and the Renaissance, the age of humanism, opera and church music, the age of Enlightenment, the age of Beethoven, and the modern age. The volumes

are each divided chronologically, geographically, and topically. Many musical illustrations as well as a few place photographs are included. A chapter-oriented bibliography and an index are appended to each work. Still to be published in the series are two volumes dealing with the growth of instrumental music and Romanticism. In addition, volume 11 (pending) will provide a general index and chronological tables to complement the entire set.

v.1 Wellesz, Egon, ed. *Ancient and Oriental Music.* 1957.

v.2 Hughes, Dom Anselm, ed. *Early Medieval Music to 1300.* 1954.

v.3 Hughes, Dom Anselm, and Gerald Abraham, eds. *Ars Nova and the Renaissance, c. 1300–1540.* 1960.

v.4 Abraham, Gerald, ed. *The Age of Humanism, 1540–1630.* 1968.

v.5 Fortune, Nigel, and Anthony Lewis, eds. *Opera and Church Music, 1630–1750.* 1975.

v.7 Wellesz, Egon, and Frederick W. Sternfeld, eds. *The Age of Enlightenment, 1745–1790.* 1975.

v.8 Abraham, Gerald, ed. *The Age of Beethoven, 1790–1830.* 1982.

v.10 Cooper, Martin, ed. *Modern Age, 1890–1960.* 1974.

Yet to be published:

v.6 *The Growth of Instrumental Music.*

v.9 *Romanticism.*

Strunk, Oliver. *Source Readings in Music History.* New York: Norton, 1950. Paperback ed. in 5v.: v.1, *Antiquity and the Middle Ages;* v.2, *The Renaissance;* v.3, *The Baroque Era;* v.4, *The Classic Era;* v.5, *The Romantic Era.*

Intended to provide teachers and musicians with a source book on important works in the history of music, this edition is a reissue of the original one-volume work published in 1950 by Norton. Each volume contains the writings, in translation, of historians, composers, or critics of music such as Plato, St. Jerome, Boethius, William Byrd, Martin Luther, Claudio Monteverdi, Joseph Addison, J. J. Rousseau, E. T. A. Hoffmann, and Richard Wagner. A brief biography and discussion of the writer's views on music precedes each essay. Each volume is fully indexed.

MUSIC HISTORY IN PICTURES

Kinsky, George, ed. *A History of Music in Pictures.* New York: Dover, 1951. 363p.

Kinsky's work surveys some 4500 years of music history from Babylonia, Assyria, and Egypt to the masters of impressionism. While there are a few pictures relating to the Orient, Africa, and America, the emphasis is overwhelmingly on Europe. The pictures are divided chronologically and usually geographically as well. Persons, both as individuals and as representative types; instruments; music; buildings; and pages from books all figure as subjects. One finds, for example, pictures of eighteenth-century French operatic singers, of nineteenth-century wind instruments, of music incunabula, and of sixteenth- and seventeenth-century lyres. Reproductions of artistic works are common. Indexes to instruments, places, and persons are included.

CHRONOLOGIES

Slonimsky, Nicolas. *Music since 1900.* 4th ed., New York: Scribner's, 1971. 1595p.

This reference work consists mainly of a descriptive chronology that records international events in the musical world. Entries are given for days of each month and extend from 1900 to 20 July 1969. Events recorded were chosen for their potential contribution to the future of music rather than their significance at the time of occurrence. The author was thus not highly selective in choosing material but sought to include as many potentially important events as possible. A separate section of letters and documents is included, along with a dictionary of terms and a common index of names and terms. The latter three sections are all alphabetically arranged.

Bibliographies of Music Literature

GENERAL

Besterman, Theodore. *Music and Drama: A Bibliography of Bibliographies.* Totowa, N.J.: Rowman & Littlefield, 1971. 365p.

Besterman's guide contains sections for music, drama, and special subjects, such as persons and instruments related to the two former fields. Numerous subdivisions for countries, periodicals, history, manuscripts, and so forth are employed. Within each subdivision, the arrangement is chronological by the date of publication. Besterman has not provided extensive annotations, but he has noted the number of items included in each bibliography and has made explanatory comments regarding titles, series, and editions when he deemed them necessary.

Marco, Guy A. *Information on Music: A Handbook of Reference Sources in European Languages.* v.1– . Littleton, Colo.: Libraries Unlimited, 1975– .

This annotated bibliography lists reference works of use to students and researchers in the field of music. General reference sources, such as the *New York Times Index* and the *Oxford English Dictionary*, as well as more specialized tools, are included. These annotations seek to describe the features and special uses of each source. In addition to bibliographical information and annotations, many entries have citations to other bibliographic descriptions of the works.

Volume 1 of this work lists sources that are universal in scope. It is divided into chapters by forms, such as direct information sources, universal biographical sources, lists of music, and general discographies. Volume 2 covers the Americas and is arranged by country. Subsequent volumes are promised for Europe; Africa, Asia, and Oceania; specific topics; and individual musicians. The final volume is to be a "Guide to Musical Editions."

Works relating to classical music, folk music, jazz, and popular forms are included. Each volume is separately indexed and contains, in an appendix, revisions for the previous volumes of the set.

CURRENT OR ANNUAL

Music Article Guide. An Annotated Quarterly Reference Guide to Significant Signed Feature Articles in American Music Periodicals. Philadelphia: Music Article Guide, 1966– .

This guide indexes articles appearing in approximately 175 American music periodicals. Each quarterly issue cites, with brief explanatory annotations, the articles under a variety of subject headings ranging from bugle and Dorian Woodwind Quintet to Modeste Mussorgsky and theory. Each issue also gives a directory of American music periodicals.

Music Index. Detroit: Information Coordinators, 1949– .

Music Index is published monthly with annual cumulations. Approximately 300 journals from all over the world are indexed. Within each volume are author, proper name, and subject entries in one alphabetical order. Geographical headings may be main entries or subdivisions. A work with a text is entered under the name of the composer with a cross-reference from title. Book reviews and specific recording reviews are grouped alphabetically under those divisions, whereas reviews of compositions are listed under works. Reviews of performance may be found under the name(s) of the performer(s), either individuals or groups. It is the most comprehensive index to music journals.

RILM Abstracts of Music Literature. International Musicological Soc., International Assn. of Music Libraries, American Council of Learned Societies, 1967– .

These abstracts, with their author and subject indexes, are published quarterly, with the fourth issue being a cumulative index to the three preceding. Books, articles, essays, reviews, dissertations, catalogs, and other ephemera of international provenance are included. Titles in foreign languages appear both in the original and in English, and all abstracts are in English. The summaries are signed and include the notation of key words for indexing. *RILM Abstracts* is the single such service in music and aims at comprehensiveness.

SPECIAL AND SUBJECT BIBLIOGRAPHIES

AMERICAN MUSIC

Hixon, Donald L. *Music in Early America: A Bibliography of Music in Evans.* Metuchen, N.J.: Scarecrow, 1970. 607p.

Hixon has compiled a finding list or index to those publications containing printed musical notation recorded in Charles Evans's *American Bibliog-*

raphy and in the microprint edition by Readex Corporation of *Early American Imprints, 1639–1800*. The first portion of the book is an alphabetical composer/editor/compiler key to the latter publication, and the second portion is a key to those works recorded in Evans but which have not yet appeared in *Early American Imprints*. Anonymous works have been entered under their titles. Since Hixon's work is primarily an index, its entries do not contain a great deal of descriptive cataloging material. They do note, however, the serial numbers that Evans assigned. A third section of the book provides brief biographical sketches with personal and career data on the composers, musicians, compilers, and editors noted in the previous sections. Composer, title, and numerical indexes are included.

Horn, David. *The Literature of American Music in Books and Folk Music Collections: A Fully Annotated Bibliography*. Metuchen, N.J.: Scarecrow, 1977. 556p.

More than 1300 monographs, anthologies, and reference books relating to American music are listed in this bibliography, which has a subject arrangement. Biographies, musicological works, books about musical genres, collections of songs, and works of criticism are among the types of book included. Each entry consists of a bibliographic citation, often to more than one edition, and an extensive, critical annotation. Typical chapters are "The Cultivated Tradition in the 19th Century," "The Music of the American Indian," "Folk Music," "Black Music," and "Jazz." Each chapter is divided further by topic and/or form. An index of subjects and names is provided; the appendix is an unannotated list of 300 additional books of marginal interest.

BLACK MUSIC

de Lerma, Dominique-René. *Bibliography of Black Music*. v.1, *Reference Materials;* v.2, *Afro-American Idioms;* v.3, *Geographical Studies*. Westport, Conn.: Greenwood, 1981– . 124p.

These are the first three volumes of a projected ten-volume set. Volume 1 lists more than 2600 reference works, including monographs, articles, and dissertations; the entries are not annotated. Instead of employing "see" or "see also" references, items relevant to more than one subject area are given full entry in each area. Twelve broad subject headings are employed; the works are listed alphabetically within each section by author. Volume 2, which contains 6000 citations, is organized under eleven subject headings corresponding to types of black music (e.g. Jazz, Blues). Again, the citations in volume 2 are not annotated.

McCabe, Jane A., comp. "Music and the Black American." In *Fine Arts and the Black American*, pp. 21–33. Comp. by Betty Jo Irvine. Bloomington: Indiana Univ. Libraries, 1969. 33p.

This is a bibliography of the monographic holdings, both general and specific, of the library, which contain material on black American musicians. Most of the items listed were published since World War II. The arrangement is alphabetical under modified Library of Congress subject headings. Also included is a list of subject headings useful in searching periodical indexes.

Skowronski, JoAnn. *Black Music in America: A Bibliography.* Metuchen, N.J.: Scarecrow, 1981. 723p.

This bibliography covers books and articles about black music and musicians in the United States from colonial times to 1979. It is divided into three sections: "Selected Musicians and Singers," "General References," and "Reference Works." The first section is the largest, with an alphabetical listing by musician's name followed by chronologically arranged citations of the books and articles. The second section lists general material on black music and musicians chronologically. Some specific subjects and dissertations are included. The final section is a bibliography of reference works that treats the subject of black music or musicians in depth. There is an author index with reference to the citation number.

CANADIAN MUSIC

Jarman, Lynne, ed. *Canadian Music: A Selected Checklist, 1950–73.* Buffalo: Univ. of Toronto Pr., 1976. 170p.

The entries in this work were adapted from lists of Canadian music in the journal, *Fontes artis musicae,* and the Canadian national bibliography *Canadiana.* Most of these items, which are arranged by Dewey decimal numbers with Library of Congress classification numbers also provided, are songbooks and scores. Books about Canadian music, biographies, reference books, and works of music theory are also included. These entries provide the information in card catalogs, such as indications of bibliographies, analytics, and designations of the number of players for which compositions are scored. Access to this volume is provided by author and title indexes.

DISSERTATIONS

Adkins, Cecil, and Alis Dickinson. *Doctoral Dissertations in Musicology.* 7th N. American ed.; 2nd international ed. Philadelphia: American Musicological Soc.; International Musicological Soc., 1984. 545p.

A comprehensive listing by author of approximately 6000 dissertations and other musicological works in progress. It combines the seventh cumulative listing of American-Canadian doctoral dissertations and the second cumulative listing of international doctoral dissertations in musicology, thus superseding both the *International Index of Dissertations and Musicological Works in Progress* (Adkins-Dickinson, 1977) and the *American-Canadian Supplement* (same editors, 1979). Includes indexes. Most universities and graduate divisions will not approve dissertation topics that duplicate, or nearly duplicate, works already listed in Adkins.

Dissertation Abstracts International. Ann Arbor, Mich.: Xerox Univ. Microfilms International, 1935– .

A listing of dissertations available from Xerox University Microfilms. Includes author abstracts of doctoral dissertations from over 350 cooperating institutions; nearly 30,000 entries are added each year. Monthly compilations are published in two sections: "A" (humanities and social sciences) and "B" (natural sciences and engineering); music appears in "A." Author and subject indexes are cumulated annually. Volumes 1–11 (1935–51) appeared as *Microfilm Abstracts;* volumes 12–29 (1952–69) appeared as *Dissertation Abstracts.*

ETHNOMUSICOLOGY

Nettl, Bruno. *Reference Materials in Ethnomusicology. A Bibliographic Essay.* 2nd ed., rev. Detroit: Information Coordinators, 1967. 40p.
Addressed to the student and the librarian, Nettl's work stresses materials on primitive and Asian ethnomusicology. Most of the works cited are surveys and compendia rather than primary research studies. A series of bibliographic essays examine surveys, collections, periodicals, directories, bibliographies, and publications on research techniques, elements of music, instruments, and special approaches. A single bibliography of publications cited is appended.

JAZZ

Carl Gregor, Duke of Mecklenburg. *International Jazz Bibliography: Jazz Books from 1919 to 1968.* Strasbourg: P. H. Heitz, 1969. 198p.
————. *1970 Supplement to International Jazz Bibliography and International Drum and Percussion Bibliography.* Graz: Universal Edition, 1971. 109p.
————. *1971/72/73 Supplement to International Jazz Bibliography and Selective Bibliography of Some Jazz Background Literature and Bibliography of Two Subjects Previously Excluded.* Graz: Universal Edition, 1975. 246p.
The 1969 volume lists books and pamphlets from the United States and other countries dealing with all aspects of jazz. It includes biographies, monographs, histories, theories and analyses, reference works, bibliographies, dissertations and theses, discographies, works on the subject of ragtime, rhythm and blues, rock and pop, and many more. Altogether over 1500 items, including translations and reprint editions, are featured in the volume. Full bibliographic data are provided for each entry. Annotations are not provided. The arrangement is alphabetical by author, and several indexes provide further access.
Two supplements to the *International Jazz Bibliography* have since been published that attempt to gather together any titles overlooked in the original edition. Together the supplements also include new titles that appeared from 1968 to 1973. They are arranged by subject, then alphabetically by author. Additional areas covered by the supplements include an international drum and percussion bibliography, a selective bibliography of jazz background literature, and a bibliography dealing with poetry, fiction, cartoons, and drawings. Material listed in all volumes of the series was sent by many different collaborators and was mostly left unchecked by the author because of the lack of information to be found for the titles in any other reference sources.

Kennington, Donald, and Danny L. Read. *The Literature of Jazz; A Critical Guide.* 2nd ed. Chicago: American Library Assn., 1980. 236p.
This is a list of significant books on the subject. It has chapters on general background, the histories of jazz, the lives of jazz performers, analysis, theory, and criticism, reference sources, the periodical literature, jazz and literature, and organizations.

JEWISH MUSIC

Sendrey, Alfred. *Bibliography of Jewish Music.* New York: Columbia Univ. Pr., 1951. 404p.
Sendrey began his work with a historical survey of the bibliography of Jewish music and then divided his work into two principal parts. The first part contains citations to works about Jewish music with chronological, form, and subject subdivisions. The second part contains citations to the actual musical compositions, both sacred and secular. The works cited are those that in some sense convey a Jewish theme or feeling or that relate to Jewish life. Those works composed by Jews that have none of the above characteristics are not included. Popular Yiddish theater songs are also excluded. Separate indexes for both sections appear at the end of the book. Annotations are provided only if the contents of the work are unclear from the title.

OPERA AND THEATER MUSIC

Drone, Jeanette Marie. *Index to Opera, Operetta and Musical Comedy Synopses in Collections and Periodicals.* Metuchen, N.J.: Scarecrow, 1978. 171p.
Drone has indexed English-language collections containing synopses of operas, operettas, and musical comedies. First, the seventy-four different collections are numbered along with four periodicals. Next, opera titles are given in alphabetical order with a number or numbers referring to the books or periodicals where synopses of the operas can be found. A third feature is an index of composers listing the operas that have been summarized in the collections. Finally, a list of additional sources includes books treating the operas, operettas, and musical comedies of individual composers.

SACRED MUSIC

Von Ende, Richard C. *Church Music: An International Bibliography.* Metuchen, N.J.: Scarecrow, 1980. 453p.
This bibliography includes 5445 entries in twenty-five languages. The materials are chiefly books but include articles, catalogs, and lists of music. The work, covering many aspects of ecclesiastical music, is arranged under 284 alphabetical categories from "abbeys" to "yearbooks." "See also" references send the reader to related entries under other topics. An index of authors, editors, and compilers completes the volume.

Bibliographies of Music

GENERAL

Berkowitz, Freda Pastor. *Popular Titles and Subtitles of Musical Compositions.* 2nd ed. Metuchen, N.J.: Scarecrow, 1975. 209p.
This is an alphabetical listing by title of the nicknames and subtitles that have been given since 1600 to compositions such as sonatas and symphonies known formally only by their key and opus number. The listings are in English and in the original language. Information on the origin of the popular names and subtitles is provided whenever possible. A bibliography and an index of composers are included.

Bibliographic Guide to Music: 1977. Boston: G. K. Hall, 1977. 477p.
Intended as a reference, acquisition, and cataloging tool, this computer-produced supplement to the *Dictionary Catalog of the Music Collection, The Research Libraries of the New York Public Library* (G. K. Hall, 1964) includes materials cataloged between September 1, 1975 and August 31, 1976. Arranged as a dictionary catalog, the work includes Americana, periodicals, folk songs, eighteenth- and nineteenth-century librettos, opera and scores, vocal music, record catalogs, manuscripts, literature on the voice, and symphonic music. Full Library of Congress cataloging information for each title is provided.

British Broadcasting Corporation. Central Music Library. *BBC Music Library Catalogues.* London: British Broadcasting Corporation, 1965– .
These volumes list the manuscript and printed music holdings of the BBC. The arrangement is alphabetical by composer or by title with dates, broadcast timings, and principal thematic catalogs used noted when possible. Classified indexes, bibliographies, and lists of publishers are frequently provided. To date, the catalogs cover chamber music, composer lists for piano and organ music and for songs, song title lists, and composer and title lists for choral and opera music.

De Charms, Desiree, and Paul F. Breed. *Songs in Collections; An Index.* Detroit: Information Service Inc., 1966. 588p.
De Charms and Breed have provided an index to the songs in over 400 collections published primarily between 1940 and 1957. The names of the collections are listed at the front of the volume. The songs included are primarily classical, folk, and sacred with a few popular ones. Most have piano accompaniments. Those songs for which a composer could be determined are listed in the first section under her or his name. Folk and several other anonymous songs are listed geographically by country. Listings of carols and sea chanties comprise the third and fourth portions. At the end are indexes to titles, first lines, and authors.

Fuld, James J. *The Book of World-Famous Music; Classical, Popular, and Folk.* New York: Crown, 1971. 688p.

This bibliography brings together for the first time historical information concerning hundreds of the most popular musical compositions in the history of Western music. Works from over twenty-five countries are included and cover a period of 500 years of music history. Entries are listed alphabetically by title and reproduce the first few bars of each composition along with the lyrics. Composers are given for each composition when known, along with biographical information. The author used the first printing of each musical composition as the chief source of historical information whenever possible. Includes an extensive introduction, which outlines research methods, lists abbreviations of the principal works consulted, and more. The index includes composers, titles listed in the original language and in English translation, and alternative titles whenever available.

Hodgson, Julian. *Music Titles in Translation: A Checklist of Musical Compositions.* London: Clive Bingley, 1976. 370p.
A listing in one alphabet of both the original title, giving the English translation, and the English translation, giving the original title. Composers' names are given in the entries. Alternate titles and titles of works from which some pieces are derived are also given.

Performing Arts Books 1876–1981. New York: Bowker, 1981. 1656p.
A retrospective bibliography of 50,000 titles published or distributed in the United States from 1876 to 1981. All aspects of the performing arts are treated. Full entries are arranged alphabetically by Library of Congress subject headings and are cited from both author and title indexes. Under each subject, entries are arranged chronologically. They include full bibliographic information, classification, notes, and tracings as well as cataloging and some publishing information. Some 2431 current serials published internationally are indexed by primary subject. Cross-references from secondary subjects and titles appear in a separate section.

Peterson, Carolyn Sue, and Ann D. Fenton. *Index to Children's Songs: A First Line and Subject Index.* New York: Wilson, 1979. 318p.
This index provides access to 5000 songs for children located in 298 books likely to be found in school and public libraries. The three main sections of this work include indexes to titles and first lines of songs, subjects, and a list of the books indexed, which provides full bibliographic information and location codes for each work. Variations on titles and first lines are also found. Each of the three sections is arranged alphabetically; after the song titles the user is led to books containing the desired song.

Sears, Minnie Earl. *Song Index.* New York: Wilson, 1926.
———. *Supplement.* 1934. 2v. in 1. 403p.
Almost 20,000 songs are indexed in the *Song Index* and its *Supplement.* There are entries under title, composer, and author; but only the first contains the reference to the collection in which the song may be found. Only those collections likely to be found in a medium-sized public library have been indexed; and certain specialized hymns and folk dances, as well as most foreign collections and collections of individual composers, have been ex-

cluded. Foreign songs are entered under their original title except for certain "exotic" and non-Roman alphabet languages. Although there is no subject classification, there is a classified list of collections indexed. At the end of each volume is a directory of publishers.

CURRENT OR ANNUAL

The British Catalogue of Music: A Record of Music and Books about Music Recently Published in Great Britain, Based upon the Material Deposited at the Copyright Receipt Office of the British Library, Arranged according to a System of Classification with a Composer and Title Index, a Subject Index, and a List of Music Publishers. London: British Library, 1957– .
This work has been published annually for some twenty years, and its scope and format are well indicated by its expanded title. The classified section is divided into two main parts. The musical literature section lists works under form and subject divisions. The music section is subdivided by genres and by instruments. The catalog excludes certain popular music compositions published in Great Britain but includes foreign music available there through a sole agent. Prices are noted when known.

Nardone, Thomas R., ed. *Music in Print.* Philadelphia: Musicdata, 1974–79. 4v.
To date, the Music-in-Print Series consists of six volumes that individually cover a variety of topics: choral music (sacred and secular), organ music, classical vocal music, orchestral music, and string music. Volumes in the series are updated annually by supplements. The set lists 225,000 editions included in the catalogs of some 900 international publishers of music. Entries for each composition include the title, composer, arranger, instrumentation, and publisher. The title of each work appears in the original language and any translated titles are listed below with cross-references to the original. The catalogs utilize standard musical abbreviations to enable worldwide usage. Includes a special list of explanatory notes to the abbreviations and also a directory of publishers.

United States. Copyright Office. *Catalog of Copyright Entries.* 3rd Series. Pt. 5: *Music.* Washington, D.C.: Copyright Office, 1947– .
This work lists all musical compositions entered for copyright registration in the United States. Issued twice a year, the catalog consists of a list of current and renewal registrations, arranged by registration number and providing full bibliographic information, in addition to an index. The latter provides access to the list by title, composer, and publishing company.

———. Library of Congress. *Music, Books on Music, and Sound Recordings.* 1977– . (formerly *Music and Phonorecords: 1953–72.*)
This catalog is a reproduction of information contained on cards of the Library of Congress and other North American libraries. The entries listed represent a wide variety of music collections and include music scores, sheet music, librettos, works on music and musicians, and sound recordings of all

types. Volumes are published semi-annually with annual and five-year cumulations. The bibliography is designed as a reference and acquisitions tool. It is also an aid to individual libraries wishing to order Library of Congress printed cards for music, musicology, and sound recordings.

SPECIAL AND SUBJECT BIBLIOGRAPHIES

AMERICAN MUSIC

Sonneck, Oscar George Theodore. *A Bibliography of Early Secular American Music (18th Century)*. Rev. and enl. by William Treat Upton. n.p.: Library of Congress, Music Division, 1945. 616p.

The major portion of this bibliography consists of an alphabetical listing by title of eighteenth-century songs, published and unpublished, by native and naturalized Americans. Several details, such as the composer, the text of the first line, the content and format, publishing details, and the location, are noted. Both individual songs and collections are included. Following this section is a bibliography of secondary materials published during the same century. Appendixes include an alphabetical list of composers and their works, with brief biographical data also included; a list of songsters; a list of first lines, with title and composer; a list of opera librettos; and both a general index and an index to publishers, printers, and engravers. All of these latter features assist the user in gaining access to the main bibliography. To be used with Wolfe, *Secular Music in America*.

Wolfe, Richard J. *Secular Music in America, 1801–1825: A Bibliography*. New York: New York Public Library, 1964. 3v.

These volumes provide information about almost 10,000 musical compositions published in America during a quarter century. The work represents a continuation of Sonneck and Upton's *Bibliography of Early Secular American Music*. The arrangement is alphabetical by composer, with anonymous works entered by their titles. Short biographical sketches are provided for many of the lesser-known composers. Detailed descriptive cataloging information has been supplied for the various editions and imprints of the compositions, and note has been made as well of locations in libraries. The third volume contains appendixes that update Sonneck and Upton's work and list unrecorded eighteenth-century imprints, redated imprints, and additional copies of eighteenth-century imprints. The volumes conclude with indexes for titles and first lines; for publishers, engravers and printers; for publishers' plate and publication numbering systems; and with a general index. To be used with Sonneck.

BLACK MUSIC

Tischler, Alice. *Fifteen Black American Composers: A Bibliography of Their Works*. Detroit: Information Coordination, 1981. 328p.

This work provides performance and recording citations to the works of fifteen twentieth-century black American composers of classical music. The author provides for composers a complete list of the titles, dates, publication data, and library holdings of their compositions. There are "see also" references, and both title and medium of performance indexes. Brief biographical data for the composers are also provided.

CANADIAN MUSIC

Canadian Music Library Association, comp. *Musical Canadiana. A Subject Index*. Ottawa: Canadian Library Assn., 1967. 62p.

This work is a catalog of approximately 800 instrumental and vocal pieces published before 1921 and composed by Canadians and/or associated with Canada. The works are listed under general and detailed subject headings that include persons, places, sports, the military, types of transportation, groups of people, buildings, and historical events, among others. For each title, the names of the composers or sources of words and music are supplied as well as the date of composition and the instrument for which it was composed, if applicable.

MUSIC FOR PERFORMANCE

ASCAP Symphonic Catalog 1977. Ed. and comp. by the American Society of Composers, Authors, and Publishers. 3rd ed. New York: Bowker, 1977. 522p.

This third edition of the *Symphonic Catalog* of the American Society of Composers, Authors, and Publishers lists 26,000 musical works for symphonies, chamber groups, and choral groups, by American and foreign composers whose works are licensed for performance in the United States. The catalog is organized alphabetically by composer and arranger, with titles of works following the composer's name. Entries include instruments required for performance, authors of texts, and publishers and publication date. Keys to instrument abbreviations and to publishers' abbreviations are included. The work is not indexed.

Farish, Margaret K. *String Music in Print*. 2nd ed. New York: Bowker, 1973. 464p.

Addressed both to the performer and the teacher, Farish's book provides a guide to available published music for the violin, viola, violon-cello, double-bass, and viol. The volume is based on sales and rental catalogs issued by publishers. The first nine chapters list music available for from one to ten instruments; and they are subdivided by various groups of instruments. Other chapters list music for various combinations of instruments, for voice and instruments, chamber music, music for instruments and electronic tape, music for solo stringed instruments and orchestra, orchestral study scores, and study materials. Within each section, the arrangement is alphabetical by composer with the title and an abbreviation for the publisher noted. A composer index and a directory of publishers are included.

Hinson, Maurice. *Music for Piano and Orchestra: An Annotated Guide*. Bloomington: Indiana Univ. Pr., 1981. 327p.

A guide to compositions for piano and orchestra written from 1700 to the present. The compositions are arranged chronologically by composer. The works are described and graded by difficulty. Editions of these works are listed in order of preference. Entries include bibliographies; and an annotated bibliography and indexes of works for piano and orchestra, strings, and band are included. Addresses of music publishers and agents are given.

McGraw, Cameron. *Piano Duet Repertoire: Music Originally Written for One Piano, Four Hands*. Bloomington: Indiana Univ. Pr., 1981. 334p.
A guide to piano duets. These compositions are listed alphabetically by composer. The entries give the full title of the work, dates of composition, and publication and publisher. The level of difficulty is given and the characteristics and style are discussed. The indexes list library locations and names and addresses of music publishers. The appendixes list collections and anthologies of four-hand music.

JAZZ AND POPULAR MUSIC

Shapiro, Nat, ed. *Popular Music: An Annotated Index of American Popular Songs*. New York: Adrian Pr., 1964– .
To date, this series is composed of six volumes and covers the period 1920–69. Included are songs that have garnered a modicum of popular acceptance, were exposed to the public in exceptional circumstances, or were put forward by well-known musicians. Each volume is divided into yearly segments, and songs are listed alphabetically by title under these. Variant titles are noted next to used titles, and there are cross-references from the former to the latter as well. Each main entry also lists the author(s)/composer(s) and the current publisher and indicates country of origin if not the United States, the type of production in which the song was introduced and by whom if important, and first or best-selling recordings. Other data may be included if relevant and important. At the end of each volume is a list of titles and year under which they may be found and a list of publishers of songs indexed. Addresses are included.

EARLY MUSIC IN MODERN EDITIONS
(INCLUDING COLLECTIONS AND MONUMENTS)

Bryden, John R., and David G. Hughes, comps. *An Index of Gregorian Chant*. Cambridge: Harvard Univ. Pr., 1969. 2v.
These two volumes provide an index to Gregorian chants to be found in almost twenty printed collections and manuscripts. The first volume lists the chants in alphabetical order according to opening words or textual incipits; and the second volume lists the chants according to a numerical representation of the opening melodies. Both volumes include for each chant information on its mode, the category to which it belongs, sources where it may be found, the first note, textual and melodic incipits, and the finale.

Charles, Sydney Robinson. *A Handbook of Music and Music Literature in Sets and Series*. New York: Free Pr., 1972. 497p.

This work was written as a guide to the intricacies of sets and series of music and music literature. The four parts detail the contents and contain explanatory notes for sets and series of monuments, complete works, monographs, and periodicals. The index covers personal and corporate names, titles, and some subjects.

Heyer, Anna Harriet, comp. *Historical Sets, Collected Editions and Monuments of Music.* 3rd ed. Chicago: American Library Assn., 1980. 2v.
This work provides a list of and an index to 1300 major collections of music published in the Western world before 1980. It is of value to musicians and scholars wanting to locate scores of composers in anthologies and collected editions. Works were selected for their historical significance, musical value, quality of editing, or contribution to music research. Entries follow the standard format of the Library of Congress card. They are arranged alphabetically by name of composer or compiler of a collection when known, and otherwise by title of the work. Complete cross-references are provided. Every attempt is made to include full bibliographic information and a content summary for each work. Some categories specifically excluded from the listing are folk music, collections of songs, and microfilm copies of works. An extensive index of composers, compilers, editors, and titles makes up volume 2 of the set. It is the most comprehensive index to music in sets and anthologies.

PRIMARY SOURCES OF EARLY MUSIC:
MANUSCRIPTS AND PRINTED BOOKS

Census-Catalog of Manuscript Sources of Polyphonic Music 1400–1550. Comp. by the Univ. of Illinois Musicological Archives for Renaissance Manuscript Studies. v.1, A–J; v.2, K–O; v.3, P–U. Renaissance Manuscript Studies, 1. Neuhausen-Stuttgart: Hänssler-Verlag, American Institute of Musicology, 1979– .
Catalog of current library location of all known manuscripts containing polyphonic music composed between 1400 and 1550, excepting: tablatures, manuscripts containing only anonymous "primitive" polyphony already described in RISM B IV/3–4, and most sources copied after 1700. Each entry gives a siglum, a manuscript designation by city, library and call number, a summary list of contents by genres, a list of composers whose works are found in the manuscript, a physical description, information on date, provenance and subsequent history, and a bibliography. Volume 4 (V–Z and supplement) is in preparation.

Répertoire International des Sources Musicales (International Inventory of Musical Sources or RISM). München: G. Henle, 1960– .
This multivolume work is a catalog of musical works produced up to 1800, including writings about music, liturgical sources, treatises, songbooks, textbooks, and monodic music. It is intended to list the known editions of such works in circulation between these years. The work is divided into two series: A, Alphabetical, and B, Systematic or Classified.
Series A, which has more than 200,000 entries, includes individual edi-

tions of music works in circulation during the period 1500 to 1800. The works are arranged alphabetically according to composer or editor.

Series B is arranged chronologically by category, such as the "theories of music" or "manuscripts." Series B compiles collections of music between 1500 and 1801, listing basically the same material as Series A according to genre, with, in most cases, more detail and more thorough annotations. These volumes have been published:

B:1. Recueils Imprimés, 16ᵉ–17ᵉSiècle.

    v.1, Liste Chronologique. (This set, when finished, is to replace Eitner's *Bibliographie der Musiksammelwerke.*)

B:2. Recueils Imprimés, 18ᵉ Siecle.

B:3. The Theory of Music from the Carolingian Era up to 1400.

    v.1, Descriptive Catalog of Manuscripts.

    v.2, Italy: Descriptive Catalog of Manuscripts.

B:4. Manuscripts of Polyphonic Music.

    v.1, 11th-Early 14th Century.

    v.2, Ca. 1320-1400.

    v.3, 4, 14th-16th Century.

B:5. Tropen- und Sequenzenhandschriften. (Lists tropes and sequenas.)

B:6. Écrits Emprimes Concernant la Musique. (A bibliography of writings about music in monographs and periodicals to 1800.)

B:8. Das Deutsche Kirchenleid. (A catalog of traceable printed sources of German hymns.)

    v.1, Verziechnis der Druke von den Aufängen bis 1800.

B:9.

    v.2, Hebrew Writings Concerning Music in Manuscripts and Published Books from Geonic Times up to 1800.

For each item, bibliographical descriptions are given, with the locations in libraries throughout the world. Each volume or group of volumes is indexed. *RISM* is the most broadly based and comprehensive bibliographic effort in musical scholarship.

SACRED MUSIC

Cunningham, W. Patrick. *The Music Locator.* Saratoga, Calif.: Resource Publications, 1976. 187p.

The purpose of *The Music Locator* is to assist those people who select music for worship to make choices appropriate to the occasions, to expand the range of potential decisions, and to assist in locating publishers. This computer-generated listing of over 12,500 published titles is broken down in four ways: (1) a categorized index of titles, including music for liturgies, seasonal music, and thematic music; (2) an alphabetical index of titles; (3) a composer index; and (4) an alphabetical index of publishers of religious music. Articles on aspects of planning music for the church precede the indexes.

BALLET

The Simon and Schuster Book of the Ballet. New York: Simon & Schuster, 1979. 323p.

A lengthy discussion on the evolution of ballet from 1581 to 1979 is followed by a chronological "catalog of ballets." This selective group of ballets represents significant developments in the history of ballet. Each entry includes a list of credits for the first performance, a synopsis, and a signed, critical assessment of the work. There are many illustrations in both black-and-white and color. There are indexes to both the ballets and the choreographers.

Catalogs of Music Libraries and Collections

Brunnings, Florence E. *Folk Song Index: A Comprehensive Guide to the Florence E. Brunnings Collection.* New York: Garland, 1981. 357p.

By indexing her personal collection of records, books, and magazines, the author has provided access to over 50,000 titles. Listed are work songs, chanties, traditional ballads, love songs, nursery rhymes, and folk songs. Songs are listed alphabetically, followed by a number or numbers referring to a numerical list of abbreviated book and journal titles. A bibliography giving full title, publisher, and publication date is included. An underlined number refers to a numerical list of recordings, which is followed by an alphabetical list of records and performers. The entries for lead performers include record titles, record companies, and catalog numbers. "See" references for variant titles are provided.

International Association of Music Libraries. Commission of Research Libraries. *Directory of Music Research Libraries: Including Contributors to the International Inventory of Musical Sources (RISM).* Comp. by Rita Benton et al. Iowa City: Univ. of Iowa, 1967– . 3v. to date.

This directory of institutions in North America and Europe includes not only musical research libraries but also collections in archives, museums, seminaries, monasteries, and private homes. Those libraries have cooperated in the preparation of the *Répertoire International des Sources Musicales* (*RISM*), a bibliography of music and works about music being compiled by the International Association of Music Libraries. The first volume covers Canada and the United States, while the second and third volumes are devoted to Europe. Volumes for Eastern Europe and Russia are in progress. For each country, a list of music bibliographies and works pertaining to music collections is provided for additional reference. Maps of the European countries are also included. The arrangement is alphabetical by geographic location within each country. For each institution within the country, these data are given: types of catalogs, a brief description of the collection, photocopying services available, days open, and references to materials published by and about the library. About 1900 institutions are represented, with Italy contributing the highest number. Each volume has its own index, which is arranged in separate lists by country. In progress.

New York Public Library. Music Division. *Bibliographic Guide to Music.* Boston: G. K. Hall, 1975– .
This annual supplement combines the New York Public Library's new acquisitions with additional entries from the Library of Congress. LC cataloging is given for each title, as well as the NYPL call number. Authors, titles, subject, and added entries are all arranged in a single alphabet.

———. Reference Dept. *Dictionary Catalog of the Music Collection.* Boston: G. K. Hall, 1964. 33v.
———. *Cumulative Supplement, 1964–1971.* 1973. 10v.
These volumes consist of reproductions of the cards describing and providing access to one of the world's outstanding collections of music. All cards are arranged in one alphabetical order. The supplementary volumes are arranged in the same manner.

Sibley Music Library Catalog of Sound Recordings. Boston: G. K. Hall, 1977. 14v.
The Sibley Music Library, which serves the Eastman School of Music at the University of Rochester, contains one of the larger collections of music and musical literature in the United States. The catalog of this distinguished library has been reproduced in book form to provide researchers with access to 25,000 disc and tape recordings. The catalog has a dictionary arrangement. Western recordings of classical music make up the greater portion of this work; but entries for jazz, ethnic music, spoken word recordings, and contemporary rock and popular music are also included. This set would be of use to larger public, academic, and musical libraries.

U.S. Library of Congress. Music Div. *Catalogue of Opera Librettos Printed Before 1800.* Prep. by Oscar George Theodore Sonneck. Washington, D.C.: Library of Congress, 1914. 2v.
The first volume of this set is a listing by title of opera librettos printed before 1800. The citations frequently include notes on the first performance, the text, the number of acts, and the authorship. The second volume contains author and composer lists and an aria index. Although Sonneck is still the central bibliography for opera librettos, it is in need of revision.

Discographies

Allan, Daniel. *Bibliography of Discographies.* Vol. 2: *Jazz.* New York: Bowker, 1981. 239p.

This work covers several types of popular music—gospel, ragtime, blues, and jazz—for the period 1935–80. More than 3500 discographies are listed alphabetically by artists' names. A coding system identifies the particular features of each item. The index provides both author and title access. "See" references are provided for artists whose popular names differ from their legal names.

Foreman, Lewis. *Systematic Discography.* London: Clive Bingley, 1974. 144p.
A guide for collectors and librarians for the cataloging, classification, and preservation of sound recordings. Also includes lists of dealers, pirate labels, journals, and sources of reviews. It contains a bibliography and an index.

Schwann-1, Record and Tape Guide. v.1– . Monthly. Boston: Schwann, 1973– .
This guide lists more than 45,000 selected tapes and records available in the United States at retail stores. Included in each issue are new listings, classical listings, electronic, jazz, soundtracks and original cast recordings of movies, musicals, and television shows, collections, such as anthologies, ballet, organ, quadrophonic records and tapes, and current popular recordings. A record price list is also included. The *Schwann-2, Semi-annual Supplementary Record and Tape Guide,* published spring and fall, lists mono records, electronically reprocessed stereo, international, noncurrent pop, religious, spoken, and miscellaneous recordings, many of which are not included in *Schwann-1.*

Yearbooks and Directories

The Music Yearbook: A Survey and Directory with Statistics and Reference Articles for 1972–3– . London: Macmillan, 1972– .
Oriented primarily toward the United Kingdom, *Music Yearbook* provides essays and statistics on notable musical events, compositions, and persons. The reference section contains short articles on such areas as law, copyright, and postage as they relate to musicians and on musical careers. A directory provides addresses for organizations, vendors, educational institutions, and other music groups. A briefer directory for overseas organizations is also included.

Pavlakis, Christopher. *The American Music Handbook.* New York: Free Pr., 1974. 836p.
This work provides descriptions and directory information on many types of musical organizations in the United States, including societies, orchestras and other instrumental ensembles, opera and dance companies, academic and professional vocal groups, music festivals, schools with music programs, music periodicals, and companies in the music industry. Biographical information on performers and composers as well as data on contests, awards,

and grants are also included. The coverage is restricted to the United States, although a brief "Foreign Supplement" lists foreign music festivals and publishers and international competitions.

Zalkand, Donald. *Contemporary Music Almanac 1980/81–* . New York: Schirmer Books, 1980– .
The *Contemporary Music Almanac*, a biennial publication, provides current information about the hits, personalities, events, trends and business aspects of the contemporary musical scene. A weekly list of top singles and albums for the year, events, a calendar, awards, biographies of individual artists and groups, and articles on trends in contemporary music make up most of the almanac. Some black and white photographs of artists and groups will be found along with the biographies. The rock business directories include stations, promoters, agents, managers, record companies, facilities, organizations and publications. The work is designed for the amateur and the music professional.

Miscellaneous Bibliographical Tools

GUIDES TO MUSIC LIBRARIANSHIP AND RESEARCH

Bradley, Carol J., ed. *Manual of Music Librarianship*. n.p.: Music Library Assn., 1966. 140p.
This book consists of a series of signed essays and outlines with appended bibliographies. Articles were written by music librarians in both academic and public library settings to assist colleagues in organizing and administering music libraries. Originally intended as a procedural manual for the novice, this work is useful to a much broader audience with a wide variety of background and experience in librarianship. Individual authors were selected to contribute articles on the basis of their expertise in certain subject areas. The editor sought to maintain a balance of information between public and academic library practices and to cover as wide a geographic distribution as possible. The chapters deal with such diverse topics as budgeting, cataloging and classification, acquisitions, preservation, recording equipment, and more. A subject index concludes the volume.

McColvin, Lionel Roy, and Harold Reeves. *Music Libraries, Including a Comprehensive Bibliography of Music Literature and a Select Bibliography of Music Scores Published Since 1957*. Rewritten, revised, and extended by Jack Dove. London: André Deutsch, 1965. 2v.
This two-volume work is directed to the questions of establishing and managing music libraries. A general survey of musical activity introduces the first volume and is followed by annotated lists of periodicals and catalogs, articles on dealers, binding, storage, and display, instructions and tables for

classifying and cataloging, and finally by listings of music libraries around the world together with information on their holdings and special features. The second volume is a compilation of titles of musical scores and of bibliography with indexes to both sections.

Watanabe, Ruth T. *Introduction to Music Research*. Englewood Cliffs, N.J.: Prentice-Hall, 1967. 237p.
Watanabe's guide is addressed to the graduate student and takes several different approaches. The first part is designed to orient the student to general library use in such areas as the catalog, interlibrary loan, and photoreproduction. The second part contains bibliographic essays with appended bibliographies for books, periodicals, music, and discography. It also advises on research methods and writing. The final section deals with types of research materials and surveys contemporary music periodicals. Separate indexes are appended for names, titles, and subjects.

BIBLIOGRAPHIES OF BIBLIOGRAPHIES

Brook, Barry S. *Thematic Catalogues in Music: An Annotated Bibliography*. Hillsdale, N.Y.: Pendragon, 1972. 347p.
More than 1400 entries with brief annotations make up this bibliography. Listed are thematic catalogs, that is, indexes that identify musical works through citation of their opening notes. Works dealing with a single composer are entered under the composer's name, the remainder under the compiler or publisher. The arrangement is alphabetical. Works in many languages are included.

Coover, James. *Music Lexicography, Including a Study of Lacunae in Music Lexicography and a Bibliography of Music Dictionaries*. 3rd ed., rev. and enl. Carlisle, Pa.: Carlisle Books, 1971. 175p.
This work is primarily an alphabetical listing by main entry of musical dictionaries. Brief textual, explanatory annotations are occasionally included. Some attempt has been made to indicate libraries that possess the works. The bibliography proper is introduced by an essay dealing with gaps in the literature of musical dictionaries. Appended to this introduction are various lists of dictionaries and other works with glossaries of musical terms published before 1700. At the end of the volume are indexes to personal names, to topics and types, and by date of publication.

Duckles, Vincent, comp. *Music Reference and Research Materials: An Annotated Bibliography*. New York: Free Pr., 1974. 526p.
Duckles' work is largely a classified bibliography of bibliographies, although it also includes citations to some standard histories as well as to key reference dictionaries and encyclopedias. It was designed as a teaching tool and as a guide to the literature. Foreign language as well as English works are included. Each citation contains full bibliographic information and a brief annotation that indicates the scope of the work and frequency of publi-

cation if it is a serial. There are bibliographies of both music and music literature as well as information on discographies. Very general reference works that deal only in part with music and works dealing with related arts are excluded. At the end are indexes of authors, editors, and reviewers; of subjects; and of titles. Most comprehensive and balanced guide to music research titles.

Meggett, Joan M. *Music Periodical Literature: An Annotated Bibliography of Indexes and Bibliographies.* Metuchen, N.J.: Scarecrow, 1978. 125p.
   Although this work is classified into six parts, the annotated descriptive citations of indexes and bibliographies of music periodical literature are numbered in one continuous sequence. Within the classifications the items are listed alphabetically by author or by title. The addition of an "R" to the identification number indicates that the title indexes music articles appearing before 1949. General, retrospective, special and nonmusic periodicals are covered. Separate indexes for author, editors and compilers; for subjects; and for titles provide further access.

Mixter, Keith. *General Bibliography for Music Research.* 2nd ed. Detroit: Information Coordinators, 1975. 135p.
   This work is designed to point out features of musical interest in general bibliographic tools; and it is addressed both to music students and researchers. Books only are discussed, with the emphasis on North American and European publications. The bibliographic essays included in the work discuss such types of works as encyclopedias, dictionaries, union lists and catalogs, indexes, and directories. A final chapter deals with indexes and editions of vocal texts arranged by languages. Mixter highlights features directly pertinent to music and notes features from cognate areas of interest as well. Both a title index and one of authors, compilers, and editors are provided.

Annotated Listing of Selected Music Periodicals

American Musicological Society. *Journal.* Richmond, Va., 1948– .
   Published triannually in the spring, summer, and fall, this journal consists mainly of a series of scholarly articles on specialized topics in such areas as music history, theory and composition, composers and their works, and musical themes and forms. Articles are signed and present detailed analyses of the subject in question; the essays are the result of advanced scholarly research. Also included are reproductions of manuscripts and musical scores, as well as illustrations of musical notations, charts, diagrams, and tables.
   A section devoted to reviews provides in-depth responses to recent publications in the field of music. All reviews are signed and include complete bibliographic citations for the material discussed. In addition, a listing of

recent publications is appended. An editorial section of responses to articles and reviews from previous issues also appears.

Association for Recorded Sound Collections. *Journal*. New York, 1967– .
Issues of this *Journal* are published two to three times a year and contain several scholarly articles dealing with specific topics in the area of sound recordings. Articles deal variously with technical aspects as well as with content of recordings. Illustrations are generally not provided. A section devoted to discographies of various distinguished musicians and vocalists, along with discussion and commentary, is included. A companion section also appears in many issues that provides a current bibliography for publications dealing with some aspect of recorded sound.
Book and record reviews are included in most issues with in-depth discussions and analyses of several recently published works. Bibliographic as well as order information is provided for each entry. Space is also given to editorial comment concerning previous issues, and recent announcements pertaining to the field of recorded sound.

Early Music. London: Oxford Univ. Pr., 1973– .
Published quarterly, each issue of *Early Music* begins with a series of scholarly articles devoted to various aspects of premodern music. Articles deal with a variety of topics related to musical developments of Western Europe. Discussions are not highly technical and focus on specific aspects of such areas as musical instruments, vocal and instrumental performance, composers, music history, and even dance. Texts are highly illustrated with black and white photographs of manuscripts, instruments, and paintings of the period showing instruments and their use. Also included are musical notations, charts, and diagrams illustrating various instruments and their parts.
A section devoted to reviews of recent books in the field of early music follows. All reviews are signed and present lengthy discussions of the work in question. Two companion sections provide similar types of reviews for recent issues of printed music and sound recordings. Concluding each issue is a section for comment concerning previous reviews and discussion of upcoming conferences and performances of early music.

Ethnomusicology. Ann Arbor, Mich.: Soc. for Ethnomusicology, 1953– .
Published triannually in the winter, spring, and fall, this journal is mainly composed of original articles of a scholarly nature. They cover a wide variety of topics dealing with such aspects of ethnomusicology as history, theory and composition, instrumental and vocal performance, sociocultural implications, and more. Articles focus on cultures that generally have not been influenced by the musical developments of Western Europe. This includes peoples of such diverse geographical areas as Asia, Africa, Oceania, India, the Middle East, and Central and South America. Illustrations of musical notations, charts, diagrams, and some photographs of musicians and their instruments are provided but are not abundant.
A section devoted to reviews of publications relating to the field of ethnomusicology is included. All reviews are signed and discuss in some detail the works in question, which range in date of publication anywhere from one to five years previous to the issue. A companion section follows for reviews of

sound recordings. Recent issues have added a section devoted to the review of films. A current bibliography and discography serves each issue with an updated listing of current materials in ethnomusicology. Each entry provides basic bibliographic information.

Fontes Artis Musicae. Kassel: Bärenreiter-Verlag, 1954– .
Each volume consists of a variety of reports and papers dealing with current issues in the field of music librarianship and music publishing. Articles are international in scope and are presented in the language in which they were written. Representative languages include mainly German, French, and English, although articles deal with developments in all major centers of music throughout the world. Some of the topics discussed include the history of music libraries, selection and acquisition of materials, cataloging systems, and bibliographic research.
Articles vary in length and detail. Illustrations, such as reproductions of manuscripts, are provided for some articles but are not numerous. Also included are reports on the activities of major conferences, such as the International Association of Music Libraries (IAML), and reports from other groups such as the Cataloguing Commission. A section devoted to recent publications in the field of music also appears.

International Musicological Soc. *Acta Musicologica.* Basel: Bärenreiter-Verlag, 1928– .
A semiannual publication, the *Acta Musicologica* is a scholarly journal that presents a series of highly advanced essays written in one of several languages, primarily German, French, or English. Illustrations, mostly in the form of musical notations, diagrams, and tables, are provided. Topics presented are very specific and represent the results of detailed research. They deal with various aspects of music theory and composition, musicology, musical forms, and historical studies. Scholarship focuses mainly on the history and development of the music of Western European culture, although an occasional article is devoted to a topic of ethnomusicological interest. Concluding each issue is a section that provides current announcements, such as major new publications, important acquisitions of rare materials by archives or research libraries, and upcoming conferences of interest to the community of music scholars. Of special value is the continuing series of articles that survey the current state of musicology in the United States and other countries, with close attention to recent bibliography.

Journal of Musicology; A Quarterly Review of Music History, Criticism, Analysis, and Performance Practice. St. Joseph, Mich.: Imperial Printing Co., 1982– .
The *Journal of Musicology* is a comprehensive scholarly periodical that aims to provide a forum equal in quality to that of the *Journal of the American Musicological Society* and *Acta Musicologica.* The range of articles covers all aspects of music history and the methodology of musical research. Supplementing the several scholarly articles in each issue are conference reports and detailed reviews of recently published books, scholarly editions of music, and music journals.

Journal of Music Theory. New Haven, Conn.: Yale Univ., 1957– .

Published semiannually in the spring and fall, this journal is comprised of a series of four to five scholarly articles dealing with very advanced subjects in the field of music theory. The language is highly technical and discussions of specific topics are very detailed. Included are musical notations, diagrams, charts, and tables to illustrate many of the ideas expressed in the text. A section of lengthy critical reviews gives a series of very detailed analyses of musical publications. All reviews are signed and deal with books published anywhere between one to five years previous to the issue. A section containing letters to the editor provides critical response to book reviews and articles appearing in previous issues.

A brief section entitled "Communications" lists announcements of upcoming conferences, musical societies, and a variety of other information of interest to scholars in the field of music. Also included in each issue is a listing of recently published books and articles dealing with music theory and composition. Entries are arranged alphabetically by author and provide only standard bibliographic citations. Concluding each issue are advertisements of individual contributors.

Musica Disciplina: A Yearbook of the History of Music. Rome: American Inst. of Musicology, 1946– .

Originally published as the *Journal of Renaissance and Baroque Music,* each annual issue of *Musica Disciplina* is composed mainly of lengthy articles written by scholars in the field and also provides a bibliography of books related to the history of music. Articles deal with specific topics within such categories as music history, types and forms of music, evolution of musical styles, composers and leading figures in the field of music, and more. Articles are supplemented by photographic reproductions of manuscripts and musical notations where appropriate. A list of forthcoming and current publications of the American Institute of Musicology concludes each volume. Entries for publications are listed according to the AIM journal in which they appear and citations include price, order numbers, and descriptive information of varying length and detail.

The Musical Quarterly. New York: G. Schirmer, 1915– .

Essays covering a wide variety of such subjects as music history, composers, manuscripts, musical forms and pieces, musical themes, and music theory make up the major part of this journal. Topics are not highly technical in nature and are accessible to a wide range of readers. Essays are signed and include illustrations and reprints of manuscripts, musical notations, charts, and sections of musical pieces where appropriate.

A section devoted to reviews of recently published books dealing with various aspects of music is provided. Each review is signed and discusses the volume in question in considerable detail. A companion section is also included for reviews of sound recordings. A more comprehensive listing of music books contains titles recently published in major languages. It is arranged alphabetically by author and includes standard bibliographic information.

Music and Letters. London: Oxford Univ. Pr., 1920– .

A series of scholarly articles is the primary focus of this quarterly publication. Essays deal with specific topics in the field of Western European music for such areas as music history, composers and their works, and musical themes. Special attention is given to research devoted to historical manuscripts. Essays are fairly lengthy and discuss individual topics in detail. Although scholarly in nature, most articles do not deal with highly technical aspects of the music field, such as theory and composition. Illustrations consist mainly of musical notations, charts, and photographs of original manuscripts.

Concluding each issue are two companion sections that provide in-depth reviews of relatively recent publications of books and printed music. Following are sections for editorial correspondence and listings of books and printed music recently received for review.

Music Library Association. *Notes*. Canton, Mass., 1934– .

This journal is a quarterly publication devoted mainly to reviews and listings of music, books and periodicals on music, and scholarly articles. Topics discussed in the articles include special collections and exhibitions, music publishing, bibliography, various aspects or periods of music history, and reports on the activities of the association. Specific sections of the journal deal with music-related news and events, book reviews of selected titles, and a more comprehensive listing of books recently published. The latter includes volumes in English and many foreign languages along with standard bibliographic information. A comprehensive list of new and current music publishers' catalogs of international scope also appears. Arrangement is alphabetical by publishers' name and addresses of publishers are included.

The "Index to Record Reviews" provides access to critical commentaries of recorded works found in other periodicals. It is primarily an alphabetical arrangement by composer, with composite works listed also under name of the manufacturer. Entries for each musical recording include descriptive details followed by a list of review sources with symbols indicating the reviewer's judgment of the performance. Other features of the journal are the "Music Reviews," devoted to review of musical scores published within the last few years, and a section on "Music Received," a listing of musical scores arranged alphabetically by composer with brief descriptions and basic bibliographic information about the pieces. "Communications" is an editorial section that provides comment and discussion of previous reviews for a publication that reviews more music and books on music than any other journal.

Music Theory Spectrum. Bloomington, Ind.: Soc. for Music Theory, 1979– .

Approximately ten scholarly essays on some aspect of music theory or composition are found in each annual issue of this journal. Essays are fairly extensive and treat in considerable detail subjects of a highly technical nature. They are submitted mainly by professors of music affiliated with particular colleges or universities. In addition, numerous musical notations, diagrams, charts, and tables are provided to help illustrate many of the proposed theories.

A lengthy section devoted to reviews and commentaries appears after the major articles. Reviews of recent publications of musicological importance are very thorough and highly critical. Each review and commentary is signed and often includes musical notations and charts to illustrate major points. Issues conclude with a section for correspondence addressed to the editor as well as a section that lists authors of the various articles and their credentials.

The Musical Times. London: Novello, 1844– .
Published monthly, the *Musical Times* consists of several relatively brief articles generously illustrated with portraits, photographs, manuscripts, and musical notations. Articles are of a scholarly, though not a highly technical, nature and are accessible to the general reader as well as interesting to the music specialist. These articles deal with a wide variety of subjects, mostly in connection with the history and development of Western European music.
Three separate sections devoted to brief reviews of recent books, sound recordings, and printed music follow. Most issues provide space for editorial comment concerning previous articles and reviews, discussions of major upcoming musical events in London, reports on international happenings in the field of music, and discussions of television performances. Listings of appointments and awards, competitions, courses, and new publications, conclude each issue.

Nineteenth-Century Music. Berkeley, Calif.: Univ. of California Pr., 1977– .
Published semiannually, this journal mainly consists of scholarly essays devoted to various aspects of the music of the nineteenth century. Essays deal with specific topics of musicological importance. The length of individual essays varies but treatment of the material is thorough and in-depth. Illustrations are provided to supplement the text and include photographic reproductions of original manuscripts, musical notations and sections from musical scores, charts, relevant drawings from the period, and more.
A section devoted to reviews of recently published books is also included. Each review is signed and provides a detailed analysis and discussion of the work in question. Concluding each issue is a section entitled "Comment and Chronicle," which contains editorial responses to current writings, both in short article and book form, dealing with various aspects of music.

Recorded Sound. Journal of the British Institute of Recorded Sound. London: British Institute of Recorded Sound, 1961– .
In addition to the normal range of scholarly articles dealing with broad subjects and persons related to the field of music, this publication frequently contains book reviews and discographies of British composers. Some of the early issues also contain abstracts. Photographs of musical personages discussed in some of the articles are reproduced in black and white. Listings of recent publications dealing with the field of music are included. Each issue also concludes with a list of publications of the British Institute of Recorded Sound that provides order and price information on current as well as back issues. This journal is published semiannually and provides limited space for advertisements and announcements of other musical organizations, journals, music publishers, record and book shops, and audio systems.

AUTHOR-TITLE INDEX

Compiled by Dickerson-Redd Indexing Systems

19th-Century Music, 91–92, 93
40,000 Years of Music, J. Chailley, 31

Abert, H. W. *A. Mozart,* 85
Abraham, G. *Slavonic and Romantic Music,* 92
Acta Musicologica, International Musicological Society, 12, 143
Adkins, C. and A. Dickinson, *Doctoral Dissertations in Musicology,* 125
Adler, G. *Methode der Musikgeschichte,* 12; *Der Stil in der Musik,* 12, 27; "Umfang, Methode, und Ziel der Musikwissenschaft," 12, 27
Adorno, T. *Philosophy of Modern Music,* 30
After 100 Years, H. W. Hitchcock, 100, 103
"The Aims of Baïf's *Académie de Poésie et de Musique,*" D. P. Walker, 65, 68
Alessandro Scarlatti, D. J. Grout, 77
All American Music, J. Rockwell, 104
Allan, D. *Bibliography of Discographies,* 137–38
Allen, W. D. *Philosophies of Music History,* 30
Allgemeine Geschichte der Musik, J. N. Forkel, 18–19, 31
The American Composer Speaks, G. Chase, 97, 99, 103
American Music, 103
The American Music Handbook, C. Pavlakis, 138–39
American Musical Theatre, G. Bordman, 120
American Musicological Society. Journal, 141–42

"American Musicology and the Social Sciences," G. Chase, 13
American Studies and American Musicology, R. Crawford, 103
America's Music, G. Chase, 22, 31, 100, 103
"Analysis," I. Bent, 28, 31
Analysis and Value Judgment, C. Dahlhaus, 31
"Analytical Thinking in the First Half of the Nineteenth Century," I. Bent, 92
Anderson, R. E. *Contemporary American Composers,* 112
Anderson, W. D. *Ethos and Education in Greek Music,* 49, 50
Andrew Law, R. Crawford, 103
Anglès, H. "Gregorian Chant," 52, 56
The Anthropology of Music, A. Merriam, 14
Annals of Opera 1597–1940, A. Loewenberg, comp., 117
The Anthropology of Music, A. Merriam, 14
Antonio Caldara, U. Kirkendale, 77
Apel, W. *Gregorian Chant,* 34, 39, 52, 56; *Harvard Dictionary of Music,* 115; *The History of Keyboard Music to 1700,* 64, 66, 73, 76; *The Notation of Polyphonic Music,* 34, 39, 53, 56
"Applications of the History of Ideas to Music (II)," M. R. Maniates, 14
Arnold, D. *Monteverdi,* 76; "The Profession of Musical Scholarship," 12
———, and N. Fortune, eds. *The Monteverdi Companion,* 77
Arnold, F. T. *The Art of Accompaniment from a Thorough-Bass,* 73, 77

147

The Art of Accompaniment from a Thor-ough-Bass, F. T. Arnold, 73, 77
"The Artusi-Monteverdi Controversy," C. Palisca, 70, 78
ASCAP Biographical Dictionary, 112
ASCAP Symphonic Catalog 1977, 132
Aspects of Schenkerian Theory, D. Beach, 31
Aspects of Twentieth Century Music, G. Wittlich, ed., 100
Association for Recorded Sound Collections. *Journal*, 142
Atlas, A. W. *The Capella Guilia Chansonnier*, 36, 39, 66
"Atti del Congresso internazionale sul Tema 'Manierismo' in arte e musica," 66–67
Aufführungspraxis der Musik, R. Haas, 43, 45
Die Ausbreitung der Historismus der Musik, W. Wiora, ed., 33
Austin, W. W. *Music in the Twentieth Century*, 94, 98, 103; "*Susanna*," "*Jeanie*," and "*The Old Folks at Home*," 103
The Authentic English Editions of Beethoven, A. Tyson, 37, 40

Babbitt, M. "Contemporary Music Composition and Music Theory," 98–99; "Who Cares If You Listen," 97
Bach, C. P. E. *Essay on the True Art of Playing Keyboard Instruments*, 74, 77
The Bach Reader, H. T. David and A. Mendel, eds., 38, 40
"Die Bachforschung seit etwa 1965," W. Blankenburg, 75, 77
Badura-Skoda, E. and P. Badura-Skoda. *Interpreting Mozart on the Keyboard*, 44
Baker's Biographical Dictionary of Musicians, N. Slonimsky, rev., 111–12
Barlow, H. and S. Morgenstern. *A Dictionary of Musical Themes*, 119. *See also* Morgenstern, S.
"Baroque," C. Palisca, 78
The Baroque Concerto, A. Hutchings, 77
Baroque Music, C. Palisca, 71, 78
Baroque Music, V. Rangel-Ribeiro, 74, 78

"The Baroque Oratorio," H. E. Smither, 78
"Baroque—Is It Datum, Hypothesis, or Tautology," J. H. Mueller, 78
Bartha, D. and L. Somfai, eds. *Haydn als Opernkapellmeister*, 83, 85
Barzun, J. *Berlioz and the Romantic Century*, 89–90, 92; "The Meaning of Meaning in Music," 92
Battcock, G., ed. *Breaking the Sound Barrier*, 97, 99
BBC Music Library Catalogues, British Broadcasting Corp., 128
Beach, D. *Aspects of Schenkerian Theory*, 31
Beckwith, J. *See* MacMillan, K.
Beethoven, H. C. R. Landon, 38, 40
"Beethoven," J. Kerman and A. Tyson, 32
Beethoven, R. H. Schauffler, 26
Beethoven, M. Solomon, 85, 86
Beethoven and His Nephew, E. Sterba and R. Sterba, 84, 86
"Beethoven and His Nephew," M. Solomon, 86
The Beethoven Quartets, J. Kerman, 85
"Beethoven Scholars and Beethoven's Sketches," D. Johnson, 37, 40
Beethoven Studies I, A. Tyson, ed., 37, 40
Beethoven's Compositional Choices, J. Levy, 84, 86
"Beethoven's Instrumental Music," E. T. A. Hoffmann, 87, 93
Beiträge zur Chronologie der Werke J. S. Bachs, G. von Dadelsen, 26, 31
Beiträge zur Geschichte des Musikanschauung um 19. Jahrhundert, W. Salmen, ed., 93–94
Beiträge zur Musiktheorie des 19. Jahrhunderts, M. Vogel, ed., 91, 92, 94
Bent, I. "Analysis," 28, 31; "Analytical Thinking in the First Half of the Nineteenth Century," 92
———, ed. *Source Materials and the Interpretation of Music*, 44
Bent, M. "*Musica recta* and *musica ficta*," 56; "*Resfacta* and *Cantare super librum*," 67
Berkowitz, F. P. *Popular Titles and Subtitles of Musical Compositions*, 128
Berlioz and the Romantic Century, J. Barzun, 89–90, 92

Bernstein, L. F. "Notes on the Origin of the Parisian Chanson," 64, 67

Berry, M. "The Restoration of the Chant and Seventy-Five Years of Recording," 52, 56

Besseler, H. and M. Schneider, eds. *Musikgeschichte in Bildern,* 39

The Best of the Music Makers, G. T. Simon, 113

Besterman, T. *Music and Drama,* 122

Between Romanticism and Modernism, C. Dahlhaus, 89, 92–93

Beyond Schenkerism, E. Narmour, 29, 32

Bibliographic Guide to Music, New York Public Library, 137

Bibliographic Guide to Music: 1977, 128

Bibliography of Black Music, D. R. de Lerma, 124

Bibliography of Discographies, D. Allan, 137–38

A Bibliography of Early Secular American Music, O. G. T. Sonneck, 131

Bibliography of Jewish Music, A. Sendrey, 127

A Bio-Bibliographical Finding List of Canadian Musicians, Canadian Music Library Association, 112

Biographical Dictionary of Afro-American and African Musicians, E. Southern, 113

Biographical Dictionary of American Music, C. E. Claghorn, 112–13

Biographical Dictionary of Dance, B. N. Cohen-Stratyner, 110

Biographie universelle des musiciens et bibliographie générale, F. J. Fétis, 19, 31

Black Music in America, J. Skowronski, 125

Blacking, J. *How Musical Is Man?* 12

Blankenburg, W. "Die Bachforschung seit etwa 1965," 75, 77; "Zwölf Jahre Bachforschung," 76, 77

Blume, F. *Classic and Romantic Music,* 85, 89, 92; "Historische Musikforschung in der Gegenwart," 12–13; "Musical Scholarship Today," 13; *Protestant Church Music,* 77

Boethius, A. M. "De institutione musica," 50; *The Principles of Music,* 56–57

"Boethius," C. M. Bower, 50

Boetticher, W. *Orlando di Lasso und seine Zeit,* 64, 67

The Book of World-Famous Music, J. J. Fuld, 128–29

Boorman, S. "The 'First' Edition of the *Odhecaton A,*" 67

Bordman, G. *American Musical Theatre,* 120

Boretz, B. and E. T. Cone, eds. *Perspectives on American Composers,* 99, 103; *Perspectives on Contemporary Music Theory,* 96, 99; *Perspectives on Schoenberg and Stravinsky,* 96, 99

Bower, C. M. "Boethius," 50

Bowles, E. *La pratique musicale au Moyen-Age,* 39

Boyden, D. D. *The History of Violin Playing from Its Origins to 1761,* 73, 77

Bradley, C. J., ed. *Manual of Music Librarianship,* 139

Breaking the Sound Barrier, G. Battcock, ed., 97, 99

Breed, P. F. *See* De Charms, D.

Brett, P. *The Songs, Services and Anthems of William Byrd,* 67. *See also* Kerman, J.

Brindle, R. S. *The New Music,* 99

British Broadcasting Corp. *BBC Music Library Catalogues,* 128

The British Catalog of Music, 130

Britt, S. *See* Case, B.

Brook, B. *La symphonie fran;ahcaise dans le seconde motie de XVIIIe siècle,* 85

———, ed. *Perspectives in Musicology,* 13

Brook, B. S. *Thematic Catalogues in Music,* 140

Brown, H. M. *Embellishing Sixteenth-Century Music,* 44; "The Genesis of a Style," 63, 67; *Instrumental Music Printed before 1600,* 64, 67; *Music in the Renaissance,* 60, 67

———, and J. Lascelle. *Musical Iconography,* 38, 39

———, and J. McKinnon. "Performing Practice," 44

"Brunelleschi's Dome and Dufay's Motet," C. Warren, 60, 68

Brunner, L. "The Performance of Plainchant," 57

Brunnings, F. E. *Folk Song Index,* 136

Bryden, J. R. and D. G. Hughes, comps. *An Index of Gregorian Chant*, 133
Bücken, E., ed. *Handbuch der Musikwissenschaft*, 21, 31
Budden, J. *The Operas of Verdi*, 90, 92
Buelow, G. J. *Thorough-Bass Accompaniment according to Johann David Heinichen*, 73, 77
Bukofzer, M. *Music in the Baroque Era*, 69–70, 75, 77; *The Place of Musicology in American Institutions of Higher Learning*, 13
Burney, C. *A General History of Music*, 18, 31

Cage, J. *Silence*, 97–98, 99
"The 'Camerata Fiorentina'," C. Palisca, 65, 68, 78
Canadian Music, L. Jarman, ed., 125
Canadian Music Library Association. *A Bio-Bibliographical Finding List of Canadian Musicians*, 112; *Musical Canadiana*, 132
Cannon, B. C. *Johann Mattheson*, 31, 77
Cantus Firmus in Mass and Motet, 1420–1530, E. Sparks, 58
The Capella Guilia Chansonnier, A. W. Atlas, 36, 39, 66
Carl Gregor, Duke of Mecklenburg. International Jazz Bibliography, 126
Case, B. and S. Britt. *The Illustrated Encyclopedia of Jazz*, 113
Catalog of Copyright Entries: Music, U.S. Copyright Office, 130
Catalogue of Opera Librettos Printed before 1800, U.S. Library of Congress, 137
Census-Catalog of Manuscript Sources of Polyphonic Music 1400–1550, 134
Chailley, J. *40,000 Years of Music*, 31
———, ed. *Précis de musicologie*, 13
The Chansons of the Troubadours, H. Van der Werf, 54, 58
"Character and Purposes of American Musicology," E. E. Lowinsky, 14
Charles, S. R. *A Handbook of Music and Music Literature in Sets and Series*, 133–34
Charles Ives Remembered, V. Perlis, 103, 104
Chase, G. *The American Composer*

Speaks, 97, 99, 103; "American Musicology and the Social Sciences," 13; *America's Music*, 22, 31, 100, 103; "Musicology, History and Anthropology," 13
Chew, G. "Notation," 98, 99
Childs, B. *See* Schwartz, E.
Chrysander, F. "Vorwort und Einleitung," 13
Church Music, R. C. Von Ende, 127
Churgin, B. "G. B. Sammartini and the Symphony," 85
Claghorn, C. E. *Biographical Dictionary of American Music*, 112–13
Classic and Romantic Music, F. Blume, 85, 89, 92
Classic Music, L. Ratner, 81, 86
"Classic Period," E. Wolf, 81, 86
"Classical," D. Heartz, 79, 85
The Classical Style, C. Rosen, 79–80, 84, 86
Cohen, A. *International Encyclopedia of Women Composers*, 110
Cohen-Stratyner, B. N. *Biographical Dictionary of Dance*, 110
The Collegium, E. Kottick, 8, 13
The Commonwealth of Art, C. Sachs, 47, 50, 55, 57
A Companion to the Opera, R. May, 117
Compendium musicae, R. Descartes, 77
The Compositional Matrix, A. Forte, 32
The Compositional Process of J. S. Bach, R. Marshall, 76, 78
"The Concept of Baroque in Literary Scholarship," R. Wellek, 78
The Concise Encyclopedia of Music and Musicians, M. Cooper, ed., 107
The Concise Oxford Dictionary of Music, M. Kennedy, 108
Concise Oxford Dictionary of Opera, H. Rosenthal and J. Warrack, 118
Conductors on Record, J. L. Holmes, 110–11
Cone, E. T. *See* Boretz, B.
The Consort and Keyboard Music of William Byrd, O. W. Neighbour, 68
Contemporary American Composers, R. E. Anderson, 112
Contemporary Canadian Composers, K. MacMillan and J. Beckwith, eds., 113
Contemporary Composers on Contemporary Music, E. Schwartz and B. Childs, eds., 97, 100

Contemporary Music Almanac 1980/81– , D. Zalkand, 139
"Contemporary Music Composition and Music Theory," M. Babbitt, 98–99
Cook, D. *Vindications,* 92
Cooper, M., ed. *The Concise Encyclopedia of Music and Musicians,* 107
Coover, J. *Music Lexicography,* 140; "Music Theory in Translation," 31
"The Corded Shell," P. Kivy, 13
Corpus Mensurabilis Musicae, 36, 39
Corpus of Early Keyboard Music, 36, 39
Corpus Scriptorum de Musica, 36, 40
Coussemaker, E. *de Scriptorum de musica medii aevi novam seriem,* 31
Crawford, R. *American Studies and American Musicology,* 103; *Andrew Law,* 103
The Creative World of Beethoven, P. H. Lang, ed., 86
The Creative World of Mozart, P. H. Lang, ed., 86
Crevel, M. van "Introduction," in Jacob Obrecht, *Opera omnia,* 61, 67
"Critical Years in European Musical History," International Musicological Society, 79, 85
Crocker, R. *The Early Medieval Sequence,* 52, 57; *A History of Musical Style,* 31, 52, 57
Cunningham, W. P. *The Music Locator,* 135
"Current Historiography and Music History," D. J. Grout, 22, 32
Current Thought in Musicology, J. Grubbs, ed., 13

Dadelsen, G. von. *Beiträge zur Chronologie der Werke J. S. Bachs,* 26, 31
Dahlhaus, C. *Analysis and Value Judgment,* 31; *Between Romanticism and Modernism,* 89, 92–93; *Esthetics of Music,* 13; *Foundations of Music History,* 23, 24, 31; "Harmony," 75, 77; *Die Musik des 19. Jahrhunderts,* 93; *Richard Wagner's Music Dramas,* 91, 93; "Tonality," 75, 77; "Zu Marcus van Crevels neuer Obrecht Ausgabe," 61, 67
———, ed. *Das Drama Richard Wagners als musikalisches Kunstwerk,* 93; *Studien zur Trivialmusik des 19. Jahrhunderts,* 91, 93

David, H. T. and A. Mendel, eds. *The Bach Reader,* 38, 40
Day, J. *See* Le Huray, P.
De Charms, D. and P. F. Breed. *Songs in Collections,* 128
"De institutione musica," A. M. Boethius, 50
de Lerma, D. R. *Bibliography of Black Music,* 124
Dean, W. *Handel's Dramatic Oratorios and Masques,* 72, 77
Denis, A., ed. *The New Oxford Companion to Music,* 107
Denkmäler altgriechischer Musik, E. Pöhlmann, 49, 50
Dent, E. J. *Mozart's Operas,* 83, 85
Descartes, R. *Compendium musicae,* 77
Deutsch, O. E. *Handel,* 38, 40; *Mozart und seine Welt in Zeitgenössischen Bildern,* 38, 40; *Schubert,* 38, 40
Dickinson, A. *See* Adkins, C.
Dickinson, G. S. *A Handbook of Style in Music,* 31
Dictionary Catalog of the Music Collection, New York Public Library, 137
The Dictionary of Composers, C. Osborne, ed., 111
Dictionary of Contemporary Music, J. Vinton, ed., 110
Dictionary of Early Music, J. Roche, 108
Dictionary of Music, J. J. Rousseau, 17, 33
A Dictionary of Musical Themes, H. Barlow and S. Morgenstern, 119
A Dictionary of Opera and Song Themes, S. Morgenstern and H. Barlow, comps., 119
Directory of Music Research Libraries, International Association of Music Libraries, 136–37
Dissertation Abstracts International, 125–26
Doctoral Dissertations in Musicology, C. Adkins and A. Dickinson, 125
Dodecachordon, H. Glarean, 67
Donakowski, C. L. *A Muse for the Masses,* 93
Donington, R. *The Interpretation of Early Music,* 43, 44; *A Performer's Guide to Baroque Music,* 36, 40, 43, 45; *The Rise of Opera,* 77
Das Drama Richard Wagners als musikalisches Kunstwerk, C. Dahlhaus ed., 93

Dreyfus, L. "Early Music Defended against Its Devotees," 13, 45

Drone, J. M. *Index to Opera, Operetta and Musical Comedy Synopses*, 127

Duckles, V. "Johannes Nicolaus Forkel," 31; "Musicology at the Mirror," 31; "Patterns in the Historiography of 19th-Century Music," 31
———, comp. *Music Reference and Research Materials*, 140–41

Dufay, D. Fallows, 56, 57, 64, 67

"Dufay at Cambrai," C. Wright, 38, 41

Dunsby, J. "Music and Semiotics," 30, 31

E. T. A. Hoffmann and Music, R. M. Schafer, 88–89, 94

Early Jazz, G. Schuller, 102, 104

The Early Medieval Sequence, R. Crocker, 52, 57

Early Music, 44, 45, 91, 142

"Early Music Defended against Its Devotees," L. Dreyfus, 13, 45

Eastern Elements in Western Chant, E. Wellesz, 50, 51

Editions and Musicians, W. Emery, 36, 40

Eggebrecht, H. H. "Historiography," 31

Einführung in die gregorianischen Melodien, P. Wagner, 52, 58

Einstein, A. *The Italian Madrigal*, 64, 66, 67; *Mozart*, 85; *Music in the Romantic Era*, 89, 92, 93

Elders, W. *Studien zur Symbolik in der Musik der alten Niederländer*, 61, 67

Electronic Music, E. Schwartz, 100

The Elizabethan Madrigal, J. Kerman, 64, 66, 68

Embellishing Sixteenth-Century Music, H. M. Brown, 44

Emery, W. *Editions and Musicians*, 36, 40

Emotion and Meaning in Music, L. Meyer, 14

The Encyclopedia of American Music, E. Jablonski, 107

The Encyclopedia of Jazz in the Seventies, L. G. Feather, 114

The Encyclopedia of Jazz in the Sixties, L. G. Feather, 114

The Encyclopedia of the Music Business, H. Rachlin, 118–19

Encyclopedia of the Musical Film, S. Green, 120

"Das Ende der Ars nova," U. Günther, 54, 57

English Chamber Music, E. H. Meyer, 30, 32

Epstein, D. *Sinful Tunes and Spirituals*, 103

Essay on the True Art of Playing Keyboard Instruments, C. P. E. Bach, 74, 77

Essays in Musical Analysis, D. Tovey, 33

Essays on Music in the Byzantine World, O. Strunk, 50

Essays on the Viennese Classical Style, H. C. R. Landon, 86

Esthetics of Music, C. Dahlhaus, 13

The Ethnomusicologist, M. Hood, 13

Ethnomusicology, 142–43

Ethos and Education in Greek Music, W. D. Anderson, 49, 50

"Evidence and Explanation," A. Mendel, 22–23, 32

Fallows, D. *Dufay*, 56, 57, 64, 67

Farish, M. K. *String Music in Print*, 132

Feather, L. G. *The Encyclopedia of Jazz in the Seventies*, 114; *The Encyclopedia of Jazz in the Sixties*, 114

Fenton, A. D. See Peterson, C. S.

Fétis, F. J. *Biographie universelle des musiciens et bibliographie générale*, 19, 31; *Histoire générale de la musique*, 19, 31

Fifteen Black American Composers, A. Tischler, 131–32

Fink, R. and R. Ricci. *The Language of Twentieth-Century Music*, 115

"The 'First' Edition of the *Odhecaton A*," S. Boorman, 67

Folk Song Index, F. E. Brunnings, 136

Fondements d'une sémiologie de la musique, J. J. Nattiez, 30, 32

Fontes Artis Musicae, 143

Foreman, L. *Systematic Discography*, 138

Forkel, J. N. *Allgemeine Geschichte der Musik*, 18–19, 31; *Ueber Johann Sebastian Bachs Leben, Kunst und Kunstwerke*, 19, 31

Forte, A. *The Compositional Matrix*, 32;

The Structure of Atonal Music, 32, 95, 99

———, and S. E. Gilbert. *Introduction to Schenkerian Analysis*, 32

Fortune, N. "Italian Secular Monody from 1600 to 1635," 71, 77; "Monody," 71, 77; "Solo Song and Cantata," 77. *See also* Arnold, D.

Foundations of Music History, C. Dahlhaus, 23, 24, 31

The Four Ages of Music, W. Wiora, 15, 33

Free Composition, H. Schenker, 28–29, 33

The French Encyclopedists as Critics of Music, A. Oliver, 33

French Song from Berlioz to Duparc, F. Noske, 89, 94

"From Garrick to Gluck," D. Heartz, 85

La Frottola, K. Jeppesen, 64, 67

Fugue and Fugato in Rococo and Classical Chamber Music, W. Kirkendale, 76, 78, 85

Fuld, J. J. *The Book of World-Famous Music*, 128–29

"G. B. Sammartini and the Symphony," B. Churgin, 85

Gaffurio, F. *Practica musicae*, 67

Gammond, P. *The Illustrated Encyclopedia of Recorded Opera*, 116

Garey, H. *See* Perkins, L.

Geiringer, K. *Johann Sebastian Bach*, 77

General Bibliography for Music Research, K. Mixter, 141

A General History of Music, C. Burney, 18, 31

A General History of the Science and Practice of Music, J. Hawkins, 18, 32

"The Genesis of a Style," H. M. Brown, 63, 67

George Fridric Handel, P. H. Lang, 78

Georgiades, T. *Greek Music, Verse, and Drama*, 49, 50; *Music and Language*, 32

Geschichte der Musik, A. W. Ambros, 20, 30–31

Gesualdo, G. Watkins, 65–66, 69

Gilbert, S. E. *See* Forte, A.

Girolamo Mei, C. Palisca, 65, 68

Glarean, H. *Dodecachordon*, 67

Gold, R. S. *A Jazz Lexicon*, 115

The Great Dr. Burney, P. Scholes, 33

"Greece. I: Ancient," R. P. Winnington-Ingram, 48, 51

"Greek Music," R. P. Winnington-Ingram, 49, 51

Greek Music, Verse, and Drama, T. Georgiades, 49, 50

Green, S. *Encyclopedia of the Musical Film*, 120

"Gregorian Chant," H. Anglès, 52, 56

Gregorian Chant, W. Apel, 34, 39, 52, 56

Griffiths, P. *Modern Music*, 99

Grout, D. J. *Alessandro Scarlatti*, 77; "Current Historiography and Music History," 22, 32; *A History of Western Music*, 21, 32, 55, 57; *A Short History of Opera*, 77

Grubbs, J., ed. *Current Thought in Musicology*, 13

Grundlage einer Ehren-Pforte, J. Mattheson, 17–18, 32

Grundriss der Musikwissenschaft, H. Riemann, 14

Guidelines for Style Analysis, J. LaRue, 28, 32

Gunther, R. *Musikkulturen Asiens, Afrikas und Ozeaniens im 19. Jahrhundert*, 91

Günther, U. "Das Ende der Ars nova," 54, 57; "Zitate in französischen Liedsätzen der Ars nova und Ars subtilior," 54, 57

Haar, J. "Lassus," 64, 67; "Music History and Cultural History," 32

Haas, R. *Aufführungspraxis der Musik*, 43, 45

Hamm, C. "Manuscript Structure in the Dufay Era," 40; *Music in the New World*, 99, 101–2, 103; *Yesterdays*, 102, 103

A Handbook of Music and Music Literature in Sets and Series, S. R. Charles, 133–34

A Handbook of Style in Music, G. S. Dickinson, 31

Handbuch der Musikwissenschaft, E. Bücken, ed., 21, 31

Handel, O. E. Deutsch, 38, 40

Handel and the Pastoral Tradition, E. Harris, 77

Handel's Dramatic Oratorios and Masques, W. Dean, 72, 77

"Harmony," C. Dahlhaus, 75, 77

Harmony, W. Piston, 33

Harris, E. *Handel and the Pastoral Tradition,* 77

Harrison, F. L. *Music in Medieval Britain,* 56, 57. See also Westrup, J. A.

———, M. Hood and C. Palisca. *Musicology,* 5, 8, 10, 13

Harvard Dictionary of Music, W. Apel, 115

Hawkins, J. *A General History of the Science and Practice of Music,* 18, 32

Haydn, A Documentary Biography, H. C. R. Landon, 86

Haydn als Opernkapellmeister, D. Bartha and L. Somfai, eds., 83, 85

Haydn: Chronicle and Works, H. C. R. Landon, 38, 40, 83, 86

Haydon, G. *Introduction to Musicology,* 6, 13

Hays, W., ed. *Twentieth-Century Views of Music History,* 99

Heartz, D. "Classical," 79, 85; "From Garrick to Gluck," 85; *Pierre Attaingnant,* 64, 67

Henderson, I. and D. Wulstan. "Introduction: Ancient Greece," 48, 50

Heyer, A. H., comp. *Historical Sets, Collected Editions and Monuments of Music,* 134

Hinson, M. *Music for Piano and Orchestra,* 132–33

Hirschhorn, C. *The Hollywood Musical,* 120

Histoire générale de la musique, F. J. Fétis, 19, 31

Historical Musicology, L. Spiess, ed., 14

Historical Sets, Collected Editions and Monuments of Music, A. H. Heyer, comp., 134

"Historiography," H. H. Eggebrecht, 31

"Historische Musikforschung in der Gegenwart," F. Blume, 12–13

A History of Byzantine Music and Hymnography, E. Wellesz, 34, 40, 49, 51

The History of Keyboard Music to 1700, W. Apel, 64, 66, 73, 76

A History of Music in Pictures, G. Kinsky, ed., 121

History of Music Theory, Books I and II, H. Riemann, 33

A History of Musical Style, R. Crocker, 31, 52, 57

History of the Art of Antiquity, J. Winckelmann, 82

The History of Violin Playing from Its Origins to 1761, D. D. Boyden, 73, 77

A History of Western Music, D. J. Grout, 21, 32, 55, 57

Hitchcock, H. W. *After 100 Years,* 100, 103; *Music in the United States,* 99, 103

Hixon, D. L. *Music in Early America,* 123–24

Hodeir, A. *Jazz, Its Evolution and Essence,* 102, 103

Hodgson, J. *Music Titles in Translation,* 129

Hoffmann, E. T. A. "Beethoven's Instrumental Music," 87, 93

The Hollywood Musical, C. Hirschhorn, 120

Holmes, J. L. *Conductors on Record,* 110–11

Holoman, D. K. and C. Palisca, eds. *Musicology in the 1980s,* 10, 13, 29

Hood, M. *The Ethnomusicologist,* 13. See also Harrison, F. L.

Hoppin, R. *Medieval Music,* 52, 53, 55, 57

Horn, D. *The Literature of American Music in Books and Folk Music Collections,* 124

How Musical Is Man? J. Blacking, 12

Hubbard, F. *Three Centuries of Harpsichord Making,* 44, 45

Hucke, H. "Toward a New Historical View of Gregorian Chant," 52, 57

Hughes, A. *Manuscript Accidentals,* 55, 57; *Medieval Liturgical Manuscripts for Mass and Office,* 53, 57; *Medieval Music,* 56, 57

Hughes, D. G. See Bryden, J. R.

Huglo, M. *Les Tonaires,* 52, 57

Hugo Riemann's Theory of Harmony, W. C. Mickelsen, 32

Huizinga, J. *The Waning of the Middle Ages,* 55, 57

A Humanistic Philosophy of Music, E. A. Lippman, 13

Husmann, H. "The Origin and Destination of the *Magnus liber organi,*" 53, 57

Hutchings, A. *The Baroque Concerto,* 77

Iconographie musicale, 40
"The Iconology of Musicology," E. Winternitz, 40
The Illustrated Encyclopedia of Jazz, B. Case and S. Britt, 113
The Illustrated Encyclopedia of Recorded Opera, P. Gammond, 116
The Illustrated Encyclopedia of Rock, N. Logan and B. Woffinden, 114
An Index of Gregorian Chant, J. R. Bryden and D. G. Hughes, comps., 133
Index to Children's Songs, C. S. Peterson and A. D. Fenton, 129
Index to Opera, Operetta and Musical Comedy Synopses, J. M. Drone, 127
Information on Music, G. A. Marco, 122–23
Instrumental Music Printed before 1600, H. M. Brown, 64, 67
International Association of Music Libraries. *Directory of Music Research Libraries,* 136–37
The International Cyclopedia of Music and Musicians, O. Thompson, ed., 109–10
International Encyclopedia of Women Composers, A. Cohen, 110
International Jazz Bibliography, Carl Gregor, Duke of Mecklenburg, 126
International Musicological Society. *Acta Musicologica,* 12, 143; "Critical Years in European Musical History," 79, 85; "Musicology Today," 14; *Report of the Eighth Congress, New York 1961,* 13
International Who's Who in Music and Musician's Directory, 111
The Interpretation of Early Music, R. Donington, 43, 44
Interpreting Mozart on the Keyboard, E. Badura-Skoda and P. Badura-Skoda, 44
"Interrelationships between Poetic and Musical Form in Trouvère Songs," T. Karp, 57
"Introduction: Ancient Greece," I. Henderson and D. Wulstan, 48, 50
"Introduction," in Jacob Obrecht, *Opera omnia,* M. van Crevel, 61, 67
Introduction to Music Research, R. T. Watanabe, 140
Introduction to Musicology, G. Haydon, 6, 13

Introduction to Schenkerian Analysis, A. Forte and S. E. Gilbert, 32
L'istitutioni harmoniche, G. Zarlino, 69
The Italian Madrigal, A. Einstein, 64, 66, 67
"Italian Secular Monody from 1600 to 1635," N. Fortune, 71, 77

Jablonski, E. *The Encyclopedia of American Music,* 107
Jacobs, A. and S. Sadie. *Opera,* 116
Jacques Moderne, S. Pogue, 64, 68
Jacquot, J., ed. *La luth et sa musique [Colloque],* 67
Jahn, O. *W. A. Mozart,* 19, 32
Jarman, L., ed. *Canadian Music,* 125
Jazz, F. Tirro, 102, 104
Jazz, Its Evolution and Essence, A. Hodeir, 102, 103
A Jazz Lexicon, R. S. Gold, 115
Jeppesen, K. *La Frottola,* 64, 67; *The Style of Palestrina and the Dissonance,* 27, 32, 63, 67
Johann Mattheson, B. C. Cannon, 31, 71
"Johann Mattheson on Affect and Rhetoric in Music," H. Lenneberg, 78
Johann Sebastian Bach, K. Geiringer, 77
Johannes Gabrieli und sein Zeitalter, C. Winterfield, 19, 34
"Johannes Nicolaus Forkel," V. Duckles, 31
Johnson, D. "Beethoven Scholars and Beethoven's Sketches," 37, 40
Johnson, H. E. *Operas on American Subjects,* 116
Josquin des Prez, E. E. Lowinsky, ed., 64, 68
Josquin Desprez, H. Osthoff, 64, 68
Journal of Music Theory, 32, 144
Journal of Musicology, 143

Karkoschka, E. *Notation in New Music,* 98, 99
Karp, T. "Interrelationships between Poetic and Musical Form in Trouvère Songs," 57. *See also* Stevens, J.
Kennedy, M. *The Concise Oxford Dictionary of Music,* 108
Kenney, S. *Walter Frye and the Contenance angloise,* 56, 57
Kennington, D. and D. L. Read. *The Literature of Jazz,* 127

Kerman, J. *The Beethoven Quartets,* 85; *The Elizabethan Madrigal,* 64, 66, 68; *Ludwig van Beethoven,* 37, 40; *The Masses and Motets of William Byrd,* 68; *Opera as Drama,* 93; "A Profile for American Musicology," 13; "Viewpoint," 92, 93
————, and A. Tyson. "Beethoven," 32
————, and P. Brett. *The Music of William Byrd,* 64
"Key Relations in Verdi's *Un Ballo in Maschera,*" S. Levarie, 92, 93
Kinsky, G., ed. *A History of Music in Pictures,* 121
Kirkendale, U. *Antonio Caldara,* 77; "The Source for Bach's *Musical Offering,*" 75–76, 77–78
Kirkendale, W. *Fugue and Fugato in Rococo and Classical Chamber Music,* 76, 78, 85; "New Roads to Old Ideas in Beethoven's *Missa Solemnis,*" 86
Kivy, P. "The Corded Shell," 13
Knight, W. F. J. *St. Augustine's "De Musica,"* 50
Kottick, E. *The Collegium,* 8, 13
Kraeling, C. H. "Music in the Bible," 50

Landon, H. C. R. *Beethoven,* 38, 40; *Essays on the Viennese Classical Style,* 86; *Haydn, A Documentary Biography,* 86; *Haydn: Chronicle and Works,* 38, 40, 83, 86; "The Operas of Haydn," 83, 86
————, and D. Mitchell, eds. *The Mozart Companion,* 86
Lang, P. H. *George Fridric Handel,* 78; *Music in Western Civilization,* 21, 32, 82, 86, 90, 93
————, ed. *The Creative World of Beethoven,* 86; *The Creative World of Mozart,* 86
The Language of Twentieth-Century Music, R. Fink and R. Ricci, 115
LaRue, J. *Guidelines for Style Analysis,* 28, 32
Lascelle, J. *See* Brown, H. M.
"Lassus," J. Haar, 64, 67
Le Huray, P. and J. Day, eds. *Music and Aesthetics in the Eighteenth and Early-Nineteenth Centuries,* 82, 86
Lenneberg, H. "Johann Mattheson on Affect and Rhetoric in Music," 78

Lester, J. "Major-Minor Concepts and Modal Theory in Germany: 1592–1680," 78
Levarie, S. "Key Relations in Verdi's *Un Ballo in Maschera,*" 92, 93
Levy, J. *Beethoven's Compositional Choices,* 84, 86
Liber de arte contrapuncti, J. Tinctoris, 68
The Liber Usualis, 40
The Life and Activities of Sir John Hawkins, P. Scholes, 33
The Life of Richard Wagner, E. Newman, 91, 93
Lippman, E. A. *A Humanistic Philosophy of Music,* 13; *Musical Thought in Ancient Greece,* 48, 50; "What Should Musicology Be?" 14
The Literature of American Music in Books and Folk Music Collections, D. Horn, 124
The Literature of Jazz, D. Kennington and D. L. Read, 127
The Lives of the Great Composers, H. C. Schonberg, 111
Lockwood, L. "Renaissance," 62, 68
Loewenberg, A., comp. *Annals of Opera 1597–1940,* 117
Logan, N. and B. Woffinden. *The Illustrated Encyclopedia of Rock,* 114
Longyear, R. M. *Nineteenth-Century Romanticism in Music,* 93
Lovejoy, A. O. "On the Discriminations of Romanticisms," 93
Lowens, I. *Music and Musicians in Early America,* 103; *Music in America and American Music,* 104
Lowinsky, E. E. "Character and Purposes of American Musicology," 14; *The Medici Codex of 1518,* 36, 40; "Music in the Culture of the Renaissance," 58, 68; *Secret Chromatic Art in the Netherlands Motet,* 61, 68; "Secret Chromatic Art Re-Examined," 68; *Tonality and Atonality in Sixteenth-Century Music,* 63, 68
————, ed. *Josquin des Prez,* 64, 68
Ludwig van Beethoven, J. Kerman, 37, 40
Ludwig van Beethoven's Leben, A. Thayer, 19, 33
La luth et sa musique [Colloque], J. Jacquot, ed., 67

MacClintock, C., ed. *Readings in the History of Music in Performance*, 44, 45

MacMillan, K. and J. Beckwith, eds. *Contemporary Canadian Composers*, 113

The Madrigal, J. Roche, 66, 68

"Major-Minor Concepts and Modal Theory in Germany: 1592–1680," J. Lester, 78

Maniates, M. R. "Applications of the History of Ideas to Music (II)," 14; *Mannerism in Italian Music and Culture, 1530–1630*, 66, 68

Manual of Music Librarianship, C. J. Bradley, ed., 139

Manuscript Accidentals, A. Hughes, 55, 57

"Manuscript Structure in the Dufay Era," C. Hamm, 40

Marco, G. A. *Information on Music*, 122–23

Marcuse, S. *Musical Instruments*, 114–15

Marshall, R. *The Compositional Process of J. S. Bach*, 76, 78

Martin, G. *The Opera Companion*, 117; *The Opera Companion to Twentieth Century Opera*, 117

Martini, G. B. *Storia della Musica*, 18–19, 32

The Masses and Motets of William Byrd, J. Kerman, 68

Mattheson, J. *Grundlage einer Ehren-Pforte*, 17–18, 32; *Der vollkommene Capellmeister*, 17, 32

May, R. *A Companion to the Opera*, 117

McCabe, J. A. "Music and the Black American," 124

McColvin, L. R. and H. Reeves. *Music Libraries*, 139–40

McGraw, C. *Piano Duet Repertoire*, 133

McKinnon, J. See Brown, H. M.

"The Meaning of Meaning in Music," J. Barzun, 92

The Medici Codex of 1518, E. E. Lowinsky, 36, 40

"Medieval," N. Pirrotta, 57, 68

Medieval Liturgical Manuscripts for Mass and Office, A. Hughes, 53, 57

Medieval Music, A. Hughes, 56, 57

Medieval Music, R. Hoppin, 52, 53, 55, 57

Meggett, J. M. *Music Periodical Literature*, 141

Mellers, W. *Music in a New Found Land*, 99

The Mellon Chansonnier, L. Perkins and H. Garey, 68

Les mélodies grégoriennes, J. Pothier, 52, 57

Mendel, A. "Evidence and Explanation," 22–23, 32. See also David, H. T.

Merriam, A. *The Anthropology of Music*, 14

"Metastasio, Pietro," M. F. Robinson, 83, 86

Methode der Musikgeschichte, G. Adler, 12

Meyer, E. H. *English Chamber Music*, 30, 32

Meyer, L. *Emotion and Meaning in Music*, 14; *Music, the Arts and Ideas*, 99

———, ed. *Studies in the Criticism and Theory of Music*, 84

Mickelsen, W. C. *Hugo Riemann's Theory of Harmony*, 32

Mitchell, D. See Landon, H. C. R.

Mixter, K. *General Bibliography for Music Research*, 141

"Mode," H. Powers, 62, 68

Modern Music, P. Griffiths, 99

Modern Musical Scholarship, E. Olleson, ed., 14

"Monody," N. Fortune, 71, 77

Monteverdi, D. Arnold, 76

Monteverdi, L. Schrade, 26, 33

The Monteverdi Companion, D. Arnold and N. Fortune, eds., 77

Monuments of Renaissance Music, 40

Morgenstern, S. and H. Barlow, comps. *A Dictionary of Opera and Song Themes*, 119. See also Barlow, H.

Mozart, A. Einstein, 85

The Mozart Companion, H. C. R. Landon and D. Mitchell, eds., 86

Mozart und seine Welt in zeitgenössischen Bildern, O. E. Deutsch, 38, 40

Mozart's Operas, E. J. Dent, 83, 85

Mueller, J. H. "Baroque—Is It Datum, Hypothesis, or Tautology," 78

A Muse for the Masses, C. L. Donakowski, 93

Music and Aesthetics in the Eighteenth

and Early-Nineteenth Centuries, P. Le Huray and J. Day, eds., 82, 86
Music and Drama, T. Besterman, 122
Music and Language, T. Georgiades, 32
Music and Letters, 145
Music and Musicians in Early America, I. Lowens, 103
"Music and Semiotics," J. Dunsby, 30, 31
"Music and the Black American," J. A. McCabe, 124
Music and the Middle Class, W. Weber, 94
Music Article Guide, 123
Music, Books on Music, and Sound Recordings, U.S. Library of Congress, 130–31
Music for Piano and Orchestra, M. Hinson, 132–33
"Music History and Cultural History," J. Haar, 32
Music in a New Found Land, W. Mellers, 99
Music in America and American Music, I. Lowens, 104
Music in Early America, D. L. Hixon, 123–24
Music in Medieval Britain, F. L. Harrison, 56, 57
Music in Print, T. R. Nardone, ed., 130
Music in the Baroque Era, M. Bukofzer, 69–70, 75, 77
"Music in the Bible," C. H. Kraeling, 50
Music in the Classic Period, R. Pauly, 86
"Music in the Culture of the Renaissance," E. E. Lowinsky, 58, 68
Music in the Medieval World, A. Seay, 55, 58
Music in the Middle Ages, G. Reese, 21, 33, 54, 57
Music in the New World, C. Hamm, 99, 101–2, 103
Music in the Renaissance, G. Reese, 21, 33, 59–60, 68
Music in the Renaissance, H. M. Brown, 60, 67
Music in the Romantic Era, A. Einstein, 89, 92, 93
Music in the Twentieth Century, W. W. Austin, 94, 98, 103
Music in the United States, H. W. Hitchcock, 99, 103
Music in the Western World, P. Weiss and R. Taruskin, 51

Music in Western Civilization, P. H. Lang, 21, 32, 82, 86, 90, 93
Music Index, 123
Music Industry Directory, 118
Music Lexicography, J. Coover, 140
Music Libraries, L. R. McColvin and H. Reeves, 139–40
Music Library Association. *Notes*, 145
The Music Locator, W. P. Cunningham, 135
Music Notation in the Twentieth Century, K. Stone, 98, 100
The Music of Black Americans, E. Southern, 102–3, 104
"The Music of Post-Biblical Judaism," E. Werner, 50, 51
The Music of William Byrd, J. Kerman, P. Brett and O. W. Neighbour, 64
Music Periodical Literature, J. M. Meggett, 141
Music Reference and Research Materials, V. Duckles, comp., 140–41
Music since 1900, N. Slonimsky, 100, 122
Music, the Arts and Ideas, L. Meyer, 99
"Music Theory in Translation," J. Coover, 31
Music Theory Spectrum, 32, 145–46
Music through Sources and Documents, R. H. Rowen, 48, 50, 87, 93
Music Titles in Translation, J. Hodgson, 129
The Music Yearbook, 138
Musica Disciplina, 144
"*Musica recta* and *musica ficta*," M. Bent, 56
Musica Canadiana, Canadian Music Library Association, comp., 132
"Musical Humanism in the 16th and Early 17th Centuries," D. P. Walker, 68
Musical Iconography, H. M. Brown and J. Lascelle, 38, 39
Musical Instruments, S. Marcuse, 114–15
Musical Instruments and Their Symbolism in Western Art, E. Winternitz, 40
Musical Instruments of the Western World, E. Winternitz, 41
The Musical Quarterly, 144
"Musical Scholarship Today," F. Blume, 13
Musical Thought in Ancient Greece, E. A. Lippman, 48, 50

The Musical Times, 146
"The Musicologist and the Performer,"
    R. Taruskin, 15
Musicology, F. L. Harrison, M. Hood
    and C. Palisca, 5, 8, 10, 13
Musicology, D. Stevens, 14
"Musicology at the Mirror," V. Duckles,
    31
"Musicology, History and Anthropol-
    ogy," G. Chase, 13
"Musicology in the 1980s," 14
Musicology in the 1980s, D. K. Holo-
    man and C. Palisca, eds., 10, 13, 29
"Musicology Today," International Mu-
    sicological Society, 14
Die Musik des 19. Jahrhunderts, C.
    Dahlhaus, 93
*Die Musik in Geschichte und Gegen-
    wart,* 108
*Musikkulturen Asiens, Afrikas und Oz-
    eaniens im 19. Jahrhundert,* R.
    Gunther, 91

Nardone, T. R., ed. *Music in Print,* 130
Narmour, E. *Beyond Schenkerism,* 29,
    32
Nattiez, J. J. *Fondements d'une
    sémiologie de la musique,* 30, 32
Neighbour, O. W. *The Consort and
    Keyboard Music of William Byrd,*
    68; "Schoenberg, Arnold," 99
Nettl, B. *Reference Materials in Ethno-
    musicology,* 126; *The Study of Eth-
    nomusicology,* 14; *Theory and
    Method in Ethnomusicology,* 14
Neue Zeitschrift für Musik, 87–88
Neumann, F. *Ornamentation in Baroque
    and Post-Baroque Music,* 43, 45,
    74, 78
*The New College Encyclopedia of Mu-
    sic,* J. A. Westrup and F. L. Harri-
    son, 110
*The New Grove Dictionary of Music
    and Musicians,* S. Sadie, ed., 108–9
The New Music, R. S. Brindle, 99
New Oxford History of Music, 33,
    120–21
"New Roads to Old Ideas in Beetho-
    ven's *Missa Solemnis,*" W. Kirken-
    dale, 86
"The New World," L. Rosenstiel, 104
*New World Records, Recorded Anthol-
    ogy of American Music,* 102
New York Public Library. *Bibliographic

Guide to Music,* 137; *Dictionary
    Catalog of the Music Collection,*
    137
Newman, E. *The Life of Richard
    Wagner,* 91, 93
Newman, W. S. *Performance Practices
    in Beethoven's Piano Sonatas,* 44,
    45; *The Sonata in the Baroque Era,*
    73, 78; *The Sonata in the Classic
    Era,* 80, 81, 84, 86; *The Sonata
    since Beethoven,* 93
Nineteenth-Century Music, 146
*Nineteenth-Century Romanticism in Mu-
    sic,* R. M. Longyear, 93
Noblitt, T. "Textual Criticism of Se-
    lected Works Published by Pe-
    trucci," 68
Northouse, C. *Twentieth Century Opera
    in England and the United States,*
    117–18
Noske, F. *French Song from Berlioz to
    Duparc,* 89, 94
"Notation," G. Chew, 98, 99
Notation in New Music, E. Karkoschka,
    98, 99
The Notation of Polyphonic Music, W.
    Apel, 34, 39, 53, 56
Notes, Music Library Association, 145
"Notes on the Origin of the Parisian
    Chanson," L. F. Bernstein, 64, 67

Oliver, A. *The French Encyclopedists as
    Critics of Music,* 33
Olleson, E., ed. *Modern Musical Schol-
    arship,* 14
On Criticising Music, K. Price, ed., 14
"On Historical Criticism," L. Treitler, 33
On Playing the Flute, J. J. Quantz, 73,
    78
"On the Discriminations of Romanti-
    cisms," A. O. Lovejoy, 93
Opera, A. Jacobs and S. Sadie, 116
Opera as Drama, J. Kerman, 93
The Opera Companion, G. Martin, 117
*The Opera Companion to Twentieth
    Century Opera,* G. Martin, 117
The Operas of Alban Berg, G. Perle, 99
"The Operas of Haydn," H. C. R. Lan-
    don, 83, 86
The Operas of Verdi, J. Budden, 90, 92
Operas on American Subjects, H. E.
    Johnson, 116
The Oratorio in the Baroque Era, H. E.
    Smither, 72, 78

"The Origin and Destination of the
Magnus liber organi," H. Husmann,
53, 57
Orlando di Lasso und seine Zeit,
W. Boetticher, 64, 67
Ornamentation in Baroque and Post-
Baroque Music, F. Neumann, 43,
45, 74, 78
Osborne, C., ed. The Dictionary of
Composers, 111
Osthoff, H. Josquin Desprez, 64, 68
Oxford History of Music, 21, 33

Palisca, C. "The Artusi-Monteverdi Con-
troversy," 70, 78; "Baroque," 78;
Baroque Music, 71, 78; "The 'Cam-
erata Fiorentina'," 65, 68, 78;
Girolamo Mei, 65, 68; "Reflections
on Musical Scholarship in the
1960s," 14. See also Harrison, F.
L.; Holoman, D. K.
"Papers of the Colloque at Saint-Ger-
main-en-Laye," 91, 93
"Patterns in the Historiography of
19th-Century Music," V. Duckles,
31
Pauly, R. Music in the Classic Period, 86
Pavlakis, C. The American Music Hand-
book, 138-39
"The Performance of Plainchant," L.
Brunner, 57
Performance Practice, M. Vanquist and
N. Zaslaw, 43, 45
Performance Practices in Beethoven's Pi-
ano Sonatas, W. S. Newman, 44,
45
A Performer's Guide to Baroque Music,
R. Donington, 36, 40, 43, 45
Performing Arts Biography Master In-
dex, 111
Performing Arts Books 1876-1981, 129
"Performing Practice," H. M. Brown
and J. McKinnon, 44
Perkins, L. and H. Garey. The Mellon
Chansonnier, 68
Perle, G. The Operas of Alban Berg, 99;
Serial Music and Atonality, 95, 99
Perlis, V. Charles Ives Remembered,
103, 104
Perspectives in Musicology, B. Brook,
ed., 13
Perspectives of New Music, 96, 99
Perspectives on American Composers, B.
Boretz and E. T. Cone, eds., 99, 103

Perspectives on Contemporary Music
Theory, B. Boretz and E. T. Cone,
eds., 96, 99
Perspectives on Schoenberg and Stravin-
sky, B. Boretz and E. T. Cone, eds.,
96, 99
Peterson, C. S. and A. D. Fenton. Index
to Children's Songs, 129
Philosophies of Music History, W. D.
Allen, 30
Philosophy of Modern Music, T.
Adorno, 30
Piano Duet Repertoire, C. McGraw, 133
The Piano in Concert, 108
Pierre Attaingnant, D. Heartz, 64,
67
Pirrotta, N. "Medieval," 57, 68
Piston, W. Harmony, 33
The Place of Musicology in American
Institutions of Higher Learning, M.
Bukofzer, 13
Plantinga, L. B. Schumann as Critic, 87,
93
Pogue, S. Jacques Moderne, 64, 68
Pöhlmann, E. Denkmäler altgriechischer
Musik, 49, 50
Polyglot Dictionary of Musical Terms,
115-16
"Polyphony and Secular Monophony,"
E. Sanders, 55, 57
Popular Music, N. Shapiro, ed., 133
Popular Titles and Subtitles of Musical
Compositions, F. P. Berkowitz, 128
Pothier, J. Les mélodies grégoriennes,
52, 57
Powers, H. "Mode," 62, 68
Practica musicae, F. Gaffurio, 67
La pratique musicale au Moyen-Age, E.
Bowles, 39
Précis de musicologie, J. Chailley, ed.,
13
"Present Status of Research in Byzantine
Music," M. Velimirović, 51
Price, K., ed. On Criticising Music, 14
Primmer, B. "Unity and Ensemble," 93
The Principles of Music, A. M. Boethius,
56-57
"The Profession of Musical
Scholarship," D. Arnold, 12
"A Profile for American Musicology," J.
Kerman, ed., 13
Protestant Church Music, F. Blume, 77
Protestant Church Music in America, R.
Stevenson, 104

Quantz, J. J. *On Playing the Flute,* 73, 78
Quantz and His Versuch, E. R. Reilly, 78
"A Question of Commitment," A. Ringer, 14

Rachlin, H. *The Encyclopedia of the Music Business,* 118–19
Rameau, J. P. *Treatise on Harmony,* 17, 33, 75
Rangel-Ribeiro, V. *Baroque Music,* 74, 78
Ratner, L. *Classic Music,* 81, 86
Read, D. L. *See* Kennington, D.
Read, G. *Thesaurus of Orchestral Devices,* 119
Readings in Black American Music, E. Southern, 103, 104
Readings in the History of Music in Performance, C. MacClintock, ed., 44, 45
Recorded Sound, 146
Reese, G. *Music in the Middle Ages,* 21, 33, 54, 57; *Music in the Renaissance,* 21, 33, 59–60, 68
Reeves, H. *See* McColvin, L. R.
Reference Materials in Ethnomusicology, B. Nettl, 126
"Reflections on Musical Scholarship in the 1960s," C. Palisca, 14
Reilly, E. R. *Quantz and His Versuch,* 78
"Renaissance," L. Lockwood, 62, 68
Renaissance and Baroque Music, F. Blume, 77
Renaissance Manuscript Studies, 36, 40
Répertoire International des Sources Musicales, 134–35
Report of the Eighth Congress, New York 1961, International Musicological Society, 13
"*Resfacta* and *Cantare super librum,*" M. Bent, 67
"The Restoration of the Chant and Seventy-Five Years of Recording," M. Berry, 52, 56
The Rhythm of Twelfth-Century Polyphony, W. Waite, 53, 58
Ricci, R. *See* Fink, R.
Richard Wagner's Music Dramas, C. Dahlhaus, 91, 93
Riemann, H. *Grundriss der Musikwis-*

senschaft, 14; *History of Music Theory, Books I and II,* 33
RILM Abstracts of Music Literature, 123
Ringer, A. "A Question of Commitment," 14
The Rise of Music in the Ancient World, C. Sachs, 47, 50
The Rise of Opera, R. Donington, 77
Robinson, M. F. "Metastasio, Pietro," 83, 86
Roche, J. *Dictionary of Early Music,* 108; *The Madrigal,* 66, 68
Rockwell, J. *All American Music,* 104
"The Role of Ideology in the Study of Western Music," R. R. Subotnik, 33
"Romantic," J. Warrack, 89, 94
Rosen, C. *The Classical Style,* 79–80, 84, 86; *Sonata Forms,* 81, 86
Rosenstiel, L. "The New World," 104
———, ed. *Schirmer History of Music,* 21, 33
Rosenthal, H. and J. Warrack. *Concise Oxford Dictionary of Opera,* 118
Rousseau, J. J. *Dictionary of Music,* 17, 33
Rowen, R. H. *Music through Sources and Documents,* 48, 50, 87, 93

Sachs, C. *The Commonwealth of Art,* 47, 50, 55, 57; *The Rise of Music in the Ancient World,* 47, 50; *The Wellsprings of Music,* 47, 50, 54
The Sacred Bridge, E. Werner, 49, 51
Sadie, S., ed. *The New Grove Dictionary of Music and Musicians,* 108–9. *See also* Jacobs, A.
Salmen, W., ed. *Beiträge zur Geschichte des Musikanschauung um 19. Jahrhundert,* 93–94
Salzman, E. *Twentieth-Century Music,* 94, 99
Sams, E. *The Songs of Hugo Wolf,* 88, 94; *The Songs of Robert Schumann,* 88, 94
Sanders, E. "Polyphony and Secular Monophony," 55, 57
Schafer, R. M. *E. T. A. Hoffmann and Music,* 88–89, 94
Schauffler, R. H. *Beethoven,* 26
Schenker, H. *Free Composition,* 28–29, 33
Schirmer History of Music, L. Rosenstiel, ed., 21, 33

Schneider, M. *See* Besseler, H.
Schoenberg, A. *Style and Idea*, 97, 99
"Schoenberg, Arnold," O. W. Neigh-
    bour, 99
Scholes, P. *The Great Dr. Burney*, 33;
    *The Life and Activities of Sir John
    Hawkins*, 33
Schonberg, H. C. *The Lives of the Great
    Composers*, 111
Schrade, L. *Monteverdi*, 26, 33
Schubert, O. E. Deutsch, 38, 40
Schuller, G. *Early Jazz*, 102, 104
Schumann as Critic, L. B. Plantinga, 87,
    93
Schwann-1, Record and Tape Guide, 138
Schwartz, E. *Electronic Music*, 100
——— and B. Childs, eds. *Contempo-
    rary Composers on Contemporary
    Music*, 97, 100
*Scriptorum de musica medii aevi novam
    seriem*, E. de Coussemaker, 31
Scruton, R. "The Semiology of Music,"
    30, 33
Sears, M. E. *Song Index*, 129–30
Seay, A. *Music in the Medieval World*,
    55, 58
*Secret Chromatic Art in the Netherlands
    Motet*, E. E. Lowinsky, 61, 68
"Secret Chromatic Art Re-Examined,"
    E. E. Lowinsky, 68
Secular Music in America, 1801–1825,
    R. J. Wolfe, 131
Seeger, C. *Studies in Musicology, 1935–
    1975*, 14
"Self-Analysis by Twentieth Century
    Composers," L. Somfai, 96, 100
"The Semiology of Music," R. Scruton,
    30, 33
Sendrey, A. *Bibliography of Jewish Mu-
    sic*, 127
Serial Music and Atonality, G. Perle, 95,
    99
Shapiro, N., ed. *Popular Music*, 133
Shirlaw, M. *The Theory of Harmony*,
    33
A Short History of Opera, D. J. Grout,
    77
*Sibley Music Library Catalog of Sound
    Recordings*, 137
Silence, J. Cage, 97–98, 99
Simon, G. T. *The Best of the Music
    Makers*, 113
*The Simon and Schuster Book of the
    Ballet*, 136

*The Simon and Schuster Book of the
    Opera*, 118
Sinful Tunes and Spirituals, D. Epstein,
    103
"Sketches and Autographs," A. Tyson,
    37, 40
Skowronski, J. *Black Music in America*,
    125
Slavonic and Romantic Music, G. Abra-
    ham, 92
Slonimsky, N. *Music since 1900*, 100,
    122
———, rev. *Baker's Biographical Dic-
    tionary of Musicians*, 111–12
Smither, H. E. "The Baroque Oratorio,"
    78; *The Oratorio in the Baroque
    Era*, 72, 78
Smithsonian Collection of Classic Jazz,
    102
Snow, C. P. *The Two Cultures and the
    Scientific Revolution*, 11
"Solo Song and Cantata," N. Fortune,
    77
Solomon, M. *Beethoven*, 85, 86;
    "Beethoven and His Nephew," 86
Somfai, L. "Self-Analysis by Twentieth
    Century Composers," 96, 100. *See
    also* Bartha, D.
Sonata Forms, C. Rosen, 81, 86
The Sonata in the Baroque Era, W. S.
    Newman, 73, 78
The Sonata in the Classic Era, W. S.
    Newman, 80, 81, 84, 86
The Sonata since Beethoven, W. S. New-
    man, 93
Song Index, M. E. Sears, 129–30
Songs in Collections, D. De Charms and
    P. F. Breed, 128
The Songs of Hugo Wolf, E. Sams, 88,
    94
The Songs of Robert Schumann, E.
    Sams, 88, 94
*The Songs, Services and Anthems of
    William Byrd*, P. Brett, 67
Sonneck, O. G. T. *A Bibliography of
    Early Secular American Music*, 131
"The Source for Bach's *Musical Offer-
    ing*," U. Kirkendale, 75–76, 77–78
*Source Materials and the Interpretation
    of Music*, I. Bent, ed., 44
Source Readings in Music History, O.
    Strunk, ed., 45, 48, 50, 87, 94, 121
Southern, E. *Biographical Dictionary of
    Afro-American and African Musi-*

cians, 113; *The Music of Black Americans*, 102–3, 104; *Readings in Black American Music*, 103, 104

Sparks, E. *Cantus Firmus in Mass and Motet, 1420–1530*, 58

Spiess, L., ed. *Historical Musicology*, 14

St. Augustine's "De Musica," W. F. J. Knight, 50

"Steps to Publication;emAnd Beyond," A. Tyson, 37, 40

Sterba, E. and R. Sterba. *Beethoven and His Nephew*, 84, 86

Stevens, D. *Musicology*, 14

Stevens, J. and T. Karp. "Troubadours, Trouvères," 54, 58

Stevenson, R. *Protestant Church Music in America*, 104

Der Stil in der Musik, G. Adler, 12, 27

Stone, K. *Music Notation in the Twentieth Century*, 98, 100

Storia della Musica, G. B. Martini, 18–19, 32

String Music in Print, M. K. Farish, 132

"Structuralism and Musicology," P. Tunstall, 33

The Structure of Atonal Music, A. Forte, 32, 95, 99

Strunk, O. *Essays on Music in the Byzantine World*, 50

———, ed. *Source Readings in Music History*, 45, 48, 50, 87, 94, 121

Studien zur Musikgeschichte des 19. Jahrhunderts, 91, 94

Studien zur Symbolik in der Musik der alten Niederländer, W. Elders, 61, 67

Studien zur Trivialmusik des 19. Jahrhunderts, C. Dahlhaus, ed., 91, 93

Studies in Eastern Chant, M. Velimirović, ed., 50, 51

Studies in Musicology, 1935–1975, C. Seeger, 14

Studies in the Criticism and Theory of Music, L. Meyer, ed., 84

The Study of Ethnomusicology, B. Nettl, 14

Style and Idea, A. Schoenberg, 97, 99

The Style of Palestrina and the Dissonance, K. Jeppesen, 27, 32, 63, 67

Subotnik, R. R. "The Role of Ideology in the Study of Western Music," 33

"Susanna," "Jeanie," and "The Old Folks at Home," W. W. Austin, 103

La symphonie française dans le seconde

motie de XVIIIe siècle, B. Brook, 85

Systematic Discography, L. Foreman, 138

Taruskin, R. "The Musicologist and the Performer," 15. *See also* Weiss, P.

"Textual Criticism of Selected Works Published by Petrucci," T. Noblitt, 68

Thayer, A. *Ludwig van Beethoven's Leben*, 19, 33

Thematic Catalogues in Music, B. S. Brook, 140

Theory and Method in Ethnomusicology, B. Nettl, 14

The Theory of Harmony, M. Shirlaw, 33

Thesaurus of Orchestral Devices, G. Read, 119

Thompson, O., ed. *The International Cyclopedia of Music and Musicians*, 109–10

Thorough-Bass Accompaniment according to Johann David Heinichen, G. J. Buelow, 73, 77

Three Centuries of Harpsichord Making, F. Hubbard, 44, 45

Tinctoris, J. *Liber de arte contrapuncti*, 68

Tirro, F. *Jazz*, 102, 104

Tischler, A. *Fifteen Black American Composers*, 131–32

"To Worship That Celestial Sound," L. Treitler, 15, 29, 33

Tomlinson, G. "The Web of Culture," 15

Les Tonaires, M. Huglo, 52, 57

"Tonality," C. Dahlhaus, 75, 77

Tonality and Atonality in Sixteenth-Century Music, E. E. Lowinsky, 63, 68

Tovey, D. *Essays in Musical Analysis*, 33

"Toward a New Historical View of Gregorian Chant," H. Hucke, 52, 57

Treatise on Harmony, J. P. Rameau, 17, 33, 75

Treitler, L. "On Historical Criticism," 33; "To Worship That Celestial Sound," 15, 29, 33; "What Kind of Story Is History?" 15

"Troubadours, Trouvères," J. Stevens and T. Karp, 54, 58

Tunstall, P. "Structuralism and Musicology," 33
Twentieth-Century Music, E. Salzman, 94, 99
Twentieth Century Opera in England and the United States, C. Northouse, 117–18
Twentieth-Century Views of Music History, W. Hays, ed., 99
The Two Cultures and the Scientific Revolution, C. P. Snow, 11
Tyson, A. *The Authentic English Editions of Beethoven,* 37, 40; "Sketches and Autographs," 37, 40; "Steps to Publication—And Beyond," 37, 40
————, ed. *Beethoven Studies I,* 37, 40. *See also* Kerman, J.

U.S. Copyright Office. *Catalog of Copyright Entries: Music,* 130
U.S. Library of Congress. *Catalogue of Opera Librettos Printed before 1800,* 137; *Music, Books on Music, and Sound Recordings,* 130–31
Ueber Johann Sebastian Bachs Leben, Kunst und Kunstwerke, J. N. Forkel, 19, 31
"Umfang, Methode, und Ziel der Musikwissenschaft," G. Adler, 12, 27
"Unity and Ensemble," B. Primmer, 93

Van der Werf, H. *The Chansons of the Troubadours,* 54, 58
Vanquist, M. and N. Zaslaw. *Performance Practice,* 43, 45
Velimirović, M. "Present Status of Research in Byzantine Music," 51
————, ed. *Studies in Eastern Chant,* 50, 51
"Viewpoint," J. Kerman, 92, 93
Vindications, D. Cook, 92
Vinton, J., ed. *Dictionary of Contemporary Music,* 110
"The Visual Arts as a Source for the Historian of Music," E. Winternitz, 41
Vogel, M., ed. *Beiträge zur Musiktheorie des 19. Jahrhunderts,* 91, 92, 94
Der vollkommene Capellmeister, J. Mattheson, 17, 32
Von Ende, R. C. *Church Music,* 127
"Vorwort und Einleitung," F. Chrysander, 13

W. A. Mozart, O. Jahn, 19, 32
W. A. Mozart, H. Abert, 85
Wagner, P. *Einführung in die gregorianischen Melodien,* 52, 58
Wagner, C. von Westernhagen, 91, 94
Waite, W. *The Rhythm of Twelfth-Century Polyphony,* 53, 58
Walker, D. P. "The Aims of Baïf's *Academie de Poesie et de Musique,*" 65, 68; "Musical Humanism in the 16th and Early 17th Centuries," 68
Walter Frye and the Contenance angloise, S. Kenney, 56, 57
The Waning of the Middle Ages, J. Huizinga, 55, 57
Warrack, J. "Romantic," 89, 94. *See also* Rosenthal, H.
Warren, C. "Brunelleschi's Dome and Dufay's Motet," 60, 68
Watanabe, R. T. *Introduction to Music Research,* 140
Watkins, G. *Gesualdo,* 65–66, 69
"The Webb of Culture," G. Tomlinson, 15
Weber, W. *Music and the Middle Class,* 94
Weiss, P. and R. Taruskin. *Music in the Western World,* 51
Wellek, R. "The Concept of Baroque in Literary Scholarship," 78
Wellesz, E. *Eastern Elements in Western Chant,* 50, 51; *A History of Byzantine Music and Hymnography,* 34, 40, 49, 51
The Wellsprings of Music, C. Sachs, 47, 50, 54
Werner, E. "The Music of Post-Biblical Judaism," 50, 51; *The Sacred Bridge,* 49, 51
Westernhagen, C. von. *Wagner,* 91, 94
Westrup, J. A. and F. L. Harrison. *The New College Encyclopedia of Music,* 110
"What Kind of Story Is History?" L. Treitler, 15
"What Should Musicology Be?" E. A. Lippman, 14
"Who Cares If You Listen," M. Babbitt, 97
Winckelmann, J. *History of the Art of Antiquity,* 82
Winnington-Ingram, R. P. "Greece. I: Ancient," 48, 51; "Greek Music," 49, 51

Winterfield, C. *Johannes Gabrieli und sein Zeitalter*, 19, 34

Winternitz, E. "The Iconology of Musicology," 40; *Musical Instruments and Their Symbolism in Western Art*, 40; *Musical Instruments of the Western World*, 41; "The Visual Arts as a Source for the Historian of Music," 41

Wiora, W. *The Four Ages of Music*, 15, 33

———, ed. *Die Ausbreitung der Historismus der Musik*, 33

Wittlich, G., ed. *Aspects of Twentieth Century Music*, 100

Woffinden, B. *See* Logan, N.

Wolf, E. "Classic Period," 81, 86

Wolfe, R. J. *Secular Music in America, 1801–1825*, 131

Wright, C. "Dufay at Cambrai," 38, 41

Wulstan, D. *See* Henderson, I.

Yesterdays, C. Hamm, 102, 103

Zalkand, D. *Contemporary Music Almanac 1980/81–* , 139

Zarlino, G. *L'istitutioni harmoniche*, 69

Zaslaw, N. *See* Vanquist, M.

"Zitate in französischen Liedsätzen der Ars nova und Ars subtilior," U. Günther, 54, 57

"Zu Marcus van Crevels neuer Obrecht Ausgabe," C. Dahlhaus, 61, 67

"Zwölf Jahre Bachforschung," W. Blankenburg, 76, 77

SUBJECT INDEX

Compiled by G. Fay Dickerson

1970s, 12
Absolute music, 90
Académie de Poésie et de Musique, 65
Accidentals, 55, 61
Acoustics, 4, 5, 17
  Greek science of, 48–49
Adler, Guido, 3–4, 6–7, 10–11, 23–24
Aesthetics, 4, 7, 9, 19, 80
  Classic Era, 82
  in musicology, 23
  in style analysis, 27–28
Affektenlehre, 18
Aleatoric music, 97
"Allusive" music, 90
Alypios, 48
American Institute of Musicology, 36
American music, 100–3
  bibliography, 123–25, 131–32, 138–39
American Musicological Society, 8, 10
American musicology. *See* Musicology
Anachronistic performance, 41
Analysis and method, 27–30
Analytic criticism, 8–9, 10, 63, 84, 96–97
  of 19th century music, 92
Anthropology
  in music research, 6, 46–47
Antiquity, 24, 46–50
Antirational music, 97
Archival research, 38, 75, 83
Aristotle, 48,
Aristoxenus, 48
"Ars subtilior," 54
Art history. *See* Iconography
Artusi, Giovanni Maria, 70
Atlas, Allan, 59
Atonal music, 63, 95–96
  analysis, 29

Audience
  20th century, 96–97, 98
Aufklärung, 87
Authenticity
  authoritative music scores, 34–38
  in performance practice, 7–8, 41–43
Autograph scores, 35
Avant-garde
  20th-century music, 97–98

Babbitt, Milton, 96
Bach, Johann Sebastian
  19th century rediscovery, 19
  "Art of Fugue," 69
  critical editions, 37
  focal point of research, 75
  Romantic Era appreciation, 88
  source criticism, 75
Baïf, Jean-Antoine de, 65
Balance
  in Classic music, 83
Ballet
  bibliography, 136
Bardi, Giovanni de, 65
Baroque Era, 24, 26, 42, 65
  composers, 62, 72–73
  opera, 71–72, 83
  periodicals, 91
Baroque music
  ornamentation, 43
  popularity, 73
  style in Classic Era, 79
Bartók, Béla, 98
  Allegro Barbaro, 95
Beethoven, Ludwig van, 79
  classic and romantic style, 83–84
  current research, 76

167

An die ferne Geliebte, 88
Fidelio, 83
"Ninth Symphony," 29
personal relationships, 84–85
sketchbooks, 37, 84
Benedictine monks, 51–52
Gregorian chant research, 34, 51–52
Berlin, Isaiah, 22
Berlioz, Louis-Hector, 87
Symphonie fantastique, 90
Bernstein, Leonard, 96
Bibliography
19th-century standards, 19
Classic composers, 80
medieval music, 56
music bibliographies, 140–41
music literature, 122–27
music research materials, 25
music titles, 128–36
non-critical scholarship, 8–9
Binchois, Gilles, 59
Biography
bibliography, 110–14
relevance of sketch studies, 37
standards, 83
Black Americans
musicological studies, 102–3
Black music
bibliography, 124–25, 131–32
Blacking, John, 6
Blume, Friedrich, 7, 11–12, 62
Brahms, Johannes, 88, 89, 94
Britten, Benjamin, 97
Bruckner, Anton, 89
Bukofzer, Manfred, 25
Burney, Charles, 82
Byrd, William, 72
Byzantine chant, 49–50
notation, 34
Byzantine music, 47

Cadences, 62–63
Cage, John, 97–98
Camerata, 65, 69
Canadian music
bibliography, 125, 132
Canons
puzzle canons, 61
Cantus firmus technique, 61
Catalogs and cataloging
iconographic items, 39
music libraries and collections, 136–37

Chamber music
Classic composers, 80
Chance music. *See* Aleatoric music
Character pieces, 90
Chase, Gilbert, 11, 100
Chavez, Carlos, 96
Chinese opera, 71
Chopin, Frédéric, 89
Chord progressions, 63
Chromatic scale
alteration, 61
chromaticism, 75
harmony, 94, 95
Church music
19th-century reform, 19
American, 101
bibliography, 127, 135
documents, 34–35
early church, 47, 49, 50
Classic Era, 24–25, 26, 78–85
interwoven with end of Baroque, 73
Classicism, 79
18th century, 76
Coherence
in musical functions, 84
Collegium musicum, 8
Collingwood, R. G., 22
Communication gap
among music scholars, 11
Comparative musicology. *See* Ethnomusicology
Composers
13th–14th centuries, 62
13th–15th centuries, 55, 56
17th–18th centuries, 72–73
18th–19th centuries, 87–89
19th century, 36
as music historians and critics, 86–88
authoritative editions, 34
biographical dictionaries, 110–14
biography, 26
cooperation with dramatists, 71
notes and sketches, 37
score instructions, 42–43
20th century, 95–98
see also Autograph scores; Scores
Composition
20th-century techniques, 96–97
Medieval and Renaissance, 42
sketches, 37, 84, 91
Computers, 96
Concerto
17th century, 72

Consonance and dissonance, 17, 95
  dissonance, 70, 75
Contextual history, 9, 22, 29
Controversies
  Artusi-Monteverdi, 70
Copland, Aaron, 96
Coptic plainchant, 51
Counterpoint, 27, 29, 62
Country and western music, 102
Crawford, Richard, 100
Creative processes, 37
Critical editions
  of musical texts, 35–36
Criticism. *See* Analytic criticism; Style
  criticism
Croce, Benedetto, 22–23
"Cultivated music," 101
Cultural history
  deficient in music research, 5
  music research, 46–47
Cultural-sociological method, 20, 22

Dahlhaus, Carl, 23–24
Dart, Thurston, 74
Darwinism, 22
Data synthesis, 21
Debussy, Claude, 88, 90
  Afternoon of a Faun, 94
  Pelléas and Mélisande, 94
Descartes, René, 69
Desprez, Josquin, 59, 63
Devices, musical. *See* Themes and de-
  vices, musical
Dialectical materialism, 30
Dictionaries and encyclopedias
  bibliography, 107–10, 115–16, 119
  international biography, 110–12
Discographies
  bibliography, 137–38
Dissertations
  bibliography, 125–26
Dissonance. *See* Consonance and disso-
  nance
Documents
  8th century, 51
  discoveries, 75
  for music history, 25, 34–37
  source for Bach research, 75. *See also*
    Sketches and sketchbooks
Dominant-tonic relationship, 63
Donington, Robert, 74
Drama
  liturgical, 52
  operatic, 71, 72, 82–83

Duckles, Vincent, 20
  cultural-sociological studies, 22
Dufay, Guillaume, 59, 60–61
Duparc, Henri, 88

Early music
  bibliography, 133–35
  Early Music (periodical), 91
Education. *See* Music education
Eighteenth century, 70, 73, 76
  music historiography, 16–19
  periodizing difficult, 79. *See also* Clas-
    sic Era
Electronic instruments, 96
Electronic music, 97
Emigrés
  energized American research, 7
Emotion
  in Classic music, 80
  in music, 9, 18
  in operatic drama, 83
  in Renaissance, 63
  in Romantic Era, 87
  voice and piano balance, 88. *See also*
    Expression
Emotive criticism, 9
Empfindsamer style, 74, 78
Encyclopedias and dictionaries. *See* Dictionaries and encyclopedias
Encyclopedists, French, 16
English composers
  late Middle Ages, 56
Enlightenment, 81–82, 87
  histories of music, 18
Enumerative analysis, 10
Ethical properties
  music's effect, 48–49
Ethnomusicology, 5, 6, 9, 46–47
  bibliography, 126
  false application to others, 11
European tradition. *See* Western Euro-
  pean tradition
Evolutionary concept, 24
  18th-century music history, 16–17
Experimentation
  20th-century composers, 98
Expression
  music theory, 9, 60, 81
  Renaissance music, 64
  universality in folk elements, 82
Expressionism, 89, 95

Feature analysis
  categories, 28

Fifteenth century, 58–59, 61, 62, 63
Film. *See* Musical film
Fine-art music. *See* "Cultivated music"
Finscher, Ludwig, 9
Florence
  Renaissance in, 58
Folk music
  18th century studies, 17
  American, 101
  elements in the Classic Era, 82
Folk musicians
  encyclopedias, 113–14
Forkel, Johann Nikolaus
  bibliographic standards, 19
Form, musical
  in Classic Era, 81, 83
  sonata, 80–81
Formalist analysis, 29
Formalistic-structural method, 20
Forte, Allen, 29
Fortepiano
  as used by Mozart, 41
Fortune, Nigel, 71
Fourteenth century, 58–59, 62
Frankish Gregorian chant, 52
French opera
  synthesis of music and dance, 72
Futurism, 97

Gaffurio, Franchino, 58
Galant style, 76, 78, 81
Galilei, Vincenzo, 65
Gallican plainchant, 51
Geistesgeschichte, 22
Genius, 79–80
German Enlightenment. *See Aufklärung*
German philosophy
  applied to music history, 23
Gesualdo, Carlo, 65–66
Glarean, Heinrich, 62
Gluck, Christoph Willibald von, 80
  Alceste, 83
  operatic reforms, 83
Goethe, Johann Wolfgang von, 87
Graphic analyses
  H. Schenker studies, 29
Greek music, 47–49
  contemporary recreation, 48
  in modern notation, 49
  sources, 58, 64
Gregorian chant, 34, 49, 51–52
  bibliography, 133
  Roman and Frankish relationship, 52

Gregory I, Pope, 51
Günther, Ursula, 54

Hamm, Charles, 35, 100
Handel, George Fridric
  focal point of research, 75
  oratorios, 72
Happenings, musical, 97
Harmonics
  Greek science of, 48
Harmony, 17, 27, 28, 29
  Baroque music, 75
  chromatic, 94, 95
  functional, 74–75
Harpsichord, 72
  construction and music, 44
Harvard Dictionary of Music
  no article on Classic Era, 79
Hawkins, John, 82
Haydn, Franz Joseph, 72, 73, 76, 82
  operas, 83
  Viennese Classical style, 79
Hellenism
  18th century, 82
Hempel, Carl, 22
Henderson, Isobel, 48
Hermeneutics, 24
Heroic concept, 82–83
  Romantic Era, 87, 89
Hidden elements
  in Renaissance composition, 61
Hindemith, Paul, 36, 96
Historiography, 12, 16–24
  19th- century methodology, 20
  methodology, 23
  Renaissance music, 60. *See also*
    Methodology
History
  chronologies, 73, 120–21
  Romantic Era appreciation, 88
History of ideas
  Artusi-Monteverdi controversy, 70
  music history's place, 26
  place of iconography and music, 10
Hitchcock, H. Wiley, 100, 101
Hoffmann, E. T. A., 89
  spokesman for early Romanticism, 87
Holographs, musical
  authentication of, 35
Humanism, 72
  American orientation, 12
  in music studies, 25, 58
  Renaissance, 16, 64, 65
"Hyper-Romanticism," 89

Iconography, 10
   in music research, 38–39
   music history source, 47
Impressionism, 89
Improvisation
   Baroque music, 73
Indeterminacy, 97
Industry. *See* Music industry
Institute for Studies in American Music,
   101
Instrumental music
   Baroque composers, 72
   Renaissance, 64
   Romantic Era, 89
Instruments. *See* Electronic instruments;
   Musical instruments
International Musicological Society, 91
Interpretation, 8
Intervallic structure, 63
Isorhythm, 56
Italian humanism, 58
Ives, Charles, 98, 103
   Concord Sonata, 95

Jazz, 102
   bibliography, 126–27, 133, 137
   encyclopedias, 113–14
Jeppesen, Knud
   analytical methodology, 27–28
Jewish music, 47, 50
   bibliography, 127
   Greek influence, 49

Kabuki theater, 71
Kerman, Joseph, 8, 10, 102
Kottick, Edward, 8

Landowska, Wanda, 44
Language
   in music studies, 22, 30, 60, 84. *See
   also* Linguistic analysis
Lassus, Orlande de, 63
Lessing, Gotthold
   Laoköon, 87
Lexicography, music, 140
Librarianship
   manuals, 139–40
Libraries
   music collections, 136–37
Lieder and *mélodies*
   Romantic Era, 88
Linguistic analysis
   in music research, 9, 30, 47
Lippman, Edward, 12

Liszt, Franz, 87, 89
   Faust Symphony, 90
Literature and music
   relation in the Romantic Era, 87–88
Literature, music. *See* Music literature
Liturgical chant. *See* Gregorian chant;
   Plainchant
Liturgical drama
   medieval, 52
Liturgical melodies, 51–52
Lowens, Irving, 100
Lowinsky, Edward, 8, 10, 61–62
Lyricism
   in Classic music, 83

Machaut, Guillaume de, 58–59
Madrigal, 64, 65–66, 69
Mahler, Gustave, 89
Manierismo. See Mannerism
Mankind
   opera's main theme, 83
Mannerism, 64, 65–66
Manuscript sources, 35
   bibliography, 134–35
   Gregorian, 52
   medieval, 53
   Renaissance, 36, 59–60. *See also*
   Sketches and sketch books
Markings and symbols
   historical development, 42
Marxism, 30
   historiography, 11
Mathematics
   compositional underpinning, 61
Mattheson, Johann, 69, 79
Medieval Era, 24, 51–56
   American studies, 21
   composers, 55–56
   liturgy, 52–53
Melody, 27, 28, 70
   Renaissance, 63. *See also* Liturgical
   melodies
Mendelssohn, Felix, 87
Menotti, Gian Carlo, 97
Mesopotamian music, 49
Metastasio, Pietro, 82–83
Meter
   early church music, 50
Methodology
   American musicology, 7
   Charles Seeger's, 10–11
   Gustave Reese's, 54, 59–60
   inadequacies, 5, 7

Methodology (cont.)
International Musicological Society,
1970, 91
J. Mattheson's, 18
Knud Jeppesen's, 27–28
musical iconography, 38–39
Renaissance manuscript studies, 59–
60
Robert Haas's, 43
William S. Newman's, 73
see also Historiography; Musicology
Meyer, Leonard, 9, 84
Middle Ages. *See* Medieval Era
Minimalism, 97
Modal theory, 62, 63
Monody, 65, 69
history, 71
Italian operatic, 72
Monophonic songs
Medieval Era, 34, 54
Monteverdi, Claudio, 70, 71
Mozarabic plainchant, 51
Mozart, Wolfgang Amadeus, 72, 73, 76,
79, 80, 82
The Marriage of Figaro, 83
Music dictionaries. *See* Dictionaries and
encyclopedias
Music education, 4
Music history
American studies, 101–4
methodological refinement, 25–26
periodization, 24–26. *See also* Histori-
ography; Musicology
Music industry
bibliography, 118–19
Music literature
bibliography, 122–27
Musica ficta, 55
Musical comedy, 101
Musical film
encyclopedias, 120
Musical forms, 27
Musical instruments
historical study of, 7, 38
Musicologists, 3
as historians, 5–6
Musicology, 3–12
American research, 4, 7, 8, 10, 12, 21,
101–4
applied musicology, 8
archival research, 38
Bukofzer's approach, 69–70
categories, 3–4, 5, 6
historic, 3–6

musical iconography, 38–39
Romantic Era foundation, 92
scholarship, 25
see also Ethnomusicology
Musique concrète, 97
Myth, 82

Nationalism
in Romantic music, 89
Native American music, 102
Naturalism, 89
Neo-Romanticism, 89
Neoplatonism, 72
Neue Zeitschrift für Musik, 87
Neumatic notation, 34, 52
*New World Records, Recorded Anthol-
ogy,* 102
Nineteenth century
music research, 19–20
music studies established, 88
musical language, 84
periodicals, 91–92. *See also* Romantic
Era
Notation
16th-century codification, 34
20th-century revision, 98
ancient, 34
ancient Greek, 47, 48
Byzantine, 34, 49
deciphering, 49
Middle Ages, 42, 55
neumatic, 34, 52
polyphonic, 53
Renaissance, 42
transcriptions, 49
Notre Dame polyphony, 53
Numerological symbolism, 60–61

Obrecht, Jacob, 61
Ockeghem, Johannes, 59
Old music
contemporary recreation, 7
Opera
Baroque Era, 71–72
bibliography, 116–18, 127
Classic Era, 82–83
early history, 70–72
Romantic Era, 90
Oral tradition
in American music, 102
music history documentation, 103
Oratorios, 72
Organ music, 72
Organology, 7

Organum. *See* Two-voice organum
Orientalism
  19th-century interest, 19
Origins, music, 46–47
Ornamentation
  Baroque music, 43, 73, 74

Palestrina, Giovanni Pierluigi da, 27, 63, 70
Palisca, Claude, 6, 12
Pamphleteering
  Romantic movement, 87, 88
Patronage
  Classic Era change, 86
Pattern identification
  in style analysis, 28
Paul, Jean, 87
Performance music
  bibliography, 132–33
Performance practice, 7–8, 41–44, 70
  19th century, 90
  Baroque music, 73–74
  Classic Era, 85
  use of musical iconology, 38
Peri, Jacapo
  Dafne, 70–71
  Euridice, 70–71
Periodicals
  19th century, 91–92
  annotated list, 141–46
  for performance practice, 44
Periodization, 24–26
  of music history, 46–103
  performance recreation, 41–44
Perkins, Leeman, 59
Philology
  18th-century studies, 17
  19th-century studies, 19, 49
  source criticism, 10, 35–36
Philosophy, German, 23
Philosophy, Greek, 48–49
Physiology, 5
Piano duets
  bibliography, 133
Piano *Etudes,* 94
Piano sonatas, 81
Pirrotta, Nino, 56
Pitch, 27, 55. *See also* "Sprechstimme"; Tone-row technique
Pius X, Pope
  Motu proprio, 34
Plainchant, 51, 53, 55
Plato
  philosophy of music, 48, 49

Poetry
  Romantic composers use of, 88
Political history
  in music history, 30
Polyphonic music, 70, 76
  16th-century criticism, 64–65
  medieval, 53
  notation, 34, 53–54
  Renaissance, 36, 61, 62, 66
Popper, Karl R., 22
Popular music
  American, 100–1, 102
  bibliography, 133
  Classic Era, 80, 85
  encyclopedias, 113–14
Positivism
  19th century, 89
Prima prattica, 66, 70, 72
Primitive music, 46
  18th century studies, 17
Program music. *See* Symphonic program music
Prokofiev, Sergei, 36, 97
Psychology, 4
Psychophysiology, 4
Puzzle canons, 61
Pythagoras, 48

Quantz, Johann Joachim, 79

Reception history, 24
Recitative
  in opera, 71
Reconstructionist attitude
  in music performance, 8
Recordings
  relationship to research, 43. *See also* Tapes and records
Reilly, Edward, 73
Renaissance, 16, 24–25, 58–66
  American studies, 21
  composers, 62
  influence of English composers, 56
  manuscripts, 36
  research, 27. *See also* Humanism
Répertoire international d'iconographie musicale, 39
Repertory
  expansion, 7
Research
  manuals and guides, 139–40
  musicology/ethnomusicology divisions, 5, 6
  see also Methodology

Respighi, Ottorino, 97
Revolution
    effect on music, 81
Rhetoric, 81
    in music, 18, 75–76
Rhythm, 27, 28
    composer's intention, 43
    early church music, 50
    Gregorian chant, 52
    harmonic, 76
    liturgical melodies, 51
    medieval music, 53, 54
    Renaissance proportional practice, 61
    see also Isorhythm
Riemann, Hugo, 6–7, 19–20
Ringer, Alexander, 12
Rock music, 102
Rococo, 74, 78, 82
Roesner, Edward, 54–55
Roman music, 47
Romantic Era, 24, 86–92
    composers, 87–89
Romanticism, 19, 84
    influence of Rousseau, 82
    music the supreme vehicle, 89
    style, 81
Rossini, Gioacchino Antonio, 90
Rousseau, Jean-Jacques, 82

Sachs, Curt, 46, 47
Sacred music. See Church music; Jewish
    music
Salon music, American, 101
Salzman, Eric, 98
Scales
    dominant-tonic relationship, 63
    Greek theories of, 48
Scarlatti, Alessandro, 71
Schenker, Heinrich
    musical analysis, 28–29
Schoenberg, Arnold, 36, 96
    compositional methods, 95
    Pierrot Lunaire, 95
Schola Cantorum, 51
Scholarship
    in music research, 3–12, 35–38
Scholasticism
    in music, 56
Schubert, Franz, 88
Schumann, Robert, 89
    as music critic, 87–88
    Scenes from Childhood, 90
Scores
    autograph and authoritative, 35

Baroque, 73
    instructions, 41, 42–43
    primary research source, 34
Scriabin, Aleksandr, 89
Seconda prattica, 66, 70, 72
Secular music
    14th–15th centuries, 58–59
    Middle Ages, 54–55
    Renaissance, 58–59, 64
    vocal, 71
Seeger, Charles, 6, 10–11
Semiotics, 29–30
Sensationalism
    20th-century music, 98
Serial technique, 95
Sessions, Roger, 96
Seventeenth century, 65, 66, 70, 71–72,
    73
    performance standards, 42
Shostakovich, Dmitri, 97, 98
Silence
    use in music, 97
Simplicity, melodic, 76
Sinfonia. See Symphonic program
    music
Singing. See Vocal music
Sixteenth century, 62–63, 64, 69
    first opera performances, 70–71
    see also Renaissance
Sketches and sketchbooks
    Beethoven's, 37, 84
    contemporary composers, 35
Smither, Howard E., 73
Smithsonian Collection of Classic Jazz,
    102
Social history
    music research, 30, 36, 38, 70
Solesmes, France
    St. Peter Abbey, 34, 51–52
Sonata, 72, 80–81
Song cycles
    Romantic Era, 88
Sonneck, Oscar G., 100
Sound and sounds, 28
    use in music, 97–98
Sound recordings
    bibliography, 137
Sound synthesizers, 96
Source criticism, 35–36, 59
    18th century origin, 18
    philological method, 10, 35–36
Specialization
    in music research, 11
"Sprechstimme," 98

Strauss, Richard, 89
  Thus Spake Zarathrustra, 90
Stravinsky, Igor, 96, 98
  The Rite of Spring, 95
String quartets
  Classic music, 80
Structuralism, 30
  in music history, 24
Sturm und Drang, 76
  reaction to *Aufklärung,* 87
Style analysis. *See* Style criticism
Style criticism, 6–7, 10, 21, 23–24, 27–
  28
  Baroque music, 70
Symbolism. *See* Numerological symbol-
  ism
Symphonic program music
  19th century, 90
  Baroque achievement, 72
  Classic composers, 80
Synagogue music
  source of Christian chant, 49
Synthesizers. *See* Sound synthesizers
Syrian music, 49
  plainchant, 51

Tapes and records
  bibliography, 138
Taruskin, Richard, 7–8
Texts, music
  authoritative editions, 37
  critical editions, 35
  humanistic emphasis, 58
  liturgical, 51
Themes and devices, musical
  dictionaries, 119
Theory and theorists, 70
  16th century, 62
  18th century, 81
  19th century, 91
  20th century, 96
  Baroque music, 74
  Classic composers, 81
  medieval composers, 55
  Renaissance music, 62. *See also*
    Modal theory
Thirteenth century, 62
Thorough-bass, 73
Tinctoris, Johannes, 17, 56, 58
Tonal music
  analysis, 29
  harmony, 74

Tonality, 17, 62, 63–64
  19th century, 92
  "incipient atonality," 94
Tone-row technique, 95
Traditionalist composers
  20th century, 97
Treitler, Leo, 9, 11
Troubadours, 54, 55
Tschaikovsky, Piotr, 89, 91
Tuning systems, 7
Twelve-tone music, 95
Twentieth century
  composers, 97
  historiography, 20–24
  music bibliography, 130–31
  music history, 94–98
  periodicals, 96
Two-voice organum, 53

Unified field theory, 9, 10–11, 47
Universality, 82
University presses
  scholarly editions of music texts, 36

Value expression
  in analytic criticism, 8
Vatican Library
  Renaissance song manuscripts, 59
Verdi, Giuseppe, 36
  Falstaff, 89
  operas, 90
  Otello, 89
Vernacular music. *See* Folk music
Viennese classicists, 76, 83–84
  Mozart, Haydn, Beethoven domi-
    nance, 79
Vocal music
  prehistoric origins, 46–47
  Renaissance, 62, 63
  secular, 71

Wagner, Richard, 87, 88, 89, 90–91
  Tristan and Isolde, 94
Western European tradition
  dominant in musicology, 5
Western music, 4–5
  art music, 62
  history, 47
  Middle Ages, 55
Williams, Ralph Vaughan, 97
Wolf, Hugo, 88

Yearbooks and directories
  bibliography, 138–397

James W. Pruett is a professor of music and chair of the Department of Music at the University of North Carolina, Chapel Hill. He is a past editor of *Notes, the Quarterly Journal of the Music Library Association* and a past president of the Music Library Association; he has held office also in the American Musicological Society. He has written extensively on topics in musicology, including American Moravian music and seventeenth-century European music, and has prepared music bibliographies.

Thomas P. Slavens, series editor, is a professor of library science at the University of Michigan, Ann Arbor. He is a past president of the Association for Library and Information Science Education and is active in ALA. He is the author of *Theological Libraries at Oxford* and *The Retrieval of Information in the Humanities and the Social Sciences* and he has edited *Library Problems in the Humanities* and *Reference Interviews, Questions and Sources* as well as the three previous *Guides* in this series.